ANXIOUS INTELLECTS

ANX-

Academic Professionals, Public Intellectuals, and Enlightenment Values

IOUS

JOHN MICHAEL

INTEL-

DUKE UNIVERSITY PRESS   Durham and London 2000

LECTS

© 2000 Duke University Press
All rights reserved
Printed in the United States of America on acid-free paper ∞
Typeset in Quadraat by Tseng Information Systems, Inc.
Library of Congress Cataloging-in-Publication Data appear on the last
printed page of this book.

Part of chapter 3 appeared in a very different form as "Fish Shticks:
Rhetorical Questions in *Doing What Comes Naturally*," *diacritics* 20 (summer
1990): 54–74.

Chapter 6 originally appeared in different form as "Prosthetic Gender
and Universal Intellect: Stephen Hawking's Law," in *Boys: Masculinities in
Contemporary Culture*, ed. Paul Smith (New York: Westview Press, 1996).

Chapter 7 appeared in different form as "Science Friction and Cultural
Studies: Intellectuals, Interdisciplinarity, and the Profession of Truth,"
Camera Obscura 37 (January 1996): 125–58.

FOR SHARON

CONTENTS

ACKNOWLEDGMENTS

This book has little directly to do with Eastern Europe, but I began thinking seriously about what intellectuals in democratic societies could and could not be expected to do during a year, from 1990 to 1991, that I spent as a Fulbright scholar in the Instytut Anglistyki, Uniwersytet Warszawski, in Poland. I would like to thank the Fulbright Foundation and the staff of the English Institute, especially Agatha Preis Smith, for making my stay in Poland during this difficult time productive. I would also like to thank Adam Michnik, Mira Marody, Stefan Marody, Jan Gross, Elena Gross, David Ost, and Tadeusz Kowalik for discussing the rapid transformations of Polish society and their impact on intellectuals' role in that society. If not for Ewa Hauser's consuming passion for things Polish, I would never have gone to Poland at all.

The University of Rochester offered me research support and time off while working on early and later versions of this manuscript. I would especially like to thank the great staff in the English Department, Nancy Hall, Rosemarie Hattman, Patricia Neal, Lucy Peck, Kate Walsh, and Cindy Warner, for the countless acts of kindness and efficiency that have made my scholarly and professional life possible at all over the last few years.

Many friends and colleagues have discussed these ideas and read various drafts of portions of the book as it evolved. I would like to thank Michael Levine (*mon plus que frère*), Frank Shuffelton, Jonathan Baldo, Anita Levy, Deborah Grayson, Morris Eaves, Bette London, Thomas Hahn, Sasha Torres, Lynne Joyrich, Paul Smith, Paul Piccone (who will disagree with everything I've written), Randall Halle, Thomas DiPiero (who also kept me laughing), David Tamarin (who has long been my model of intellectual and personal integrity), Sarah Higley, and Lisa Cartwright for their interest and attention. Mohammed Bamyeh offered me detailed comments on foreign policy and postcolonial politics. Rosemary Kegl took on the extraordinary chore of reading the first draft of the entire manuscript and making a detailed critique that, among other things, forced me to reconsider Gramsci's significance. These interlocutors have saved me from many errors of omission and commission, though no one could possibly have saved me from all of them.

I will always be grateful for the careful and detailed reports the manuscript received from the readers at Duke University Press and for Ken Wissoker's editorial interest and support. Ian Peddie helped prepare the final manuscript, and Corrine Arraez helped with my Spanish.

My daughters, Marta Zofia and Krystyna Rose, took a sympathetic interest in this work and endured my abstraction and bad temper when it was not going well. I hope they know how grateful I am, and how proud. My mother, Rose, and my siblings and their spouses—Saleme and Bradley, Frank and Mary, and Julia and Ken—offered me emotional support and made me feel lucky just by being there.

Sharon Willis, to whom I dedicate this book, sustained and sustains me in countless ways. I drew lavishly on her confidence, intelligence, and patience while I worked on the project. Her interest in it made me want to write this book. I look forward to a lifetime attempting to repay her.

ANXIOUS INTELLECTS

INTRODUCTION

Fundamental Confusion

Forget populism

Perhaps the most surprising thesis this book advances is the one fundamental to its project: the thesis that we need another book on intellectuals. Sociologists, literary critics, philosophers, and pundits have been generating a nearly overwhelming series of critiques and celebrations of intellectuals for many years. We have had postmodernist announcements of the intellectual's death, popular elegies of the last intellectuals, conservative and progressive attacks on intellectual apostasy from Western traditions, populist critiques of new class impositions, and even neo-Fabian celebrations of professionals as the one progressive class. After all of these books and arguments, what remains to be said on the topic?[1]

All of these dithyrambs and diatribes share a fundamental confusion about the character and role of intellectuals in contemporary society. Are intellectuals an empowered elite, or are they a vestigial organ of modernity with no function in a commodity-driven social order that no longer requires the regulative work of representation and legitimation that intellectuals once performed? Can progressive intellectuals speak for the oppressed, or does their intervention inevitably reproduce the silencing and marginalization of the oppressed for whom they purport to act? Can conservative intellectuals preserve the common grounds of a democratic social order, or can they only reproduce structures of privilege and exclusion? That these questions come so readily to hand indicates that the status of intellectuals, an issue fundamental to our work as intellectuals, remains confused.

The second, perhaps less surprising thesis of this book is that these questions cannot be resolved in any simple way. Rather, the fact that intellectuals today must write and act, take positions and make polemics, in the absence of clear answers to basic questions about their own positioning, authority, and prerogatives, is the very condition of intellectual work in the realm of popular politics today. It is this condition—which is not precisely the condition of postmodernity—and its fundamentally conflicted situations that I describe in this book. The aim is not (and cannot be) to resolve either the confusion or the conflicts I explore here but to clarify their terms. The confusions remain fundamental. They are the embattled grounds and the shifting foundations that contemporary intellectuals, especially critical intellectuals interested in popular politics, must come to understand. By assessing some of the specific battles involving publicity, pedagogy, and scholarship in which critical intellectuals of various sorts are engaged, I hope to make a contribution to that understanding.

The phrases "popular politics" and "critical intellectuals" require some explanation, and a distinction usefully formulated by Carl Boggs will help to clarify these terms. The confusions I am primarily interested in attend the work of critical intellectuals who are generally also academics, though I also want to emphasize that what it means to be a critical intellectual is not at all clear. Maintaining a distinction between critical intellectuals and the type of intellectual worker Boggs has called "the technological variant" proves difficult. Nonetheless, there does seem to be general agreement that the authority and influence of critical intellectuals is in decline and that technologists have become "the predominant intellectual type in the modern period."

As Boggs explains, the ascendancy of the technocratic intellectual "comes with advanced levels of industrial development and the rationalization of social life that accompanies it."[2] These technocrats—an elite of specialists and bureaucrats—fulfill some of the modernized functions of the traditional intellectuals Gramsci described as "the industrial technician, the political economist, the organizer of a new culture, of a new law, etc." Clerics of the information age, today's technicians furnish what Gramsci called "homogeneity and consciousness" for the dominant order.[3] As Boggs puts it, technological intellectuals are a "new class" of experts serving "to legitimate, in various ways, the smooth functioning of bureaucratic state capitalism and other forms of industrial society" and "are located primarily in the state bureaucracy, universities, corporations, the military, the media, and the culture industry" (3).

Here the confusion begins to emerge. Universities, the media, and the culture industry also provide the locations for most of the academic professionals whose work as critical intellectuals I will consider. One problem is that in a given institutional context, the critical intellectual is frequently also an accredited technician in the social sciences or the humanities. One confusion we may hope to clarify, one that Boggs himself perpetuates, is the belief that the two varieties of intellectuals he names—varieties that my reference to Gramsci should make clear have a long genealogy in leftist thought—not only represent stable and easily identified groups but also have generally clear and easily specified political tendencies.

The politics intellectuals as technicians practice is not essentially popular. As experts, their authority depends on institutionalized power or professional credentials rather than public opinion. Popular politics, the politics of opinion, is the province of another type of intellectual (or of another mode of intellectual work) that Boggs identifies as "evolving out of and against this stratum [of technicians,] . . . a critical intelligentsia situated in higher education, the media, and the arts but typically confined to local spheres of influence and therefore lacking the cohesion of the technocrats" (3). These "critical intellectuals" frequently function in sectors of the public sphere where professional credentials and institutionalized power cannot completely protect them. They often address a wider audience and claim to speak for or to represent excluded, silenced, or oppressed groups, criticizing the dominant order in the interests of a more egalitarian, just, or democratic society.

It is this critical orientation toward a more general audience on more general topics that I call popular politics. This is the politics of critical intellectuals or of intellectuals when they function critically. It is the politics toward which many academic professionals in cultural studies specifically, and in the humanities and social sciences more generally, aspire.

Yet there is widespread confusion today about the relationship between intellectuals both critical and technical and the communities they purport to represent and address. This confusion has been especially debilitating on the Left, where democratic principles and the inherent elitism of intellectuals often conflict. This conflict has caused some to advocate limiting the intellectual's role to championing the popular or playing the ventriloquist for the authentic voice of various identity groups. I will argue that attempting to impose such limits is a mistake. I also think that the appeals academics sometimes make to other academics to become "public" intellectuals are also mistaken. Such calls are, it seems to me, largely irrelevant. At the very least, as teachers and scholars, cultural intellectuals already function as public intellectuals in an important segment of the public sphere. The negative and sensationalized attention that cultural intellectuals in the university have recently received—distorted as it may be—indicates that the critical work we do still maintains a degree of ideological potency. Moreover, disentangling our roles as critical intellectuals and as academic specialists—masters of our specific disciplinary technologies—is not always easy and is sometimes quite impossible. Success within the professional parameters of literature departments or the equally professional interdisciplinary constructs of cultural studies is not without political point, as Bruce Robbins has effectively argued.[4] It is far from clear, however, what the nature, grounding, and authority of the political points we would make are. However large or small our audiences may be—and it is not clear to me that publication in the *Village Voice* or the *New Yorker* is, in itself, a token of political achievement—intellectuals generally (and Left intellectuals particularly) seem confused and at odds about what it is they are supposed, as intellectuals, to profess and why, after all, anyone should want to listen. This fundamental uncertainty about the importance of what intellectuals do is one vexed condition of their indispensable work that I want to explore.

A suggestive outline of these problems may be found in the work of George Konrad and Ivan Szelenyi, whose *Intellectuals on the Road to Class Power*, a samizdat manuscript smuggled out of Hungary, became a tremendously influential text in the West after its publication in 1979.[5] Reacting to the example of empowered intellectuals as official planners and bureaucratic functionaries in East European Leninist party states, Konrad and Szelenyi argued that intellectuals are not disembodied, "free-floating" representatives of universal values, transcendent reason, and progressive ideals. In their view, which has clearly influenced thinkers such as Boggs, intellectuals are shaped and deformed by their class positions in ways that Gramsci had already begun to explore in "The Formation of Intellectuals." Moreover, having become in their own right a "new class" of experts, planners, and cultural workers, intellectuals tend to hide their self-promoting agendas and aggrandizing self-interests behind claims to serve universalized truth, justice, or emancipation. "The intellectuals of every age have described themselves ideologically, in accordance with their particular interests, and if those interests have differed from age to age it has still been the common aspiration of the intellectuals of every age to represent their particular interests in each context as the general interests of mankind."[6] What defines modernity and distinguishes it from all the ages that preceded it is its unique empowerment of intellectuals in the social order. Thus, in modern and modernizing societies, intellectuals as the New Class—new as well in its unprecedented powers, with all the arrogance and presumption that accompanies those powers—have become the enemies of the oppressed and the foes of emancipation even and especially when they claim to serve both.

This analysis, the terms of which are by now very familiar to critics on the Left and on the Right, has been widely influential. If one were to construct a genealogy of critiques of intellectuals and power in recent decades, Konrad and Szelenyi precede and influence Foucault, Gouldner,

Ross, and Boggs (to choose only a few familiar names). The influence of their work may also be traced in the works of Zygmunt Bauman, Edward Said, and Gayatri Spivak. Bauman, for example, offers an elegant rephrasing of Konrad and Szelenyi's crucial criticism as the point of departure in an important essay on postmodernity: "As 'organic,' intellectuals remained invisible as the authors of ideological narratives. The pictures of society or history they painted seldom contained their own representation. . . . A closer scrutiny, however, would pierce the camouflage. It would reveal the uncanny resemblance the stage actors of ideological scenarios bore to the intellectual scriptwriters. Whoever happened to be named as the sitter in a given portrait-painting session, the product was invariably a thinly disguised likeness of the painter."[7] Alvin Gouldner, on the other hand, and unlike these other writers, sees the new class of empowered intellectuals as "the most progressive force in modern society and . . . a center of whatever human emancipation is possible in the foreseeable future."[8] While this assertion seems impossibly elitist and, especially in the light of Leninism's failure in the Eastern Bloc, historically doubtful, it is also not altogether without merit, as we shall see. In fact, I will hold that both Bauman and Gouldner, holding what appear to be mutually exclusive positions, are right. Which is to say that having identified the problem of intellectuals as a New Class does not point us reliably toward a solution, especially if that solution involves rehabilitating populism in the name of democratic values.[9]

One important source of confusion has been the ideal or idea (actually a metaphor) of organic relationship that has frequently expressed the desire of progressive intellectuals. Boggs's work is a case in point. His distinction between technocratic and critical intellectuals is related to (but not completely identical with) Gramsci's well-known distinction between traditional and organic intellectuals. Since I will frequently use and criticize the idea of organic intellectuals as it circulates today, and since a genealogical descent of the populist strain in cultural studies must confront Gramsci's concept of the organic intellectual, a brief consideration of Gramsci's use of these terms and their relationship to my argument will help clarify my own position.[10] Given the special authority usually accorded to Gramsci among cultural critics who have populist propensities (and that includes most critics in cultural studies), it is worth remembering that Gramsci's organic intellectual was no populist. In fact, if we on the Left are looking for practical grounds for progressive politics, then we must forget populism and the peculiar ideal of the organic intellectual with which it is often associated. This does not mean that we can or should embrace an antidemocratic vanguardism or a retrograde elitism.

One point to which I will frequently return in the following pages is that nothing in the idea of the organic intellectual or even in the ideal of the counterhegemonic serves in itself as a grounds for politics. The political orientation of intellectuals must originate and always does originate elsewhere than in a relation to any particular social group (though no political orientation can be realized without attempting to analyze, critique, and above all forge such relations). Rather, the fundamental grounding of any intellectual's politics, and the grounds of the acts of criticism and judgment that are unavoidably part of any intellectual's task, must and always do come from certain strains within the varied and vexed traditions of the Enlightenment. This is especially the case for those of us who still consider ourselves leftists. Moreover, I will suggest that intellectuals today, especially intellectuals who have "progressive" programs, may as well admit that there is little reason to assume that the progressive ideals of the Enlightenment (ideals of social and economic justice as civic responsibilities, for example) have any preexisting organic grounding (preexisting the work of intellectuals to create them, that is) in any particular group. This is true even though enlightened or progressive politics must remain democratic in principle even though they cannot in practice be grounded in the popular.

My use of the term "enlightened" is polemical. I mean to draw attention to another common, fundamental confusion related to the confusion that surrounds the term "organic." Although the influence of Adorno and Horkheimer may still be felt in a widespread tendency among intellectuals to distrust the Enlightenment and its values, it is worth remembering that this is more specifically a distrust of intellectual work after the institutional and ideological transformations that occurred at the end of the nineteenth century, coinciding with, and finding expression in, the reorganization of American universities as professional research and credentialing organizations. Thus the current suspicion of the Enlightenment is frequently a suspicion of the institutional empowerment of academic intellectuals who have claimed to speak for it.

W. E. B. DuBois may be the quintessential intellectual embodiment of these developments, as Adolph Reed, in his study of the sociologist's and reformer's work, makes clear. Reed offers the following concise formulation: "The changing shape and thrust of the university was in fact an element of a more profound sociological phenomenon involving redefinition of the roles and self-perceptions of intellectuals in response to the industrial reorganization of American society. . . . Indeed, the fundamental views of the proper organization of human society around which intellectuals tend to converge emphasize the importance of precisely those activities that are characteristic to intellectuals."[11] Reed goes on to emphasize a point made by James Gilbert that the belief that society should be a consciously organized entity and therefore the basis of modern radical and reform movements is rooted in the "collectivism" of corporate-era intellectuals. "The collectivist outlook," Reed summarizes, "entails typically an emphasis on expertise as a legitimate, decisive social force, notions of the impartiality and neutrality of the state and resonant assumptions of the neutral, guiding role of technology. In the collectivist outlook realization of social justice depends on neutrality and scientific impersonality as major weapons" (18–19).[12] Much of our suspicion these days is correctly directed against the overweening and antidemocratic tendencies of the self-serving elitism implicit in this ideology of intellectuals. Too often, however, these suspicions of intellectuals as a "new class" have come to include doubts about the nature of social justice or the value of truth or the reality of expertise. This antimodernist or neopopulist mood (which also has antecedents in the last century's end) tends, especially on the "Left," to debilitate the intellectual's ability to engage productively in public or democratic debate at all.

I am interested in what the term "organic" has come to imply and how, in critiques of New Class administrators, "organic" has come to signify the desire for an alternative to the troublesome articulations of knowledge and power that are part of the traditional intellectual's social function. For the moment, to stay with Gramsci, I agree that "all men are intellectuals. . . . but all men do not have the function of intellectuals in society" ("Formation of Intellectuals," 121). Thus, though "homo faber cannot be separated from homo sapiens," there is a specific intellectual function in society that certain groups are specifically enabled to play. For Gramsci, the "traditional type of intellectual" is represented not only by the churchman but by "the literary man, the philosopher, the artist." Over and against these clerics, Gramsci imagines a "new class of intellectuals," different from the new class of managers and specialists, a group of intellectuals intimately associated with the life world of industrial workers: "In the modern world technical education, strictly tied to even the most primitive and unqualified industrial work, must form the basis for the new type of intellectual" (122). Here is the seed of what Stuart Hall has described as the project of the Birmingham Centre, the project from which so much in contemporary cultural studies still grows. That project, Hall says, involved the production of organic intellectuals whose education and expertise were based on an authentic experience of the conditions of the class for which they spoke.

This project, already complicated for Gramsci, has become radically more so today. Gramsci found the roots of his organic intellectual in the Factory Councils and their political project of self-representation. As Hall admits, intellectuals today have found no equivalent: "The problem about the concept of an organic intellectual is that it appears to align intellectuals with an emerging historical movement and we couldn't tell then and we can hardly tell now, where that emerging historical movement was to be found" (281). Despite all the fascinating work on subcultures and fandom, intellectuals today lack an easily identifiable emergent class, a hero of historical agency—Marx's proletariat, Mao's Third World peasantry, or even Gouldner's new class planners—with which to forge an organic relationship.[13] In cultural studies, this is the gap that contemporary identity-based politics in the United States and the populist class-based politics of Britain attempt to fill. But as we shall see in the following pages, considering any of these as preconstituted groups in which a politics might be grounded poses embarrassing problems for aspiring organic intellectuals.

Like Stuart Hall and so many others, I evoke Gramsci as my authority. Like Boggs's distinction between technocratic and critical intellectuals, Gramsci's frequently cited distinction between traditional and organic intellectuals is complexly fissured and the flawed foundation of much confusion. For example, Gramsci's preferred case of traditional intellectuals, the ecclesiastics, can historically also be considered organic intellectuals in their relation to the dominant feudal class. Thus, Gramsci writes, "the category of the ecclesiastics can be considered as the intellectual category organically tied to the landed aristocracy" ("Formation of Intellectuals," 119). For Gramsci, the identity of intellectuals is always relational and dynamic. Moreover, the political valence of these categories and of the opposition they may represent cannot be decided in advance. To take a more contemporary example, Pat Robertson, minister of the 700 Club, may well be understood as an intellectual organically related to conservative Christians whose desire to saturate public institutions with Christian prayer and to abrogate the reproductive rights of women and the civil rights of gay men and lesbians does oppose what may be understood (and what is understood by the Christian Right) as a hegemonic, "humanistic," liberal and secular dominant order. That does not mean, however, that Robertson represents a viable "counterhegemonic" order that progressive intellectuals should support. As Stuart Hall remarks, Margaret Thatcher may be the most successful example of an organic intellectual anyone has seen in recent years. But where does that leave us?

Before the pathos of epochal consciousness carries us away (as it too often does in reflections on intellectuals), I would add that this was already a problem for Gramsci himself, whose links to the Factory Councils were not as simply organic, not as free of the politics of class, knowledge, and imposition, as populists today might wish. In an editorial in *Ordine Nuovo*, Gramsci wrote:

It is essential to convince the workers and peasants that it is above all in their own interest to submit to the permanent discipline of education and to create a conception of their own world and the complex and intricate system of human relations, both economic and spiritual, which shapes social life on the globe.[14]

Here Gramsci avows that intellectuals, not workers and peasants, sometimes know what is best for workers and peasants, and that what is best for workers and peasants is sometimes that they become more like intellectuals, those whose task it is to create socially active conceptions and politically useful representations of the world. Moreover, I do not offer this as a critique of Gramsci. In fact, I think Gramsci is right.[15] If intellectuals sometimes project their guild values—respect for accuracy and fairness in argument and an adherence to ideals of social and economic justice as civic virtues, for example—onto those they purport to represent, then this may be not only unavoidable but necessary for the work of recruitment and persuasion that remains the intellectual's critical task. To perform that task, we may have to forget populism.

Local transcendentals and specific universals

Today many intellectuals, and frequently those writers who are the most interesting, seem at a loss to characterize themselves as intellectuals or seem to want altogether to dispense with the burden of such an embarrassingly laden term, one freighted with the discredited hopes of the Enlightenment and the disreputable claims of Jacobin vanguards.[16] This confusion on the part of intellectuals has sometimes been called postmodernity. I think it is time we stopped our dithering. Following Benda, Edward Said has attempted to reclaim for the intellectual the task of "speaking truth to power" and has also argued that "in the outpouring of studies about intellectuals there has been far too much defining of the intellectual, and not enough stock taken of the image, the signature, the actual intervention and performance, all of which taken together constitute the very life-blood of every real intellectual." [17] I want to take some of that stock in this book, and I begin by noting that—as Said points out—certain universalizing absolutes (if not Benda's Platonic transcendentalism) are a crucial part of any intellectual's tool kit and burden:

The central fact for me is, I think, that the intellectual is an individual endowed with a faculty for representing, embodying, articulating a message, a view, an attitude, philosophy or opinion to, as well as for, a public. . . . The intellectual does so on the basis of universal principles: that all human beings are entitled to expect decent standards of behavior concerning freedom and justice from worldly powers or nations, and that deliberate or inadvertent violations of these standards need to be testified and fought against courageously. (Said, 11–12)

I like Said's frank and forthright definition, but I am also aware (as he is too) that this definition is the beginning rather than the end of the intellectual's problem.

In accruing to oneself the claim to speak truth, to represent truth, one also represents oneself as one entitled or empowered by talent, or training, or institutional position to do so. Said's self-avowed romance with the intellectual as a figure of distance, exile, and opposition somewhat blunts his own appreciation of the fact that these days intellectuals tend to be academic experts—though they are not always credentialed experts in the fields they purport to criticize. I think Said rests too much on his identification of the intellectual as an amateur, since few intellectuals in a society ruled by an ethos of professionalism could achieve any hearing or legitimacy except as credentialed experts in some field. Said's own effectiveness as an intellectual to some measure grows from his position as University Professor at Columbia University, even though his work on Palestinian rights and the history of Orientalism is not obviously connected to his more professionally delimited books on literary theory or the Victorian novel.

Intellectuals need to wrestle with such "facts" of their situation. The intellectual is neither dead nor absent. The Enlightenment, with all its problematic pretensions to universality, continues to ground any progressive politics that intellectuals can imagine. The bid for power and the inherently unpopular tendencies of the intellectual's critical task cannot be negotiated away or hidden behind general appeals to subversion or exile, the organic or democracy. And finally, these "facts" are the beginning of the intellectual's problems, not the solution to them.

Critics of intellectuals usually distrust the transcendent in exactly the same measure in which they distrust its associated term, the universal. Critics of these critics, both those self-identified as on the "Right" and those self-identified as on the "Left," unite in bemoaning this distrust of transcendent values and universal principles, which they agree is the root of all contemporary evils. Thus conservatives such as Allan Bloom, Dinesh D'Souza, and Lynne Cheney and progressives such as Terry Eagleton, Christopher Norris, and Todd Gitlin speak in one voice when they speak of relativism, perspectivism, and skepticism.[18] But this unity does not, in my view, mean that either side is right. Reinvigorating intellectual self-confidence by a virile renunciation of relativism and uncertainty is, at the present moment, neither possible nor desirable.

Here, once again, Konrad and Szelenyi seem positively apt. They argue that the tradition of transcendence is not itself eternal; it has a complex narrative history in the West since the Enlightenment:

What is to be viewed as transcendent in the knowledge of various ages depends on who is doing the viewing, and from what vantage point. Similarly, knowledge may have a different significance in different eras; at one time it may qualify as transcendent, at another as historically determined, and indeed with the passage of time it may lose its value altogether. (21)

However vexed the history of transcendence is, the appeal to transcendent values remains indispensable to the work critical intellectuals do.[19] One implication of this unimpeachable bit of common sense is that transcendence, historically determined and constantly shifting, is always with us. Without it we would be incapable not only of projecting alternatives to the world as it presses on us but even of imagining the necessity of doing so. As Bruce Robbins puts it, on the issue of transcendence, it may be less important to take sides on "philosophical absolutes" than to understand "a set of ongoing social practices."[20]

Thus, when critics like Bloom and Gitlin criticize professional academic humanists for abandoning the transcendent in favor of the political, they are, symptomatically, both right and wrong. They are right to identify widespread suspicion concerning the value and nature of universals; they are wrong to claim that universals have been abolished. They are right that abandoning the transcendent would be catastrophic for intellectuals; they are wrong to suggest that this is what intellectuals have done. Even those who claim to have done so in the name of critical relativism or enthusiastic populism have not been able to accomplish this abandonment. In fact, I doubt that it can be done without compromising the possibility of critical thought altogether.

Nonetheless, critics of an illusory relativism have real reason to be worried. We all do. For appeals to the transcendent cannot remove us from the realm of politics or the vagaries of history in which contending claims for truth and transcendence urged from antagonistic positions and points of view require adjudication. The transcendent, however contingent and conflicted it may be, remains a necessary part of, and grounding for, any politics and any political position at all. Universality and transcendence are not philosophical absolutes; they are contested terms in political disputes.[21] Moreover, in some situations, the special interests and particular values of intellectuals—respect for reasoned argument, respect for facts, respect for the objects of study or criticism—do offer useful forms of transcendence and of opposition. Konrad and Szelenyi call this local, specific, historically determined and context-dependent form of transcendence "cross-cultural significance," a reservoir of values and commitments beyond a given immediacy or popular practice that offer critical leverage or grounds. I would call them local transcendentals or specific universals. The leverage or grounds they provide are not only valuable; they are politically and intellectually indispensable.

Can one acknowledge an aspiration toward the transcendent as the basis for intellectual work in the realm of popular politics at the same time one attempts to specify the ways in which transcendence is historically determined? Can one say, with Konrad and Szelenyi, "we do not wish to deny the existence of transcendent elements in the activity of intellectuals, only to make them relative" (22), and continue to do the intellectual's work of recruitment and persuasion? If their statement paradoxically divides against itself—between relativism and the universal—that too is symptomatic of the intellectual's position, of what Konrad and Szelenyi; call a certain "schizophrenia inherent in the intellectual's role" (22). Schizophrenia is symptomatic of the intellectual's situation as a cross-cultural alien in most of the public contexts where critical intellectuals today work. Schizophrenia may indeed be the symptom that, to borrow a phrase from Žižek, we must learn to enjoy.

The intellectual's schizophrenia results from a double bind that cannot be resolved. On the one hand, history teaches again and again that appeals to universals and to transcendence—appearing in the twentieth century in the guise of world-historical classes, movements, or geists—tend to mask the impositions of self-interested elites and the victimization and silencing of troublesome or dissonant differences. Even without recourse to Adorno and Horkheimer's problematic critique of enlightened violence and the administered society, it is apparent that in social groupings whose members have become increasingly aware of their own heterogeneity, uncritical attempts to impose normative understandings as transcendent values or specific constructions of universal reason easily legitimate policies of oppression and exclusion that exacerbate rather than ameliorate the splits and conflicts within communities and the injustices that attend them.[22] On the other hand, without an appeal to the transcendent—to that which does not manifest itself clearly in a given situation and which projects an improvement in or advances a solution for a pressing problem, to that which articulates in practice principles of justice or standards of truth on which in theory at least all might imagine themselves to agree—there can be no intellectuals, no politics, and no community at all. Neither populism nor postmodernism offers an escape from this double bind.

Carl Boggs makes a persuasive case for considering the history of critical intellectuals as an ongoing conflict between Jacobin and anti-Jacobin tendencies. In particular, his readings of Marx and Gramsci document a long anti-Jacobin tradition on the Left. Yet as Boggs also shows, even the most determinedly anti-Jacobin strain in the Marxist tradition has always been marked by conceptual ambiguities and historical ambivalences (see Boggs, 37–62). The explicit or implicit populism of much contemporary work by cultural studies intellectuals continues this anti-Jacobin tradition.

In criticizing that populist strain, I intend not to take the side of Jacobin over organic intellectuals but to shift the terms of the dispute. No one at this moment is about to grant a determining role to a revolutionary vanguard of intellectuals.[23] And yet, though many have tried, no one can really imagine a politics in which critical intellectuals blend harmoniously into the communities they seek to serve and to represent. Despite the almost ubiquitous currency of the term "community" these days—especially among the anti-Jacobin Left—neither community nor democracy can ground the intellectual's work. They are instead the horizon of the intellectual's problem. Politics for intellectuals—and there can be no politics and no community without the representative and representational work of intellectuals—must always be a negotiation between or among conflicted positions. As I have already argued, this negotiation can occur—criticism itself can occur—only in the light of certain values whose transcendence is assumed and whose presence depends on the intellectuals' willingness to assume the Jacobin project as Boggs describes it and to "appear as theoretical architects who can overcome the limits of effective social reality" by appeal to a certain "universality of goals—for example, nationalism, democracy, the general will, revolution" (16). Although Boggs enumerates these elements as constitutive of "Jacobinism as an historical phenomena" (16), I offer them here more as a description of the necessary conditions of the intellectual's work. My only prescription is that intellectuals stop deluding themselves into believing that the values they seek to advance necessarily originate in the communities they address.

Unlike Alvin Gouldner, I do not look to the New Class (if it be one) as in itself a repository of progressive values. I do not believe that the New Class of intellectuals is "the most progressive force in modern society and is a center of whatever human emancipation is possible in the foreseeable future" (Gouldner, 83). Nor do I believe that the New Class, in itself, is the source of all our woes. For one thing there are too many diverse traditions of intellectuals and intellectual work with equally diverse political valences. In our society, the empowered intellectuals tend to be not cultural intellectuals but their colleagues among scientists and engineers.[24] The sort of contested and contesting universalism that I posit here does not bespeak any hope I cherish for a reconstitution of transcendence as a universal ground; rather, it represents my sense of the terms in which our struggles must be engaged, the terms in which they are engaged even when we are reluctant to acknowledge that fact.

Grand narratives and identity politics

On another level of abstraction, consider the oft repeated announcement that postmodernity means the end of the grand narratives, many of which, especially the political and secular ones, originate in the Enlightenment. The production and legitimation of these grand narratives, the grounding myths of progress and salvation, were the intellectual's most important contribution to society. Their end, we are told, means the end of intellectuals as well.[25] This account of postmodernity has become a grand narrative in itself, though what it actually tells us about our contemporary condition is not always clear.

Bernard Yack is one intellectual who finds this postmodern narrative unpersuasive. He sees postmodernity as one "fetish of modernity" rather than modernity's end.[26] In more concrete terms, Yack, like Richard Rorty, seems to think that postmodernists have misunderstood both history and the Enlightenment. I agree with much of what Yack says about the complexity of the Enlightenment. I agree with much of his critique about the oversimplified unidimensionality of contemporary attempts to describe a shift in epochal consciousness marking modernity's end. Yet there does seem to have been a shift in consciousness nonetheless, though it may be less epochal than many have claimed.

For example, Yack concludes the chapter in which he most directly addresses postmodernity (characterizing it as a "figment of a fetish") with the following remarks:

> The spectacular potency of distinctly modern ideas and practices has given rise to the illusion that new ideas necessarily lead to new epochs. . . . The worldly impact of distinctly modern forms of knowledge is completely unprecedented. To expect post-modern forms of knowledge to have a similar impact on the human condition is to lose sight of one of the most important and unique features of the modern age. (87)

Yack claims that, postmodern denials to the contrary notwithstanding, modernity continues substantially unchanged.[27] Yet his narrative reveals that from the intellectuals' point of view, something has indeed changed. For if intellectuals, attaching their hopes to the utopian aspirations of certain modern ideas of rationality and justice, might once have hoped to change the world by changing the world's mind, they can now neither cherish hopes for such an epochal change nor believe in such power lodged within ideas. This may be a shift within an epoch (which was always one available reading of Lyotard's version of the postmodern), but as a shift, it is significant. However nuanced this shift may be, few contemporary intellectuals enjoy immunity from its effects, not even those like Yack and Rorty who insist that nothing much has changed.

Here again is the intellectual's double bind. Grand narratives continue to emplot the intellectual's relation to the world while intellectuals have come to doubt the validity of such constructions. Antagonistic positions require being thought together even at the risk of a certain schizophrenia.

This schizophrenia manifests itself frequently in cultural studies and its relationship to identity politics. Here a struggle against cultural exclusion and against universalized norms of taste or judgment and a championing of identity based and communal particularities have seemed to furnish a sort of political grounding. It may be true on one level of analysis that, as Andrew Ross puts it in an influential essay, intellectual work "now draws upon many different schools of ethical action, informed not by 'universal' (i.e., Western) humanist values, but by the specific agendas of the new social movements against racism, sexism, homophobia, pollution, and militarism." [28] It is also certainly true that so-called Western humanist values are products of a particularly vexed and unsavory historical process implicated in the exploitation, expropriation, and oppression of the rest of the world. Nonetheless, the fact remains that the specific agendas of the popular movements against racism, sexism, homophobia, pollution, and militarism to which Ross refers (and we can easily add colonialism to the list) depend inevitably for their moral focus and rhetorical leverage on commitments to the very "universal," even humanistic, and traditionally intellectual values to which Ross attempts to oppose them: justice, equality, respect for facts, and freedom from domination. Moreover, the relationship between a decentered identity politics and a reliable progressive orientation seems more and more vexed. As Bill Readings suggests, a certain "pietistic leftism" structuring much work in cultural studies actually bespeaks a widespread anxiety "that there is no longer an automatic leftist orientation to the struggle against cultural exclusion." [29] Identity politics can be invoked to justify racism as well as to attack it. This is regularly done by those who want to restrict immigration or persecute Jews and African Americans in order to defend the particularity of a white Christian identity defining an organic, racist community. Readings has a point. Critics working in cultural studies have difficulty specifying what they mean by politics beyond a by now familiar and inadequate critique of exclusionary practices.

Cary Nelson's *Manifesto of a Tenured Radical* exemplifies this problem. Nelson's marching orders for cultural studies seek to mobilize its radical potential in a concerted attack on the abusive treatment of graduate students and adjunct faculty. About cultural studies, Nelson asserts that it "is the social and textual history of varying efforts to take up the problematic of the politics and meaning of culture," and that it "is concerned with the social and political meanings and effects of its own analyses." He thunders in conclusion that "to avoid facing this challenge and retreat into academic modesty . . . or claims of disinterested scholarship . . . is to hide from cultural studies' historical mission." Yet despite the Jacobin energy of his reference to a historical mission for cultural studies, he offers little direction about the actual character of its mission or the specific contents of its politics beyond the assertion that cultural studies works to discredit invidious distinctions between elite and popular cultures as well as all other forms of hierarchical exclusion.[30]

These are laudable aims, and I have no trouble endorsing them. But given the confusions and incoherences of identity positions and identity politics, it is difficult to make such tepid pluralism seem like a world-historical mission. In fairness to Nelson, he struggles hard with this problem. He says, for example, that cultural studies "needs now to critique its investment in what has been called the Left's 'mantra of race, class and gender,' categories that are properly considered both in relation to one another and to the culture as a whole" (66–67), but he doesn't allow himself to say much about what would ground such a critique. This is a problem if the identity categories that have grounded work in the field now become its object.

Nelson, I think, shies away from the answer not because he does not know it but because the answer is in itself embarrassingly simple. Interesting to note, when he turns to the substantial political analyses and concrete recommendations that provide the most bracingly radical and practically challenging sections of his book, he relies on recognizably orthodox Marxist narrativizations of labor, value, and exploitation rather than criticism of identity-based exclusionary practices. Not a postmodernist politics of identity and culture but a grand narrative, dependent not only on Marx but on the Enlightenment traditions of political economy and moral philosophy that shaped Marx's (and our) view of the world, enables Nelson's most effective polemics.

My point is not to offer class analysis as the only grounds for politics, nor to offer a Marxist critique of cultural studies. My point is that whenever we assert specific political positions, we rely on grand narratives to orient our polemics and to provide them with persuasive force. If I were to issue marching orders of my own, I would say that we must stop pretending that we have gotten beyond the vexed and conflicted Enlightenment traditions, the duplicitous and embattled grand narratives, that none of us on the Left has ever really been able to do without. We must stop distrusting the big words that make us so unhappy: justice, equality, solidarity, compassion, rationality, and the rest. But we must also remember that these large abstractions will never resolve the arguments in which we engage. They are the terms in which those arguments must be conducted, the terms that those arguments themselves must specify. The simplicity of this answer in principle (I almost wrote "in theory") does nothing to reduce the complexity of the problems that demand our attention. Without this answer, however, I do not see how we can make progress. We need to know not how to agree on these things (agreement not always being possible) but how to quarrel over them.

In this light, Readings's observations appear only partially correct. It is true that cultural inclusiveness has no particular political orientation in itself, but it is also true that prejudicial practices of exclusion take place within a cultural environment and a tradition of intellectual work where Enlightenment values like justice, equality, and self-determination still possess a great deal of force. Therefore, those who argue for or practice prejudicial exclusion in the interests, let's say, of preserving Western or European civilization betray the best traditions of the culture they purport to defend. I use the word "best" self-consciously and without apology. The ideals of the Enlightenment, the ideals of progressive politics—of a politics that seeks to make the world more just and to reduce the quantity of human suffering—are the best of the West, though they are not exclusively Western. My point is simply that we are never and cannot be freed from the grand narratives that continue to structure our understanding of the world and to furnish the grounds on which intellectuals and the communities they try to represent contest political issues. That these "universals" are the problematic grounds for local conflicts rather than the transcendental categories of common sense only means that intellectuals who seek to speak out of and for the best traditions of Western progressiveness must hold to and champion them all the more energetically.

The university and the public sphere, the two realms in which intellectuals work and are worked on by others, should function today as dissensual communities, to borrow a phrase from Bill Readings. The Enlightenment tradition to which I am referring does not provide a common identity on which communal harmony might be established, as Habermas imagines. Rather, it offers a panoply of competing perspectives in what Readings has called—following Jean-Luc Nancy and Maurice Blanchot—a "community without identity," a "community of dissensus that presupposes nothing in common" (Readings, 189–90). But the end of such a community, in the university or in our civil society, cannot simply be—as Readings puts it—"to make its heteronomy, its differences more complex" (190). Such a project sounds a lot like the tepid pluralism that Readings began by criticizing. Rather, if we critical and technical intellectuals are going to talk politics, then our project can only be to strive to make justice, truth, and goodness prevail. If we are to do that, we must first win an audience over to recognize their understanding of these terms as our own. This may be an impossible project to theorize, but in the chapters of this book, I hope to show that it is an impossible project to avoid. It is also, I believe, one clearly worth pursuing.

The work at hand

In part 1, I concentrate on some current polemics among intellectuals regarding the nature of the intellectual's task. I consider controversies surrounding the public sphere and publicity, pedagogy and emancipation, community and judgment, culture and politics, as they emerge in specific, particularly revealing contexts. These include the media celebration of "black intellectuals" (chapter 1), the assumptions of progressive education (chapter 2), the problem of community as it appears in the work of neo-pragmatists (chapter 3), and the relation of relativism to global politics in the new world order (chapter 4). Thus the first four chapters form a group in which I consider some fundamental confusions in contemporary debates about academic intellectuals. In general, I argue that none of the currently attractive intellectual positions—neither traditional models of intellectual influence and authority, nor populist appeals to participant democracy, nor evocations of community, nor theories of cultural relativism or social constructionism—can ground or orient an intellectual's fundamental and fundamentally political commitments. Each of these positions does, however, symptomatically represent a problem in the way intellectuals today must do their work.

In part 2, I consider three important figures for the intellectual in contemporary society, both within the university and in society at large: the intellectual as critic, as scientist, and as professional. In each case, as in part 1, I have focused on a specific instance of a practice or controversy that I have found especially revealing: critical studies of fandom (chapter 5), popularizations of physicist Stephen Hawking as a universal intellectual (chapter 6), and the "science wars" as a model of interdisciplinarity in democratic societies (chapter 7). In each of these chapters, and especially in the last, the figure of the organic intellectual, the ego-ideal for many Left-oriented workers in cultural studies today, wrestles perpetually with a demon double in the figure of a traditional counterpart. Science, or the figure of the scientist, figures prominently here because the scientist as expert may be the most powerful image of the intellectual today. In pop culture, the scientist appears either as the last, forlorn hope that something like a universal intellectual or a philosopher king might be found to save us from our political disputes and practical confusions, or as the evil of the New Class personified and empowered. None of these representations is simply accurate or true, but if we take them together, we can trace an ongoing, crucial negotiation between expert imposition and popular resistance.

These struggles, the necessary political conflicts of a heterogeneous democratic culture, are one sign that intellectuals are on the job and doing the vexed and conflicted interdisciplinary work that it is their special task to do. I am not suggesting interdisciplinarity—as figured in science studies, for example—as an alternative to the professionalized multiversity that Clark Kerr first named in 1963 and that, as Boggs remarks, remains "the hegemonic form of academic life in the 1990s" (111); but I am trying to describe what interdisciplinarity, professionalism, science, culture, and democracy have to do with one another in a conflicted realm where multiplicity rather than universality rules the field. In this field, the critical intellectual finds a crucial contemporary task to play in the realm of popular politics.

PART

Cultural Authority, Enlightenment Traditions, and Professional Anxiety

ONE

1

Publicity: Black Intellectuals as Inorganic Representatives

A group of African American professors who also write for a popular audience has received more sympathetic press than most academic intellectuals in the aftermath of the culture wars. Both in and beyond the university, these "black public intellectuals" have attracted notice as representatives of the "black community." They are the most recent and the most seductive avatar of a specter that has long haunted leftist intellectuals (though conservatives have their own versions): the specter of the organic intellectual. Intellectuals with progressive aspirations have long sought remedy for the schizophrenia of their status as cross-cultural aliens, elites attempting to work in the interests of "the people," in a particularly populist construction of Gramsci's notion of the organic intellectual. The desire to be organic intellectuals, as Stuart Hall, Fredric Jameson, and others have suggested, most often motivates the enterprise of cultural studies today.[1] That desire, however, is much older than cultural studies and much more widely pervasive among leftist thinkers. As a promised solution to the seemingly intractable problem of presuming to speak for another in the interests of liberation, empowerment, and democracy, the desire to be an organic intellectual may be an indispensable component of any thought that imagines itself to be progressive. For this reason, intellectuals in the West have periodically sought heroic organic models for the work they do. An examination of the small, not necessarily representative group of African American academics who have been presented in the media as candidates for the position of exemplary organic intellectual will suggest both the promises and the problems of the organic intellectual as a model for critical work.

That the organic links between identity and intellectual insight or identity and political orientation are never given but always to be forged, that in fact neither linkages nor identities are ever organic at all, would not seem to require much reflection or defense these days. Yet black intellectuals as diverse as Adolph Reed, Toni Morrison, and Michael Eric Dyson have recently felt it necessary to address the issue of their relationship to other black Americans because the desire for organic intellectuals still persists and tends to attach itself to these "authentic" voices from the African American "community." The desire to discover organic intellectuals plays out in representations of these figures (and sometimes in their self-representation) in ways that may help us to see the real conditions in which public intellectuals labor. The condition of black intellectuals today is peculiar, but it is not unique. They offer a particular perspective on the problematics of representation and power that inevitably attend the intellectual's inorganic relationship to those for and to whom he or she speaks.

In 1995 public intellectuals, long thought to be a vanishing species in the United States, suddenly appeared to repopulate the public sphere. Robert S. Boynton, in a cover story in the *Atlantic Monthly*, proclaimed that the intellectual had reappeared:

> Nearly a decade after an influential book declared the public intellectual extinct, an impressive group of African-American writers and thinkers have emerged to revive and revitalize that role. They are bringing moral imagination and critical intelligence to bear on the definingly American matter of race—and reaching beyond race to voice what one [of them] calls "the commonality of American concern." [2]

Russell Jacoby's pessimism had been unwarranted. Public intellectuals were back "in Black," as Michael Hanchard, writing in the *Nation*, put it.[3]

Boynton attempted the bizarre and, I think, symptomatic project of linking the black intellectuals to the New York intellectuals of the fifties dubbed (and fetishized) by Russell Jacoby as *The Last Intellectuals*.[4] Both Hanchard and Adolph Reed, writing in the *Village Voice*, criticized Boynton for paying scant attention to the long tradition of African American intellectual work that offers a more appropriate frame of reference. Reed in particular focused on the symptomatic status of the "black public intellectual," of whose celebrity in mainstream American culture he is deeply suspicious:

> In the last few months, the notion [of the black public intellectual] has gained greater currency. It has been addressed in successive articles by Michael Alan Bérubé in *The New Yorker* and Robert Boynton in *The Atlantic*, while Leon Wieseltier's right-for-the-wrong-reasons attack on Cornel West in *The New Republic* has spawned commentary by James Ledbetter and Ellen Willis in *The Voice*. Although these white writers obviously didn't invent the black public intellectual identity, they have certainly anointed it as a specific, notable status in upper-middlebrow American culture.[5]

That status, not wholly invented but certainly constructed in article after article in mainstream middlebrow publications around this time, is the notable status of black writers as models of organic intellectual activity.

Adolph Reed identifies a certain "racial vindicationism" that has exerted a distorting pressure in work by and about African American intellectuals, one manifestation of which has been a tendency to identify those intellectuals as organic representatives of a putative black community.[6] This alone makes them notably different from the New York intellectuals with whom they are often compared and whose mantle as public intellectuals they have, according to some especially breathless commentators, assumed. Those largely Jewish modernists were never seen—nor did they ever claim—to be organically tied to any group or identity. Rather, their most cherished self-representation and public image was, as Bruce Robbins has shown, the ideal of the "luftmensch," or free-floating intellectual: independent of, and untied to, any concept of community. The African American intellectual, by contrast, appears on the public stage—as he usually has in the United States—tethered to a burden of representationality. More recently additional weight has been added in the form of an injunction for organic linkage to, and identity with, the "community" these intellectuals are supposed to represent. Thus a Gramscian ideal rather than a Mannheimian myth furnishes the peculiar problematic—or at least the special problem—that the African American intellectual faces. Yet it may well be that this problem, while it is especially evident among black intellectuals today, is not finally special to them but the general burden any intellectual who seeks to speak to and for any "community" confronts.

Thus Henry Louis Gates Jr., Cornel West, bell hooks, Patricia Williams, Toni Morrison, Michael Eric Dyson, Stanley Crouch, Shelby Steele, and Michele Wallace—to name only a few—have been anointed authentic spokespeople for, and on behalf of, an organic community whose identity these writers both help form and must reflect. As the heterogeneity of this list suggests, the only criteria of selection here may be, as Reed witheringly suggests, "black people who write social commentary and are known to white elite institutions" ("Drums," 31). That these diverse black intellectuals must strive "to express the will of the racial collectivity," as Reed reminds us, means that they have assumed the conventional task assigned by the dominant culture to the African American intellectuals it elevates to prominence. To say this, however, is not to exhaust this phenomenon's significance, nor is it necessarily to describe what they are doing. That there should be so much attention paid to black intellectuals in the dominant popular and academic culture at this time suggests not only the depth of paranoia and the urgency of desire directed by the dominant culture toward the African American "community" but also the persistence of a longing among intellectuals both "white" and black for a more organic relationship to an audience beyond the academy that they might imagine addressing. The ways in which these desires get elicited and complicated in the present turbulent intellectual and social climate require analysis.

Race, intellectuals, and American community: identity politics and its discontents

The problem of community in U.S. society is one that presses especially hard on African American intellectuals. This is in part because black intellectuals are increasingly visible in U.S. culture and also because the African American "community" is widely assumed to be in crisis. Yet despite declining standards of living for most African Americans (and for Americans generally), the situation of black intellectuals seems never to have been better. As Gerald Early has remarked, "for the first time in African-American history there is a powerful, thoroughly credentialed and completely professionalized black intellectual class." They are, as Early describes them, "the putative leaders of a generation of other African Americans like themselves, highly literate, college-educated, fortysomething offspring of the civil rights movement and integration—Stanley Crouch, Shelby Steele, Bell Hooks [sic], Patricia Williams, Michael Eric Dyson, Michele Wallace, Stephen Carter, Glenn Loury." [7] These black intellectuals play a large role in the dominant culture's imagination as representatives of, and interpreters for, a race that still occupies a special and especially vexed place in the nation's imaginary. In addition, many progressive intellectuals have looked to these writers as organic intellectuals speaking as and for the African American community.

For this reason, the publication of The Future of the Race, a joint effort by Henry Louis Gates Jr. and Cornel West, two leading public intellectuals, was an important event. Reissuing W. E. B. DuBois's influential polemic "The Talented Tenth," each of these writers struggles with the question of intellectual responsibility and intellectual agency in communities where— from their perspective—the limits and borders are far from clear and the space of belonging is always divided and conflictual. Here issues involving divisions along shifting and blurred distinctions of gender and class as well as race and xenophobia manifest themselves with particular force. Appeals to organic commitments or communities as grounds for the intellectual's work become especially problematic. Yet while they may be problematic as grounds for action, at the present moment the identity politics associated with issues of race in the United States may also be inescapable as conditions for thought.

Certainly, as Gerald Early has suggested, the ruminations of Gates and

West on the questions raised by DuBois in "The Talented Tenth" are thin and seem both self-involved and self-serving. Yet they are symptomatic of a problem of stratification and leadership that, while it bears a particular historical and structural weight for African American intellectuals, is also a problem for all intellectuals who seek to speak for a community and champion egalitarian or democratic ideals. The problem involves the distance and difference between the character and status of intellectuals and the communities they purport to represent. This ensures that whatever the relationship between intellectuals and community may be, it can never be simply organic.

There is nothing new about this problem. What is general and what is specific in the situation of black intellectuals today both appear in Adolph Reed's examination of DuBois's complex and ambivalent thinking about elites and their relationship to, and responsibilities for, the broader community. Of DuBois's view of society as expressed at midcareer in his 1940 autobiographical memoir *Dusk of Dawn*, Reed writes:

> He proposed a pyramidal view of the status and hierarchy of the black community, in which "the poor, ignorant, sick and antisocial form a vast foundation" and whose "highest members, although few in number, reach above the average not only of the Negroes but of the whites, and may justly be compared to the better-class white culture." He expressed a need for caution, however, in assessing this stratum's actual social historical role, noting, for example, the group's propensities to "conspicuous consumption" and frivolousness. He observed that upper-class blacks felt isolated and alone as a result of segregation. They were often unable or unwilling to share in middle-class white society on the terms in which it was offered, and at the same time they tended to recoil from the vulgarity of their own lower classes. (Reed, *Du Bois*, 65)

Certainly the alienation of middle-class blacks and their intellectuals is intensified by the racism—some of it internalized—of the dominant white society, but it is similar to the alienation of critical distance that intellectuals tend to feel not only toward the groups or practices they criticize but also toward the communities they attempt to champion. This is the less attractive but inevitable seamy side of the utopianism or transcendence that in some measure, as Konrad and Szelenyi and many others have argued, structures all critical thought.

Moreover, the very ideal of a community to be represented is often a production of intellectuals rather than a given fact of their situation. We tend to use, without reflection, terms like "African-American community" in close conjunction with other terms like "organic intellectual," but it takes little historical or critical reflection to realize that such terms, while valuable in analyzing stratified and divided societies, are highly problematic. Both Gates and West, in their essays on DuBois, bemoan the increasing cultural and material distance between middle-class and poor black Americans. This phenomenon, as Reed points out, had already attracted the attention of DuBois, who, writing in *The Crisis* in 1921, remarked that "the outstanding fact about the Negro group in America, which has but lately gained notice, is that it is flying apart into opposition [sic] economic classes." DuBois continues:

> This was to be expected. But most people, including myself, long assumed that the American Negro, forced into social unity by color caste, would achieve economic unity as a result, and rise as a mass of laborers led by intelligent planning to a higher unity with the laboring classes of the world.
>
> This has not happened. On the contrary, and quite logically, the American Negro is today developing a distinct bourgeoisie bound to and aping American acquisitive society and developing an employing and a laboring class. This division is only in embryo, but it can be sensed. (quoted in Reed, *Du Bois*, 68–69)

This analysis and criticism of the black bourgeoisie, taken up and expanded by E. Franklin Frazier and Harold Cruse, is the subtext or pretext of the predicament of the African American intellectual, like all intellectuals a product of the middle classes, to which Gates, West, and so many other black academics and writers today refer.

These problems are not uniquely African American problems. "White" Americans evoke identity politics, too, and dream of organic communities as well. Thus the liberal historian Arthur Schlesinger, for example, fears the "disintegration of the national community, apartheid, Balkanization, tribalization," in the United States if intellectuals and educators lulled by the siren song of multiculturalism forget that home is a place where the "American synthesis has an inevitable Anglo-Saxon coloration."[8] Certainly, when Schlesinger goes on to claim that the "republic embodies ideals that transcend ethnic, religious, and political lines," he seems to claim the moral high ground. Nonetheless, the inevitability of the Anglo-Saxon coloration he imagines as a neutral fact of national history bespeaks a certain unwillingness to abide by the transcendent ideals of the republic that the historian evokes. In the interests of fairness and as a historian, Schlesinger would have to admit that there are other ways of narrating the nation's identity given the determinate heterogeneity of its compositeness that he himself acknowledges. Such a narration might decompose and complicate without obviating the urgent importance of the identity categories and groups—always racial and gendered and inflected by class—that divide and define our sense of communal, if not common, identity.

Identity politics and white intellectuals

The attempt of white intellectuals like Schlesinger to construct and defend an untroubled category of "Western" or U.S. identity against the incursions and contamination of various racialized "non-Western" influences bespeaks the violence and reification of what Adorno relentlessly criticized as identity logic. Romantic versions of national identity, as Ernst Renan observed more than a century ago, require a determinate forgetting and repression of history: "Forgetting, I would even go so far as to say historical error, is a crucial factor in the creation of a nation, which is why progress in historical studies often constitutes a danger for [the principle of] nationality. . . . Unity is always effected by means of brutality."[9] There is no racial or cultural purity within the violently formed and determinately composite modern nation. Schlesinger's position demands that he forget the intensely violent history of cultural and racial confrontation and negotiation that produced this nation. Nations are not organic communities spawned by similarities in blood or culture; they are forced agglomerations produced by histories of conflict and accommodation. From the first, as Frank Shuffelton has pointed out, "our mixture resulted from years of confrontation, conflict, negotiation, and cooperation between culturally varied groups of European immigrants, Native Americans, and kidnapped Africans. The winds from all quarters of the globe had been blowing for centuries."[10] For Renan, the inevitable diversities of modern nations are, despite the romantic longing after chimerical ethnic or cultural purity, the source of their strength. "The noblest countries," he claims, "are those where the blood is most mixed" (Renan, 14). Recalling the inevitable mixture of a nation's metaphoric and literal blood may challenge certain constructions of national identity and certain versions of the nation's narrative, but it can also "goad [us] . . . to narrow the gap between practice and principle" so that what Schlesinger calls the nation's "noblest ideals of democracy and human rights" may not be so often "transgressed in practice" (Schlesinger, 118).

Years before Renan made his speech at the Sorbonne, Frederick Douglass, the nineteenth century's "representative colored man" in the United States, made similar arguments. In "Our Composite Nationality," a speech which he delivered in 1869, he opposed attempts to limit the immigration of groups then considered to threaten the nation's identity, especially Germans and Asians.[11] I am not attempting to reinvent Douglass as a hero of multiculturalism. Both his Eurocentric and gender biases have been sub-jected to revealing criticism.[12] But as an African American intellectual, Douglass felt compelled to remind the nation of its conflicted complexity. As he well knew, the national fantasy of cultural or racial homogeneity and harmony is usually produced, then as now, by forgetting the presence of Africans in America. As Henry Louis Gates remarks,

> In 1970, Ellison published his classic essay "What America Would Be Like Without Blacks," in *Time;* and one reason it is a classic essay is that it addresses a question that lingers in the American political un-conscious. Commanding as Ellison's arguments are, there remains a whit of defensiveness in the very exercise. It's a burdensome thing to refute a fantasy.[13]

The refutation of deleterious fantasies should be the task of all intellectu-als. In the United States, however, the burden has fallen disproportionately on African Americans. In part, this is the result of positioning, the differ-ence between finding oneself within or beyond the pale of a still dominant narrative of Anglo-Saxon coloration. However, for those attentive to his-tory and especially to the critical voices of African American intellectuals, this national coloration has never been simply inevitable. It has never been simple at all. In 1845, introducing Douglass's *Narrative of the Life of Fred-erick Douglass, an American Slave,* Wendell Phillips reminded his largely white readers of "the old fable of 'The Man and the Lion,' where the lion com-plained that he should not be so misrepresented 'when the lions wrote history.' "[14] In the long history of African American contestation of their exclusion from the national narrative, not only the misrepresentation of blacks but the misrepresentation of whites has frequently been called into question.

A countering version of the national narrative has long existed in which the identity of its dominant coloration is complexly determined by what it has traditionally sought to exclude. Thus, imagining U.S. identity apart from the implications of African Americans in it means more than just imagining American culture without its most typical African-inflected forms of dance, music, and verbal expression. Without an African pres-ence, American identity would not, in principle, be thinkable at all. Intel-lectuals seeking to comprehend the communities within and for which they work must try to remember this.

One can trace this counternarrative about the complex implications of a supposedly natural "whiteness" in the rejected and despised "blackness" that whites have violently sought to keep at a distance. Because, as Bene-dict Anderson has shown, national identity is a product of an imagined community that depends, among other things, on the production and consumption of narratives, it is not surprising that literary intellectuals have been particularly sensitive to, and sometimes critical of, this issue. The complexity of race and national identity so clearly manifest in U.S. history is also evident in the fictional works of—to choose only a few familiar examples—Mark Twain in *Pudd'nhead Wilson*, Nella Larsen in *Passing*, and William Faulkner in *The Sound and the Fury* and *Absalom! Absalom!* Recently, Toni Morrison, perhaps the best-known living U.S. novelist and a public intellectual of great importance, has made the point again. In her reading of the national narrative, "the potent and ego-reinforcing presence of an Africanist population" has been the constitutive element from the very beginning.[15] In the formation of a national identity, "this Africanist presence may be something the United States cannot do without":

> Americans did not have a profligate, predatory nobility from which to wrest an identity of national virtue while continuing to covet aristocratic license and luxury. The American nation negotiated both its disdain and its envy in the same way. . . . through a self-reflexive contemplation of fabricated, mythological Africanism. For the settlers and for American writers generally, this Africanist other became the means of thinking about body, mind, chaos, kindness, and love; provided the occasion for exercises in the absence of restraint, the presence of restraint, the contemplation of freedom and aggression; permitted opportunities for the exploration of ethics and morality, for meeting the obligations of the social contract, for bearing the cross of religion and following out the ramifications of power. (Morrison, 47–48)

Because their positioning within the ideology of the nation's identifications is so essential and so essentially conflicted, the renarration of American identity by African American intellectuals possesses great force and significance both for those who would defend America's dominant Anglo-Saxon coloration and for those who find this idea to be a whitewashed sham.

Positioning African American intellectuals

For these complex reasons, which I have been able only to sketch here, African American intellectuals have emerged today as perhaps the most important public intellectuals we have. Their racialized identity positions them on the most persistent and persistently shifting fault line of American national identity and community. They form a diverse and frequently contentious group: Henry Louis Gates, Cornel West, bell hooks, Spike Lee, and Toni Morrison are only a few African American cultural intellectuals who have been working to interrogate and transform America's understanding of itself. From the viewpoint of Americans identified with the dominant culture, the perspectives of these other Americans—representatives of a group whose exclusion has been constitutive to that dominant culture's self-understanding—and the power of the insights they have made available are both unsettling and undeniable.

Let me take one example that fixes itself in my mind. Critical legal studies scholar Patricia Williams's *Alchemy of Race and Rights: Diary of a Law Professor* begins with the following statement: "Since subject position is everything in my analysis of the law, you deserve to know that it's a bad morning." [16] In an exposition that is more literary than traditionally legal (though her point in part is to call that opposition, along with many others, into question), she introduces the reader to the field of contract law. The case in question involves the principle of redhibitory vice, "a defect in merchandise which, if existing at the time of purchase, gives rise to a claim allowing the buyer to return the thing and to get back part or all of the purchase price" (Williams, *Alchemy*, 3). So far, the introduction of the "bad morning" seems merely a stylistic device, disarmingly unexpected in this context, but little more. The point begins to prod the reader as Williams reveals that on this particular morning, the case she reads is an 1835 Louisiana suit involving the "redhibitory vice of craziness" and that the disagreement involves the purchase of a female slave named Kate, who was either stupid, according to the seller, or crazy, according to the buyer. Contract law specifies that stupidity is an apparent defect against which the law does not warrant, while madness is a redhibitory vice entitling the deceived purchaser to restitution (3). As the narrative of this bad morning unfolds, it becomes apparent that Williams's bad mood grows from her identification with the woman who appears as merchandise in this case and the ironic juxtaposition of a contemporary news item that implicates Williams as well, which she translates as follows: "Harvard Law School cannot find one black woman on the entire planet who is good enough to teach there, because we're all too stupid" (5). By now subject position has indeed become everything. It colors, so to speak, her reaction to, and identification with, the case law and news item she juxtaposes.

Yet subject position—what Todd Gitlin and others have criticized as perspectivism—is not everything, either. Williams's subject position, like any reader's, is complex and split. She is an African American woman; she is also a law professor and a specialist in contracts. The conflicted tensions of these various positions and diverse perspectives not only inform but constitute the argument of her book. She registers with special force the irony of injustice that renders an episode in an unfolding atrocity a case in contract law in which the history of that atrocity cannot appear as part of the argument. This would be the equivalent of allowing Nazi jurisprudence to figure as precedent in German courts. The legality of specific compacts appears against a background constructed by making the illegality of the larger social context disappear. Williams struggles, as a lawyer committed to the rationality and importance of legal procedures, to demonstrate the irrationality of such regularized irregularities.

Here one is obliged to make the traditional reference to DuBois's famous formulation of double consciousness as the lot of the African American intellectual, who must live both behind and beyond the veil of the color line. For African American intellectuals, this often presents itself as a particularly pressing problem — a problem involving their identities as organic intellectuals linked to a specific "community" and their relation to their varied audiences within and beyond the pale. The splits involved are frequently multiple. Patricia Williams figures this problem as a problem of audience: "To speak as black, as female, *and* [as a] commercial lawyer has rendered me simultaneously universal, trendy, and marginal" (*Alchemy*, 7). Which of her roles at a given moment are universal or trendy or marginal is somewhat unpredictable. Without the universalizing pretensions of the legal system within which she works, her particular perspective as a black woman would not have the point in her work it does. Within the legal profession, her insistence on speaking as a black feminist may marginalize her. Within the African American community, her status as a professional, a feminist, and an intellectual poses problems of its own.

The concept of an African American community may be indispensable to our political and moral reflections these days, denoting, as it does, the collectivity of people whose identities have been categorically mythologized and systematically imposed by a persistently racist and racialized dominant culture. And yet, as the situation of African American intellectuals makes clear, within the veil of that community, intellectuals find less of a universal grounding or univocal political perspective than those identified with the dominant culture have usually supposed. Gates, writing about Louis Farrakhan's place "in the mind of black America," puts it like this: "The political theorist Benedict Anderson has defined nations as 'imagined communities,' and the black nation is even more imaginary than most. We know that thirty-six million sepia Americans do not a collective make, but in our minds we sometimes insist upon it" (*Thirteen Ways*, 153). If black intellectuals frequently insist on an African American community for which they speak and from which they draw their force, they may be making a necessary gesture toward utopia. They may be hoping, as intellectuals have always done, to bring into being the community they purport to represent.[17]

As Williams, Gates, and Cornel West indicate, bringing this community into being requires complicated negotiations. These negotiations, which involve the frequently conflicted and sometimes tormented relationship between critical intellectuals and their communities, are foregrounded in *The Future of the Race*. Yet as some reviewers of this book complained, there seems to be nothing very radical or even controversial in the program for public intellectuals that the authors want to define. West, in his essay, offers the following definition of the public intellectual's fundamental role:

> The fundamental role of the public intellectual—distinct from, yet building on, the indispensable work of academics, experts, analysts, and pundits—is to create and sustain high-quality public discourse addressing urgent public problems which enlightens and energizes fellow citizens, prompting them to take public action. This role requires a deep commitment to the life of the mind—a perennial attempt to clear our minds of cant (to use Samuel Johnson's famous formulation)—which serves to shape the public destiny of a people. Intellectual and political leadership is neither elitist nor populist, rather it is democratic, in that each of us stands in public space, without humiliation, to put forward our best visions and views for the sake of the public interest. And these arguments are presented in an atmosphere of mutual respect and civic trust.[18]

West struggles with the elitism implicit in the intellectual's function—to clear our minds of cant—yet this statement implies the principle with which DuBois began his essay on the talented tenth: "The Negro race, like all races, is going to be saved by its exceptional men." It requires an exceptional person to clear our minds of cant. It requires an intellectual to clear away the cobwebs of superstition, prejudice, and misprision.[19] West does not succeed in reconstructing the "Victorian strategies" that DuBois adapted from Carlyle, Coleridge, and Matthew Arnold) ("those cultural and political elites"); he restates them.

As the program of a self-described revolutionary, this is admittedly pretty tame, and pretty disappointing. Adolph Reed, in a sustained bit of brilliant and ungenerous invective, castigates West in particular and the current cadre of black intellectuals in general for a safe and sentimental centrism that too often blames the victim and settles for a program of cultural uplift that is "left in form, right in essence" (Reed, "Drums," 31).[20] One would certainly welcome more public voices in opposition to rapacious and inhumane fiscal and public policies. Yet Gates, West, hooks, Dyson, and the others included in the media releases surrounding the re-emergence of public intellectuals "in black" are cultural intellectuals, so they tend to lack authority and persuasive clout in those areas. Although Patricia Williams writes persuasively on the lies, misperceptions, and cruelties intertwined with the current rage for welfare reform and against affirmative action, she is unlikely to play an important role in policy making. Economic reconstruction and public policy have become the special preserve of what Foucault called "specific" intellectuals. If not "universal" in fact, the role of the public intellectual is general in its aspirations. Cultural intellectuals work most authoritatively in the realm of signs and values. This work is important and valuable in its own right. Worth considering, however, is how difficult it is to play the role of public intellectual in a democratic culture.

One crucial aspect of the problem involves elitism and the ideal of community that is often offered to oppose it. Yet elitism, as West's less-than-persuasive rhetorical maneuver around the issue indicates, is not easy to escape. Nell Painter, in a review of The Future of the Race, points out that West and Gates "are taking upon themselves the Talented Tenth's early-twentieth-century responsibility to lead the race. . . . [to] 'guide the Mass away from the contamination and death of the Worst.' " The problem, she indicates, is that this project, like similar projects, depends on "two assumptions no longer so openly embraced: that it is possible to speak of African-Americans in the singular—as what used to be called 'the Negro' and now most often appears as 'the black community'—and that the authors in question possess authority to speak for the whole African-American race."[21] As Toni Morrison suggested, surveying the aftermath of the Clarence Thomas–Anita Hill confrontation, the time for speaking of a single black community may have passed.

Nell Painter makes an important point when she suggests that the gloominess of Gates's and West's assessment of the future of the race and their role as intellectuals with reference to it may be gendered and therefore distinct from her own somewhat more hopeful assessment. Gender issues have caused friction within the African American community for at least as long as they have in the dominant culture.[22] Media fascination with the perils of black masculinity and controversies surrounding Anita Hill's accusations, the O. J. Simpson trial, and the Million Man March have foregrounded these tensions. Moreover, as we will see in a later chapter, the figure of the public intellectual, the figure of mind itself, is popularly gendered male. Yet the gender-inflected Oedipal struggle with cultural forebears like DuBois accounts for only part of the pessimistic strain evident in The Future of the Race. Something in the nature of the community that the authors must evoke to ground their identities and to give their roles meaning is also important and is not without its gendered involvement.

Bell hooks, who has written well-known, trenchant critiques of black men for attempting to assume and perpetuate patriarchal positions, introduces Cornel West in a section of *Breaking Bread: Insurgent Black Intellectual Life*, which hooks and West coauthored. She begins her remarks with the following vignette, which is also a window into a familiar problem:

> Walking the wet streets of New York after we had talked together for hours, Cornel West paused to rap with a brother in a wheelchair, handing over a few dollars. Standing at a distance observing them, Cornel in his three piece suit, meticulously shined shoes, the brother wearing a mix-match of old clothes, his legs covered by a tattered blanket, I listened as they talked about how the struggle has changed since "We lost Malcolm." Cornel nods his head as the brother says, "We need more Malcolms." They stand talking in the wet, Cornel nodding his head, commenting. As we walk away, the brother calls out, "You're as good as Malcolm." Cornel responds, "I wish. I just do the best I can."[23]

This is a complicated moment that manages to be moving and unsettling at the same time. Hooks means to offer a moment of authentication and celebration, representing West as a truly organic spokesperson for "the fate of Black men" committed "to eradicating structures of domination that create and maintain suffering" by offering testimony concerning his "solidarity," his "sense of brotherhood," and "the knowledge that he must sustain his connection to the oppressed as it is that bond which brings him to the deepest level of history" (*Breaking Bread*, 22). She stands aside, a black woman who assumes the power to authenticate this vision of authentic community. On some level, this moment does all these things. A vision of organic community and an intellectual within it begins to coalesce around this scene.

Yet on closer consideration, the significance of this scene seems less clear. The man in the wheelchair gets enlisted as a poster child for the oppressed. What is he saying anyway? The casual reference to the few dollars exchanged for a moment of authentic conversation with a "brother," the complex mixing of condescension and kindness in West's gesture, the discomfiting suspicion that what has been purchased here is the right to use this man's image in the intellectual's campaign of self-promotion: these disrupt the vision that hooks means to evoke of an organic intellectual making contact with his community. Moreover, it is no disrespect to West's achievements and importance to note that the comparison between the Harvard professor and Malcolm X raises questions about just how deep the levels of history accessed here actually go. More poignantly, one wonders what West was talking about with this man. What had the lecturer at

"Harvard, Yale, Princeton, and countless other colleges and universities" (hooks, *Breaking Bread*, 21) to say to a man portrayed only as a member of the underclass? What to uplift him or help him to improve his condition? Hooks never tells us. But one is left suspecting that something like patriarchy, with West as the good black father and hooks as the approving mother, plays more of a role in the structure and content of this scene than either hooks or West would care to admit.

This is not a problem particular to hooks or West, nor to African American intellectuals in general. It is not my intention to, as Patricia Williams puts it, use the discourse of class division to slice "like a knife through the intensity and complexity of our life's connections" (*The Rooster's Egg*, 60). These divisions are problems for all intellectuals who seek to ameliorate this society's violence and cruelty. This meeting between "an extremely privileged Black man, and one of the underclass," represents a problem that confronts African American intellectuals with particular force, given the disproportionate effects of economic dislocation on black Americans, though it confronts all intellectuals at the present moment. The public intellectual's dream of addressing a community confronts an increasingly harsh reality: the forces of economic depredation and subjugation—borne disproportionately by African Americans—make any functional and inclusive model of community more and more difficult to imagine.

West and Gates spell out the material dimension of this problem in the preface to *The Future of the Race*. In the quarter century following Dr. Martin Luther King's murder,

> the size of the black middle class— . . . primarily because of affirmative action—has quadrupled, doubling in the 1980s alone. Simultaneously—and paradoxically—the size of the black underclass has grown disproportionately as well: in 1995, 45 percent of all black children are born at, or beneath, the poverty line. Economists have shown that fully one-third of the members of the African-American community are *worse off* economically today than they were the day that King was killed. (xii)

The social dislocations attendant on an increasingly unequal distribution of power, privilege, and wealth in American society generally manifest themselves with particular force among African Americans. In the face of such facts, an intellectual may well feel pretty helpless. As Gates puts it, the "black middle class has never been in better shape—and it has never felt worse about things" (Gates and West, 19). This is evidently true of those middle-class black intellectuals who now seek to take up DuBois's challenge. Gates sees that the "politics of solidarity—of unity, of 'sacred covenants'— . . . must inevitably run up against the hard facts of political economy" (36). Despite a "romantic black nationalism," which he says "has become the veritable socialism of the black bourgeoisie," the fact is that "enormous class disparities within the 'black community' . . . undermine the very concept of such a 'community' in the first place" (37). For black Americans even more than for whites, the viability of belief in an effective intellectual and political leadership is compromised by these developments.

Yet even the black middle class does not offer a secure grounding for those progressive middle-class intellectuals who would speak to and for it. Black leadership has always, as Gates points out, been in crisis mode with reference to its own constituency:

> Pollsters have long known of the remarkable gap between the leaders and the led in black America. A 1985 survey found that most blacks favor the death penalty and prayer in public schools while most black leaders opposed these things. Most blacks opposed school busing, while most black leaders favored it. Three times as many blacks opposed abortion rights as their leaders did. Indeed, on many key social issues, blacks are more conservative than whites. If the number of black Republicans is on the rise, as these opinion surveys suggest, it would be unwise to dismiss the phenomenon. (Gates and West, 33)

In fact, one need only mention Stanley Crouch, Shelby Steele, or the many African American critics cited in opposition to Gates and West and hooks to recall that there is no more reliable agreement among black intellectuals and between black intellectuals and their constituencies than there is for other intellectuals. Given these dismal facts, the role of the progressive black intellectual seems less importantly to explain "the mysteries of black America" for a white audience, as Adolph Reed mockingly claims (though such a project in a society still largely characterized at all levels by racial misprision is, despite Reed's sneering, still important). Rather, their primary function may have to be the attempt to lay down the law for a black "community" that seems less and less inclined to listen and increasingly unlikely to offer imaginable grounds for political action understood as organic commitment to a preconstituted and popular stand. If this task is inherently elitist, that may be the least of its problems.

If the identity and social positioning of black intellectuals offer no secure grounds for the intellectual's critical work, the perspectives these afford represent an important point of departure for his or her work, though no one should assume to know what that work should be, nor how it should be done. Gerald Early ends his review of *The Future of the Race* by evoking Oscar Wilde. "Would that some black might say," he wishes, " 'I have little interest in speaking to the poor and absolutely none in speaking for them, so how am I to be my brother's keeper as I must be?' " (Early, 7). It is a fine, twisted epigram. The burden of the poor and oppressed, the task to speak to and for them, can be neither fulfilled nor avoided. The knife of these divisions cannot cut us free, but it can make us bleed. The image of Cornel West hovering over the man in the wheelchair both evokes and obscures this fact. Progressive intellectuals can not afford too much sentimentality. Nor can they do without the hopes for connection and organic union this sentimentality sometimes inflects. For the intellectual, the perspective of a poor person is invaluable especially when the character of the poor is so often defamed by U.S. policy makers who work so hard to ensure that poverty will remain a problem. As he listens to this man, West may be performing an important task, one that will help him forge representations that might in turn help make a difference.

Poverty, however, is no proof against error. The poor cannot simply authorize the intellectual, nor can the intellectual simply represent the dispossessed. If, as Zygmunt Bauman has claimed, the role of the intellectual in a postmodern era is not to hand down the law but to interpret across the boundaries of different communities, one interpretation that intellectuals must make is where the boundaries of community fall, what they exclude and what they include within their limits. As indicated by the confrontation between progressive black intellectuals and those who would still forget the determinate Africanist presence at the nation's origins, who—in defiance of the historical record and the present moment—would still define an American community culturally, racially, or economically by its Anglo-Saxon coloration, these interpretations are likely to be conflictual. As the disjunctions that vex the notion of community among diverse African Americans in differing situations suggest, these conflicts happen within as well as between the groups or groupings that intellectuals address.

If African American identity offers no particularly secure grounds for intellectual action at the present moment, it does afford an indispensable perspective on the paradoxical and perilous groundlessness of intellectual work. This work may not be the revolutionary program of an organic spokesperson for an identity position or a world-historical vanguard. It is, however, the crucial intervention of critical intellectuals hoping to bring into being the more civil society they need to address and to move. In this struggle, one must assume the burden and privilege of whatever authority and prestige society affords. This is a struggle all progressive intellectuals share, and therefore black intellectuals speak to all of us despite the attempts of critics on the Right and on the Left to drown them out, to ignore them, or to appoint them representatives.

Robin Kelley, for example, begins *Yo' Mama's disFUNKtional!* with a telling description of representations of blacks and especially of black women in mainstream academic and popular media as a version of "playing the dozens," a game of exaggerated and frequently surrealistic insult associated with black urban youth culture. The depiction of African American life in the media and among "experts" often seems to be similarly grotesque, derogatory, and divorced from recognizable reality. As Kelley notes, having grown up in a world where "talking about somebody's mama was a way of life," he was surprised on reaching college to discover that "many academics, journalists, policy makers, and politicians had taken the 'dozens' to another level":

> I have had kids tell me that my hair was so nappy it looked like a thousand Africans giving the Black Power salute, but never has anyone said to my face that my whole family—especially my mama—was a tangle of "pathology." Senator Daniel Patrick Moynihan's "snap" has been repeated by legions of analysts and politicians, including Dinesh D'Souza, the boy wonder of the far Right. D'Souza has snapped on black people in such a vile manner that his version of the dozens dispenses with all subtlety. In *The End of Racism*, he says in no uncertain terms that African Americans have ushered in "a revival of barbarism in the midst of Western Civilization."[24]

Along with D'Souza and Moynihan, Kelley also cites Murray and Herrnstein—authors of *The Bell Curve*—and a host of still prevalent racial stereotypes ranging from welfare queens (who always seem to be black) and their numerous progeny to "naturally" talented musicians and athletes who might otherwise be depraved gang bangers and killers. The range of representations will surprise no one.

Although Kelley claims some ironic expertise at this agon of insults to which he compares the derogative, one-sided pictures of black pathology produced by intellectuals (not all of them white) in academia and the media, and though he offers his mother's mother, his mother, and his sister as counterexamples, representations of brilliantly functional black women, he adds a telling note on the limits of personal experience, of authenticity, to the work he has undertaken of offering a different representation, an other understanding of black urban life, one based on the struggles of a large, diverse, hardworking working class. "Unlike most writers these days," he says,

> I am not claiming absolute authority or authenticity for having lived there. On the contrary, it is because I did *not* know what happened to our world, to my neighbors, my elders, my peers, our streets, buildings, parks, our health, that I chose not to make this book a memoir.

Indeed, if I relied on memory alone I would invariably have more to say about devouring Good and Plentys or melting crayons on the radiator than about economic restructuring, the disappearance of jobs, the resurgence of racism, and the dismantling of the welfare state. (Kelley, 4–5)

For Kelley, as he undertakes the intellectual's task of representation, authenticity is not an issue. He might have pressed the point to remind us that by its very nature, representation can never be authentic, can never be the thing itself. Politics—given diverse modern societies and an unevenly globalizing local and world economy—does not occur on the level of the authentic. Although the effects of decisions and policies are excruciatingly real, the legitimation of those policies, the work that makes them seem palatable, plausible, or possible, occurs on the level of representations, the level on which intellectuals work and contend. And thus it is that Kelley joins what he calls "the ongoing battle over representations of the black urban condition" (8). This battle is an example of the work intellectuals do. In this work, questions of authenticity should not distract us from the real task at hand. Remembering this could clarify many issues that provoke useless debate these days, including arguments about the authenticity of various popular forms like hip-hop (about which Kelley also has a lot to say) and about the organic relations that may or may not exist between intellectuals and the various communities they address or seek to serve.

Unlike populist critics like John Fiske who tend to recognize types of resistance in any form of popular entertainment from watching television to shopping, Robin Kelley, even while championing the skill and commitment of black teenagers in the inner-city enclaves (youths who in the absence of jobs work at basketball, hip-hop, or prostitution), is careful to specify that these entrepreneurs tend to work within the dominant system, even when they work extralegally. They do not, as some populist theorists of various subcultures have argued, "challenge the structures of capitalism" (Kelley, 74). Nevertheless, Kelley is able to recognize and to represent the achievements and the agency in a variety of activities too often disparaged as the symptomatic pastimes of a population too easily characterized as merely "pathological." Therefore, while the economic and emotional survival strategies and even the triumphs of talent, skill, and will among the young people he describes do not effectively challenge the systems that oppress them (how, in fact, could they?), Kelley's intellectual work, the work of representation he so persuasively accomplishes, does. It challenges the accuracy and the adequacy of accepted understandings and familiar representations of "inner-city" life that circulate in the public sphere and in the professional discourse of social scientists and government experts. This may not be total revolution, but it is certainly worth something. It is the work that intellectuals can and do do, and it may well have an effect. It does, however, require that the writer assume without undue modesty an active and critical role interpreting the world he or she attempts to describe.

These splits, conflicts, and alienations we have noted in the situation of these African American writers are an unavoidable portion of the intellectual's lot. Intellectuals as a class cannot simply disappear into populist reconstructions or unproblematically claim authority as expert elites. Both populism and elitism are themselves quintessentially intellectual constructions, the sorts of legitimation that intellectuals like to hide behind. Andrew Ross gives a brief inventory of some contradictions interior to the functioning of intellectuals as a class that is

> elitist in its protection of the guild privileges secured by cultural capital, but also egalitarian in its positivist vision of social emancipation for all. Anti-capitalist in its technocratic challenge to the rule of capital, but also contemptuous of the "conservative," anti-intellectual disrespect of the popular classes. And lastly, of course, internally divided by antagonisms between administrative-managerial fractions and those aligned in some way with the value-oriented, anti-pragmatic codes of action and belief associated with liberal or radical humanism.[25]

Internally riven and uncertain as they may be, intellectuals continue to function in the representation of culture and the formulation of alternatives to the present. These functions remain a key, even a constitutive, part of the social, moral, and political life and identities of communities. The intellectual's role and positioning may be more vexed and more compromised than it once seemed to be, but it remains necessary, perhaps more necessary than it ever was. There is no point in trying to hide this.

Today debates about education, multiculturalism, and politics show considerable confusion on all these points. Some wish to rid themselves and the world of these problems by hustling the intellectual into the grave and burying the problem once and for all. They succeed only in burying their own heads in populist sand. Others seek to resolve the problem by restoring the intellectual's lost glory as representatives of universal, transcendent principles or traditions while forgetting that these principles are frequently the points of contention. Assuming the mantle of universal values, they end up wearing the emperor's new clothes. In either case, intellectuals get caught and exposed.

Intellectuals cannot effectively hide the unpopular nature of the work they do; nor can they cover themselves in the robe of the philosopher king. There is no way out of this dilemma. Some contradictions must be held to and lived with. Transcendence without universals, universals without transcendence: these are the paradoxes of contemporary intellectual work and modern politics in the West and, I suspect, elsewhere as well.

2

Pedagogy: Enlightened Instruction as Oppressive Discipline

Crises in higher education: some common confusions

The oft bemoaned crisis of American education gets blamed for everything from the decline of the nation's ability to compete in world markets to the unraveling of its social fabric.[1] It is easier to rant about the illusory decline of liberal education than it is to confront the economic inequity, political paralysis, and social dislocations that become more marked nearly every day.[2] No one in the United States ever lost popularity by criticizing academic intellectuals. Yet the critics of the academy (and those who celebrate its subversive potential) both exaggerate. If the liberal arts were really so immediately important to personal success and political domination, if it were still true that our "socially unequal world . . . is classified hierarchically by categories of taste,"[3] then the humanities in general and literary studies in particular would not be the bedraggled institutional stepchildren of the contemporary multiversity that they are rapidly becoming.[4]

On both the Right and the Left, critics tend to agree that the problem with the academy today has to do with the philosophical positions many of its members have adopted. Specifically, they attack academic intellectuals for having abandoned the rationalistic program and method of the Enlightenment. The philosophical position that gets blamed is usually labeled cultural relativism. This, critics claim, licenses the abandonment of "standards" and the institution of multicultural curricular reforms and other identity-based programs of study that threaten to "disunite America."[5] That cultural relativism has its own Enlightenment antecedents and has in itself no political valence whatsoever and can be made to support both emancipatory and oppressive practices (as we will see in chapter 4) makes no difference in these "debates." Ethical absolutism is at least as likely to ground totalitarian dictatorships as it is to found democracies. This does not mean, however, that the Enlightenment and its ideals are irrelevant to the academy or to the political lives of our communities. But we seem generally confused about what the relevance might be. Liberals and conservatives share common ground in their confusions about these issues. To see this, let us consider the attacks on multiculturalism and identity politics—the pragmatic or programmatic expression of cultural relativism as a curricular reform—that some self-identified U.S. liberals have recently made.

Todd Gitlin is precisely the sort of tenured radical conservative critics claim to fear: a founding member and national leader of Students for a Democratic Society (SDS), a radical sociologist and community organizer, a chronicler of the sixties. Nonetheless, he is also a determined critic of multiculturalism, political correctness, and identity politics. In *The Twilight of Common Dreams*, he warns of the Balkanization of U.S. society and of lost opportunities for progressive coalitions. Like conservative critics, Gitlin wants to reclaim moral universals as the basis of American politics. Rather than focusing on the cultural particularities that divide us, he argues, we need to reclaim certain absolutes: the Enlightenment universals of reason, justice, equality, and progress that can mobilize the various suffering segments of society together into a viable majority. This is an attractive project, but his argument is often at odds with itself.

For example, in a stirring peroration near the book's end, he writes that a "diversity of customs and races is here to stay—and nowhere more than in amazingly profuse, polychrome, polyglot America" (Gitlin, 237). Here he emphasizes the local loyalties that seem best to motivate people.[6] Then, with no transition, he reaches for his final conclusion:

> Still, we will not see what lies on the other side of the politics of identity unless, unflinchingly, without illusions, we look, look again, and are willing to go on looking. For too long, too many Americans have busied themselves digging trenches to fortify their cultural borders, lining their trenches with insulation. Enough bunkers! Enough of the perfection of differences! We ought to be building bridges. (Gitlin, 237)

Yet it is not clear what Gitlin sees when he looks at the other side of cultural politics and identity divisions, nor is it clear how he gets from what he sees while looking at these particularities to what he imagines as a remedy for fragmentation.

Gitlin does not address the most interesting questions his polemic raises. Who is or could be imagined to be in a position to design the bridges he imagines? On what terms will these coalitions be formed, and who will construct them?

Perhaps he does not get around to considering these crucial issues because, like the conservative critics, he gets distracted by the specter of relativism. Like those critics, he blames a philosophical theory that he calls "perspectivism" for the present predicament. Unlike those critics, however, he does not find the academy to be uniquely at fault for the abandonment of truth and justice:

> Although alarmists of the cultural Right, claiming to speak for a single morality, trace this form of thinking variously to English empiricism, American anthropology, German Marxism, or French deconstruction, the academy has no monopoly on the decline of the claims to truth. Perspectivists creep up everywhere, from op-ed pages to the Grand Ole Oprah of daytime talk shows in which Klansmen and Afrocentrists, anorexics and abusers, rapists and rape victims all get their hearings. (Gitlin, 201)

Gitlin believes that the decline of truth results from a sort of perverse wrongheadedness, a promiscuous desire to let everyone have his or her say. Advocate of democracy and liberal freedom that he is, Gitlin finds the welter of positions, polemics, and pathologies clotting the public sphere too much and too uncontrolled. This may be, but truth itself is not in decline; nor is epistemology at the root of what ails us.

Talk shows, to take one form of popular culture that Gitlin finds especially symptomatic of a debilitating relativism, are far more complex than he imagines. Patricia Williams, who does not wholly disagree with Gitlin, remarks that these shows create false consensus and also distort division, condoning what they sometimes seem to challenge. Yet more accurately than Gitlin, she identifies the attraction of these shows as "the impression [they create] of having had a full airing of all viewpoints, no matter how weird, and of having reached a nobler plane, a higher level of illumination, of having wrestled with something till we've exhausted it."[7] Cultural or moral relativity is not where the kick is. Rather, these shows reaffirm the commonsense morality of the collective, represented almost ritualistically by the audience members rising one after the other to denounce or advise the miscreants and misfits onstage. The effect is not a relativistic carnival but a dramatic reaffirmation of community standards, something like a pillorying in the video village.

However mistaken, Gitlin is not alone. Many these days, particularly those identified with the dominant culture, worry that standards no longer hold and long for a time when they did. This, however, is not the result of— nor is it directly related to—the problem of truth or the question of relativism. The most volatile disagreements in social or in personal life within or across cultures never take place on this level of abstraction, except on occasion in seminar rooms or at academic conferences.

When the federal government, local school boards, and individual citizens quarrel over busing, no one adopts a position he or she would characterize as unfair based on arguments or evidence he or she believes to be false. Rather, each side represents its own contending and frequently internally conflicted versions of fairness and fact. Similarly, when affirmative action or reproductive rights get debated, no one adopts a position that he or she would characterize as unjust or immoral. Rather, different visions of justice and morality come into conflict. Those who fear that standards no longer hold long for the ability to adjudicate these disagreements on a higher and more decisive level of abstraction, to end disputes about particular truths from the vantage point of Truth itself, to put an end to politics and polemics. When the Truth speaks it should always have the last word. This is one definition of what an intellectual is. The intellectual is one who desires to speak the Truth and to have the last word.

This, ultimately, is Gitlin's dream. In the final analysis, it is not anything so abstract as relativism that worries him. Instead he has concrete worries that his credentials as an intellectual, his authority to plan the bridges of truth and construct the coalitions of comprehension that will unify society, are in doubt. When he ironically anticipates a counterargument to his position, he reveals something of his own anxiety. He imagines an accusing multiculturalist who says that Gitlin's defense of universals merely expresses the crisis of his own white, male, and heterosexual subjectivity: "It expresses nothing other than the lament of his caste, which needless to say feels threatened. With reason—it has lost some of its power and resents it" (Gitlin, 203). Gitlin, I think, displaces his anxiety even as he reveals it. The identity he bespeaks most poignantly at this moment is not the gendered, sexed, and raced identity he names but the modern, progressive, intellectual identity so fundamental to his view of the world and his desired place in it that he never speaks of it at all. This is particularly poignant, since the figure of the intellectual has been so hard to locate on the contemporary scene that his absence has been taken to define the very nature of our postmodernity itself.[8] Ultimately it is not the specter of relativism but the ghost of the intellectual whose death has been so widely reported that haunts Gitlin's book.

That Gitlin should mourn "the loss of the left that can no longer be— that would have given him an honorable, even central place to stand" (203) is not incidental, for the two groups, the intellectuals and the Left, have frequently been identified with each other. Intellectuals must adjust to a world where there is no clearly defined central place on which to stand. They must also realize that if such a place existed, they might not be elected to stand on it. The best of them frequently have a very difficult time making this adjustment. Intellectuals still want to have the last word.

We do not need Horkheimer and Adorno to remind us that realizing the intellectual's dream to be the final spokesperson for absolutes and universals tends to require in fact—as for Plato it did in theory—radically undemocratic measures. If, as Gitlin suggests, "The Enlightenment has had a bad century" (210), it is not because skeptics like Nietzsche or Derrida have spoken against the reality of absolutes. It is because intellectuals who believed they possessed unique access to the Truth of the world-historical *geist* or the dialectic of history attempted to administer states based on those universals, thereby silencing those whose understanding was, by this definition, less advanced. Gitlin's oft repeated commitments to democracy can be at odds with his passionate advocacy of universals. It is not merely that, as Gitlin puts it, "the century of extermination camps, Gulags, and the bombing of whole cities" (213) has discredited reason by revealing it to be an instrument of oppression; it is also that each of these atrocities was legitimated by intellectuals who believed themselves possessed of and by the truth.

Moreover, as Rey Chow points out, it is appeals to universals that have tended, in practice, to support the ghettoizing of otherness in U.S. society, offering a rationality for precisely the fragmentation that Gitlin wants to counteract:

> The debates in the U.S. on the issue of canonicity, for instance, are driven by the urge to perpetuate what has been established as the "universals" of "cultural literacy." In fact, the more frequently "minor" voices are heard, the greater is the need expressed by the likes of Allan Bloom and E. D. Hirsch for maintaining a canon, so that a Western notion of humanity can remain as the norm. . . . The rhetoric of universals, in other words, is what ensures the ghettoized existence of the other, be it in the form of a different culture, religion, race, or sex.[9]

Thus Enlightenment universals can actually contribute to the segregation of society. If one believes himself to speak for the universal, why need any other voices be heard? These others can be stigmatized and silenced as deviant or derivative, like the participants in the talk shows that Gitlin finds so offensive. If the philosopher were king, these freaks could be exiled from the republic.

Despite the Enlightenment's bad century, Gitlin is right to say that the critique of Enlightenment is itself an Enlightenment project "unimaginable were it not for the widespread acceptance of Enlightenment principles: the worth of all individuals, their right to dignity, and to a social order that satisfies it" (Gitlin, 214). I would go further and say that politics would be impossible without adherence to, and intractable disputes about, these universals. Politics, in fact, is what we call our confrontations and conflicts with those with whom we disagree about the meaning of these legacies. What characterizes this moment is a widespread suspicion and distrust of intellectuals as a group claiming to have the last word on Enlightenment. Few believe that experts or intellectuals can be trusted to have many good answers or even any helpful suggestions to make. Stripped of the power they once claimed to legislate disputes, intellectuals encounter the relativization of truth not as a theoretical construct but as a lived experience. But it is simply their own pretensions to be the ones who know the truth that have become questionable.

Pedagogy and populism

Those of us who are committed to broadening educational access and who believe in the value of multiculturalism and sex and gender equity need, I believe, to persuade Americans, as we have not successfully done, of the value of what we and our students do in colleges and universities. Many people have become skeptical of that enterprise, and indeed, in traditional American fashion, of intellectual work generally. In fact, one might argue that the real crisis of higher education has to do with the sharp decline of its authority, most particularly its cultural authority.[10]

Universities and colleges are and ought to be elitist institutions. They are institutions devoted to an elite of intelligence and cultivation and this will always be an unpopular idea in a populist democracy such as this one. This will always be an idea surrounded with resentment, distrust, and lack of respect.[11]

These two comments were originally made during a conference held at the University of Illinois in the spring of 1993 that brought both conservative and progressive academic intellectuals together to discuss the situation of higher education in America. The first speaker, Paul Lauter, is well known to Americanists as an influential proponent of canon reform and the editor of the innovative *Heath Anthology of American Literature*. The second, Jeffrey Herf, has written important histories of Nazi Germany and U.S. Cold War foreign policy and is a member of the conservative National Association of Scholars. Despite their differences in tone and orientation, they indicate a common problem: the anomalous position of intellectuals as self-declared custodians of enlightenment in a democratic society. Many of the peculiarities, frustrations, and impasses of our historical moment—as they appear to intellectuals—must be considered in light of the intellectual's uncomfortable situation. This discomfort has been particularly agonizing on the Left. In fact, this agony is part of the Left's tradition. How does a self-appointed elite democratically speak for or legitmately represent the people? Intellectuals from Marx, through Lenin, to Gramsci, and beyond have wrestled with this question. Contemporary populisms of the Right and contemporary populisms of the Left—each representing intellectual constructions of the popular—have tried to exploit or obviate the question. Yet this problem remains intractable and, for leftists in particular, inescapable.

Michael Bérubé, citing Fredric Jameson's essay reviewing the cultural studies anthology that Treichler, Grossman, and Nelson edited, explains one aspect of the problem: "Progressive academics may be populists, but populism often includes a hatred or distrust of professors and intellectuals, who are seen as upper-class regardless of their income (as in the Quayle phrase 'cultural elite')."[12] Bérubé, in a move that is symptomatic of the problem attending his appeal for greater "public access," attributes this antagonism to an "imaginary" or "exaggerated" representation of such class privileges as tenure and workplace autonomy, despite his rueful acknowledgment that the pay, for assistant professors at least, is not very good. In other words, Bérubé does not take the people's assessment of his profession very seriously, treating it as an artifact of the "manufactured 'common sense' of the 1980s," another strange example of false consciousness (21).[13]

Yet we must consider that several things are true at once. First, intellectuals and professors, especially those working and producing at research universities, are "upper-class" by most measures—tastes, habits, identifications, and in some cases even income. Second, popular antagonism to them may be rooted in a common and not wholly inaccurate perception that the modes of life and values embodied by these "cultural elites" are not popular, even or especially when their object is popular culture. Third, this situation may not, however, be simply an impediment to the functioning of critical intellectuals but may be the condition of their labors. We should not misestimate the importance, difficulties, and opportunities of this situation.

The populist fantasies and pretensions underpinning much work by leftist cultural intellectuals have been scrutinized by Rey Chow. In a scathing analysis, she characterizes their project as "a circuit of productivity that draws its capital from others' deprivation while refusing to acknowledge its own presence as endowed."[14] These populist pretensions frequently manifest themselves in an anxiety that circulates among academic leftists concerning the violence of representation and the injuries entailed by the equation of knowledge with power. Nowhere is this more evident than in the world of oppositional or critical pedagogy, and nowhere in that world is it clearer than in the work of its leading intellectual and most influential pedagogue, Paulo Freire, whose death in 1997 saddened so many progressive intellectuals—myself included—all over the world. My point will be not that these anxieties about injury are unwarranted but that the situation of power in pedagogy is unavoidable.

Paulo Freire's pedagogical theories, along with Foucault's work, helped focus much contemporary leftist anxiety concerning practical questions of power and knowledge in the academy. Freire's teaching holds to two contradictory points. The contradiction emblematizes the central paradoxes in any model of intellectual labor. In *Pedagogy of Hope*, Freire states the essential principle of progressive education: "What is ethically required of progressive educators is that consistent with their democratic dreams, they respect the educands, and therefore never manipulate them."[15] I do not want to criticize Freire, whom I admire, or his practical methods, which evidently work; I do want to indicate that his theoretical account of what he does reveals that education without manipulation is itself a manipulative illusion.

Consider what Paul Taylor has written about Freire's most famous and fundamental distinction between a kind of education that indoctrinates and oppresses its subjects and a kind of education that sets them free, "the distinction between education as an instrument of domination and education as an instrument of liberation. . . . Is it possible that Freire has rationalized a world of false dichotomies? Is it the case that education . . . is not simply *either* about liberation *or* about domination but rather about *both*?"[16] As Taylor goes on to say, Freire's famous distinction, between "Banking-Digestive Education" on the one hand and "Dialogic-Liberating Education" on the other (Taylor, 53–54), may be another false dichotomy. The former, which emphasizes the transference of knowledge and imposes itself on a passive, objectified student and therefore repeats the structure of oppression itself, finds its antidote in the nonviolent and egalitarian dynamics of the latter, where knowledge is shared between an educator who is also educated in the process and the students who are also teachers. Yet education without oppression and manipulation may not be possible. It may be that pedagogy must impose itself on its students in order, paradoxically or dialectically, to free them.

To make the point more specific: if education for liberation depends on "authentic dialogue" between learners and educators as "equally knowing subjects" and is meant to result in an improved "awareness of the real, concrete contexts of facts, that is of the social reality in which we are living," then the question often begged is "whose reality constitutes the real, concrete context of our experience?" (Taylor, 54). Raising these questions, Taylor notes that Freire does sometimes ask, "What do we mean by challenging you to think correctly?" But he tends to be interested only in the form of challenging, and he leaves unquestioned the content of the term "correctly."

In the same chapter of *Pedagogy of Hope* in which Freire speaks against pedagogical manipulation, he tells the following story. Speaking with a group of Chilean peasants, having by his own account "a lively dialogue" with them, the teacher finds the conversation interrupted first by a group silence and then by one peasant who, Freire reports, speaks for the group and says: "Excuse us for talking. You're the one who should have been talking, sir. You know things, sir. We don't" (Freire, 45). "All right," Freire responds, "Let's say I know and you don't. Still, I'd like to try a game with you" (46). The game consists of the peasant and the teacher exchanging questions from their respective life worlds. The point is to demonstrate to these peasants that they "know" things—albeit different things—as well as the teacher does. Entirely predictable results ensue. The teacher asks, "What is the Socratic maieutic?" The peasants don't know. The peasants ask, "What's a contour curve?" The teacher doesn't know. Hegel and Marx are juxtaposed to soil liming; formal grammar to erosion control; epistemology to fertilizer. The score at the evening's end is even, and presumably both teacher and students have been edified. In a second story, a bit of Socratic maieutic reveals to a group of peasants that their misery is not the will of God, "the Father of us all," because no father could so exploit and abuse the majority of his children. To which the peasants reply, "No. God isn't the cause of all this. It's the boss!" (48).

Several things should be said of these tales. First, neither seems quite credible. In the first story, one wonders how any intellectual interested in agrarian reform could fail to know or at least to have heard something about contour plowing, soil erosion, and fertilizer. He should know about these things; it is his job. On the other hand, why peasants should be familiar with Socrates, Hegel, or Marx is less obvious. It is far from clear what they will gain by knowing what these men thought. This is not to say that these philosophers are not important, only that their importance depends on and in fact constitutes the intellectual's work and world. He must forge the connection between these thinkers and the contemporary world he and the peasants inhabit. The importance of contour plowing for raising crops and conserving soil is much more readily apparent. In the second story, the ease with which the teacher intervenes in and subverts the peasants' religious explanations for their suffering, getting them with no trouble at all to substitute an incipient class analysis for an ideological obfuscation, indicates that these people had realized this for themselves. Moreover, Freire, who is alert and sensitive, must have known that they knew this.

All this leaves the reader, who finds himself positioned like one of Freire's pupils, feeling manipulated by the educator. And in fact, these tales indicate that manipulation is Freire's most common pedagogical tech-nique. The teacher sets up a game in which he establishes the rules and pre-determines the outcome. The teacher poses questions to which he already knows the answers. Equality here is merely an illusion, an illusion with the rhetorical, manipulative purpose of persuading or maneuvering the stu-dent to see the world as the teacher sees it, to receive the knowledge of the world and the calculus of options and actions that flow from it, which the teacher believes to be right, just, reasonable, true, good, useful. As John Elias remarks: "It is Freire's philosophical position that an objective reality exists, which all will inevitably come to recognize through education. This almost quixotic view fails, however, to do justice to the complex nature of reality and of human knowledge of it. It leaves little room for a relativism and a pluralism of world views." [17] Freire himself does not seem unaware of this tendency in his writing. Elias remarks that Freire's "commitment to the dialogic character of the revolution is a rather limited one" (Elias, 103). It should also be noted that the goal of "conscientizing" the peasants includes refashioning them as types of an idealized intellectual, a critically conscious subject, a version of what the teacher himself imagines himself to be.

That the teacher is manipulative and that his goal is the inevitably nar-cissistic one of transforming the student into a version of himself does not mean these ends of pedagogy are ignoble. Pedagogy always involves manipulation. A pedagogy that does not seek to transform its pupil is no pedagogy at all. The teacher's egalitarian principles are largely irrele-vant in the classroom and are sometimes antithetical to the accomplish-ment of his task. Pedagogy's goal is (as Freire, in collaboration with Henry Giroux, suggests) the overcoming of historical forgetting, which reifies the world into apparently natural and hence apparently irremediable objects and situations, "redefining historical memory, critique, and radical utopi-anism as elements of a political discourse whose central thrust must be understood primarily as a pedagogical process." [18] In pursuit of this goal, pedagogy should not adopt a pose that encourages the students to for-get the real material and historical differentials of social and institutional power and privilege that mark the teacher's relationship to them.

Elsewhere Giroux has claimed that "the aim of such a discourse is to cre-ate the ideological and material conditions for a radical public sphere." [19] But will the radicalness of that public sphere be defined formally in terms of the equality of each of its members, or will it be constituted themati-cally by the ideas that can find a hearing there and become the basis for common action? What if, when the peasants speak, they advocate unre-strained economic competition and ethnic or religious warfare instead of socialist reform and class solidarity? What if their reality is shaped not by a Marxist understanding of the world but by admiration for Western affluence and a populist legacy of romantic or religious nationalism? Would this constitute a radical public sphere that progressive educators—intellectuals whose reality is shaped by reading social, economic, and moral philosophy, whose political rhetoric and principles are legacies of the Enlightenment— could accept? If not, would they be entitled to use any means, short of physical abuse, to manipulate, cajole, or intimidate their students into seeing the error of these beliefs and accepting the imposition of better, more productive, and more just ways of viewing the world?

I would answer yes. I would also add that I am not prescribing pedagogical behavior here; I am describing what I believe pedagogues inevitably do all the time. For this reason, I believe that much of the anxiety concerning the legitimacy of pedagogy and the authority of the teacher that has become a commonplace topic among progressive academics is exaggerated and misplaced.

For example, in their contribution to the collection *Higher Eduction under Fire*, Gerald Graff and Gregory Jay critique "oppositional pedagogy" for not being democratic enough. According to oppositional pedagogues, as they describe them:

> The unleashing of critiques in the classroom ultimately leads to the unmasking of the structure of domination and disenfranchisement. The dominant groups, stripped of arbitrary or coercive power, will fail to justify their positions when thrown back solely on intellectual weaponry; the disenfranchised, liberated from material and institutional oppression, will gain the technical skills they need to understand their condition and engage in revolutionary contestation with the powers that be.[20]

This view of pedagogy is clearly influenced by Freire, but it makes more unequivocal claims for what the intellectual knows and for the critical weapons the teacher has mastered. It relies not on a mystified populism but on widely accepted canons of reason, rhetoric, and persuasion. Although Graff and Jay seek to distance themselves from this sort of critical pedagogy, I do not believe that this can be done. Whether the content is the significance of Milton's enjambments or the importance of African contributions to North American culture or the nature of truth in contemporary science or the reality of class struggle, one can base an effective pedagogy only on the belief that the version of reality one advances in the classroom is accurate, that the arguments one uses to support one's position are good ones, that those who disagree are wrong according to specifiable criteria, and that their errors can be persuasively demonstrated. Graff and Jay, like many academic leftists, are made nervous by this position. Such a view of pedagogy, they say—correctly I think—"only works . . . if one assumes in advance that no really effective arguments for injustice can be mounted that will survive critique" (207). As an alternative to this insistence on one's sense of what is right, they suggest the now famous formula of "teaching the conflicts." Yet teaching the conflicts is impossible if by teaching one means offering an impartial account of all sides in a dispute. Unless one has no position on the issues involved, one can only responsibly offer an account of what is true or right or just or accurate as one sees it. For while I too am made nervous by the position I advance here, I believe that such a position and the anxiety associated with it are inescapable.

Quite simply, I believe that "no effective arguments for injustice can be mounted that will survive critique" (Graff and Jay, 207). This is why no one on the Right or the Left ever makes an argument that sets out to defend a position admitted to be unjust. As Stanley Fish puts it, "No one in the field is aligning himself or herself with falsities" (Free Speech, 7). Rather, every- one—the National Association of Scholars and Teachers for Democracy, the Klan and the National Association for the Advancement of Colored People, William Bennett and Dinesh D'Souza and bell hooks and Catherine McKinnon—argues for, or on behalf of, what he or she believes to be just. Only some of them, however, are right.

Justice, like other enlightened abstractions, does not resolve arguments; it is the name of the field on which our battles are fought. And if one is engaged in a battle, one is in no position simultaneously to distance one- self from the fray and offer a balanced account of the positions involved. As Fish also says, "If conflict is made into a structural principle, its very nature is domesticated" (Free Speech, 36). In his contribution to Higher Educa- tion under Fire, Michael Warner makes a similar point: "Many people before me have pointed out that Western values and institutions are conflicted, not monoliths, and that the forces of evil (in the NAS scenario) in fact speak a language of value that derives from the Enlightenment." [21] If that is true, however, then we cannot responsibly disavow in our teaching those things we are persuaded are true, just, good, in order to mimic a neutrality no intellectual could ever feel or a populism no progressive intellectual could responsibly advocate.

I am, of course, not making an argument for a more authoritatively im- posing pedagogical style, nor, in fact, for any particular pedagogical style whatsoever. My own personal preference is for as open and dialectically engaged a classroom environment as possible because I believe that I am more persuasive in that setting. This, however, is beside the point. The point is that the problem Graff and Jay specify as the problem of progres- sive pedagogy is the wrong problem. Power and democracy, imposition and freedom, are the freighted and conflictual terms that define the pedagogical and intellectual enterprise. That enterprise remains, however, ineluctably violent (though the violence remains verbal) and intrinsically elitist because for pedagogy to occur, differentials of knowledge, of authority, and—often—of institutional power must exist. This, I hasten to add, is not necessarily a bad thing. I also agree with Michael Warner, who says that the "greatest political obstacle" in this culture is "a general will to ignorance," one frequently "enforced by the very people who claim to be defending knowledge and Western values" (285). He speaks of specific obstacles of ignorance faced by gay men and lesbians, but the point is generally valid. If pedagogy is to overcome these obstacles, which exist in all political realms and are internal to the subjectivities this culture constructs, then differentials of knowledge, of authority, and of institutional power may be useful tools in persuading students and opponents to see the error and ignorance of their ways. Persuasion, which Graff and Jay champion as a community-affirming pedagogical principle, is itself a conflictual and political process. It occurs across the divisions and hierarchies that divide any given group. We cannot escape from this fact, nor can we wish it away.

Thus when a progressive pedagogue like Henry Giroux argues against "the legacy of academic elitism and professionalization" in favor of a "democratization of social knowledge" (Giroux, 244) and contrasts that good democratization to a bad "Arnoldian imperative to teach the 'best that has been thought and known in the world' " (239), he mystifies the point. All of us teach what we think it best to teach, and we give each object brought under scrutiny in the classroom—from Shakespeare to MTV—our best attention and our best thought. Arnold, whose own perfectionist beliefs were explicitly progressive (and one should remember the extent to which contemporary progressive thought derives from the Victorian social conscience), might well have endorsed progressive pedagogy's critical project, its desire to make the world a closer approximation to its own best thought. The important arguments and conflicts always join at the point where the question of what is "best" gets raised.

How do we know what is best? or literary theory
is not a political position

Many intellectuals these days are confused about what cultural academics had best say about politics. As Michael Bérubé points out, this confusion, which is shared by Left academics and their critics, evidences a more fundamental confusion between "cultural" and "practical" politics. While allowing that these two political realms are "complexly intertwined," he takes a stab in *Public Access* at sorting them out:

There is a difference between the two. . . . and the failure to recognize that difference leads to a critical slippage between two meanings of "politics," broad and narrow. It leads the cultural left to think it's more subversive than it is, and it leads the cultural right to affect outrage that literary and cultural critics are engaged in "politics," as if we were interfering with trade agreements or filibustering a jobs bill. (35)

Bérubé's clarification raises at least two further questions. First, if cultural intellectuals are not to interfere with economic or social policies (presumably because they lack expertise in those areas), then what "political" issues are "cultural" intellectuals qualified to address? Second, if cultural analysis and practical politics are "different," is there any necessary link between the two? Does any specific practical politics or political position necessarily follow from one's professional practice as an academic cultural critic? To foreground the question implicit in Bérubé's own subtitle, is there any specifiable relationship between "literary theory and cultural politics"?

The answer to this last question is, I'm afraid, no. A reading of Bérubé's polemic makes this clear. The answer to the first question, as my comments in the previous section indicate, is always up for grabs and implicates many of the same issues of power and imposition imbricating pedagogical practices that understand themselves to be politically progressive.

Bérubé argues that academic cultural critics must seek a wider audience in the general public both for their own and for the public good. But one of the frustrating things about Bérubé's engaging book is its tendency to slip away from precisely the most difficult questions that his argument raises. Instead, he settles for yet another version of what Andrew Ross has called "romantic left narratives about the 'decline of the public intellectual.'" In the "classic version," Ross explains, the public intellectual "is an heroicized white male, . . . who, if he is like C. Wright Mills, still rides a Harley-Davidson to his university workplace." [22] Bérubé's amusing attempt to imagine himself through the eyes of conservative critics as a combination of puritan reformer Cotton Mather and punk rock personality Johnny Rotten, as "Rotten Mather, assistant professor of English, thirty years old and not to be trusted" (Public Access, 43), smacks a bit of this romantic heroism even in its irony. And yet he never really takes up the issue of this figure. Is he or would he like to be Rotten Mather? If he were, would he be a dangerous figure or merely another crank in costume? Does the anxiety on the Right have a point or not? If not, is it because we on the Left are harmless after all?

Perhaps he does not raise these questions because to do so would complicate his appeal to Left literary intellectuals to seek more "public access."

I have nothing against public access or the pleasure and excitement of writing for a wider and more varied audience, but why should it be my mission to do so? Bérubé consistently begs this question. Why should what cultural academics have to say be of particular interest or importance to the general community? Instead, he manifests an almost touching faith that an education in the humanities, most particularly an education in textual theory and "the possibilities of interpretation" (the work that literary critics like himself do), will make "us" and our students better—read more "progressive"—subjects and citizens. In fact, Bérubé argues the unlikely position that deficits of reading skills are at the root of most political problems today:

> the crisis of PC and the university is itself partly a crisis of reading: the PC scandals swept through the press so easily because so few of our "traditional" intellectuals and mainstream journalists are capable of reading interpretively, reading intelligently, or (in some cases) reading at all. The intellectual right is not dismayed by this, since, as many of their spokespersons have written, reading is part of the problem, not part of the solution. (*Public Access*, 265)

The problem is that reading *is* in fact part of the problem and not part of the solution. Arguing otherwise, Bérubé sounds much more like the archconservative Allan Bloom—himself a disciple of Leo Strauss and a consummate close reader—than he would probably like to admit.

Bloom, like other cultural conservatives, claims that social ills flourish because reading has withered. He writes that "whatever the cause, our students have lost the practice and taste for reading."[23] This is one important reason that their souls are "impoverished." Reading could, Bloom claims, make them better, more critical people, "able to think for themselves" with "something to think about": "The failure to read good books both enfeebles the vision and strengthens our most fatal tendency—the belief that the here and now is all there is" (Bloom, 63–64). There is every difference in the world between Bérubé's and Bloom's political positions. There are significant differences in what each means by reading—both its objects and procedures. For example, feminism and popular culture, for Bérubé, are honored objects of analysis; for Bloom they are despicable detritus that can only cloud students' minds. Each writer reads different things and reads those things differently. Yet in each writer's polemic, "reading" is an important remedy to contemporary ills, and for each writer, reading means reading as he does it. For Bloom, reading leads the student from error and distraction to a heightened appreciation of the transcendent. For Bérubé, reading frees the student from complicity and complacency to an increased awareness of the dominant's impositions.

These differences are not negligible. In fact, these differences are precisely the issue. My point is that since both antagonistic positions understand themselves to be based on reading, reading cannot be the criteria by which these battles will be decided. The criteria for decision and the protocols of persuasion lie elsewhere. Also, one notes with some uneasiness, only a cultural intellectual like Bloom or Bérubé is likely to assign so much critical importance to reading, the skill of the guild to which these intellectuals belong, the skill that defines their professional competence, the skill they are paid to teach.

I am not saying that interpretation is not important. Reading is the way each of us, professionals and nonprofessionals (Bérubé calls nonprofessionals "amateur readers"), constructs the world and our sense of possibilities within it. I am saying that reading is not the way out of our current confusions; it is another way of describing them. The addition of qualifiers such as "proper" and "advanced" or "theoretical" and "rigorous" readings of "good" or "classic" or "timeless" or "universal" texts or books does not help much, since they always beg the question. These honorific terms accrue to the type of reading and the sorts of objects that the writer has already chosen. It's always the other guy who reads incompetently or naively and whose objects are uncritically traditional or merely trendy.

When Bérubé attempts to define the links between the two realms of politics—when he attempts to link politics to reading as a way of differentiating fundamental differences between progressives and conservatives— he indulges in a bit of (perhaps necessary) wishful thinking:

> Progressive cultural politics today—the kind I analyze and practice in these pages—chiefly has to do with the creation and circulation of cultural value; and progressive cultural critics, by interpreting and reshaping the relations between culture and society, hope to forge new understandings of subjectivity—and new formulations of the status of political subjects in their interaction with other political subjects— in which "radical democracy" in the discursive realm will aid and abet the spread of radical democracy in practical policy making. (Public Access, 36)

No doubt we must work with this hope. But it does us no good to forget that in a literal and technical sense, this hope is groundless. The "creation and circulation of cultural values," reshaping of social relations, forging of new understandings of subjectivity, all of these describe not the unique work of progressive cultural critics but the practice of organic intellectuals generally. And as Bérubé himself notes, citing Stuart Hall, "Margaret Thatcher is the best Gramscian I know." If she can be this era's most effective organic intellectual—with the possible exception of Ronald Reagan—

then the work of the organic intellectual is not intrinsically progressive. Each class, the dominant classes as well as the oppressed, produces its own intellectuals, with their own interested interpretation of things.

Even more unsettling, democracy, even radical democracy, is no guarantee of progressive politics, especially if by progressive politics one means socialism, antiracism, antihomophobia, and antisexism. Ezra Pound, when he shilled for the fascists, attempted to make Mussolini a popular hero, and in fact, a certain populist appeal has always been an important part of fascism's lure. If democracy ensured progressive politics, then the American Civil Liberties Union would not have so many cases involving democratically elected and demographically representative local school boards who want to make curriculum conform to community standards by banning books or censuring teachers whose views on racial, sexual, or political issues differ from their own; if democracy ensured progressive politics, then the Supreme Court would not have had to intervene in local democratic and popular politics to ensure civil and reproductive rights for African Americans and women; if democracy ensured progressive politics, then the death penalty would not be a surefire vote getter among most constituencies in the United States.

Bérubé, of course, knows all these things, but like most of us, he tries hard to forget them at important moments so that the cultural, the social, and the political can form a comfortable democratic and populist whole.[24] This whole would be comforting because it would free the progressive intellectual from the task of trying to impose his or her views on students or on the populace at large. And yet there is no reliable unity between these realms, though Bérubé seems to assume there is. For example, writing of Philip Rahv, the quintessential New York intellectual as public figure, who celebrated T. S. Eliot's "venturesome spirit" in poetry, Bérubé writes, "But by the time Rahv wrote that sentence, Eliot was a conservative Anglican royalist on his way home from picking up the Nobel Prize" (Public Access, 129). To which the only reply, I suppose, is, so what? To assume that Eliot's political commitments flow from his aesthetic practice so that the relationship between them is self-evident and need not be forged by interpretation is to accept the modernist postulates with which Eliot himself ordered his world. The political valences of Eliot's conservatism, especially insofar as it is critical of contemporary capitalism, are not as clear as Bérubé's glib dismissal suggests. Raymond Williams, to take one example, finds Eliot's significance for progressive critique to be much more complicated. The autonomy of culture, the independence of culture from crude determinations by the economic infrastructure or by ideological tendencies, means that there is an aporia between culture and politics. This does not mean that there can be no links between culture and politics. It does mean that these links can never simply be given or effectively assumed. They must always be forged. Forging those links is one important aspect of the work cultural intellectuals do.

Thus while there is no necessary or organic link between the professional work of cultural critics and any particular practical politics, the links that one can forge may become very real indeed. If conservative critics can persuade enough people that poststructuralism is antidemocratic, then that link will have some very real effects—departments may be purged, and programs may be defunded. If progressive critics can persuade enough people that cultural relativism encourages respect and tolerance among members of a diverse community, then other real effects will follow.

The question, then, is how to forge the links one wants. Bérubé is right when he says this project depends on "an uneasy combination of stringent critique and rhetorical persuasion" (*Public Access*, 36). That crucial persuasion, however, will depend less on our academic specialization as professional interpreters and more on our principled appeals to Enlightenment values of truth, justice, and equality. Conservative critics have often claimed that academic leftists hate the Enlightenment, but in practice it is conservative positions—defending hierarchies of entrenched power and prejudice and supporting inequalities of social and economic justice—that violate enlightened principles. The universalist presumptions of the Enlightenment remain problematic, but this is a problematic from which one can not escape. It may be true, as Bérubé says, that "something there is in poststructuralist thought that does not love an Enlightenment" (*Public Access*, 201), but it is also true that the Enlightenment remains one of the most important orientations for progressive politics that we have. If, as Bérubé argues, "cultural studies engages with the popular and the 'ordinary' . . . primarily in order to understand—and thereby to *change*—the power relations that shape the most intimate and/or quotidian details of our lives, power relations that are ordinarily no more visible or remarkable to us than oxygen" (*Public Access*, 140), then the direction and political tendency of that hoped-for change—and even the hope for change itself—originate not within cultural studies or literary theory or radical democracy but in enlightened political commitments and assumptions that lie outside these fields.

I suspect that Bérubé knows that no amount of theory can fill the aporia between culture and politics. For this reason, he is unable at the end of his book to offer any but the most tepid encouragement to his colleagues:

After all, it can be useful to remember what instructive and delightful things we've done as a species while we've been butchering and maiming each other, though I seem to recall a phrase from Walter

Benjamin that suggests these things are intertwined. And training in the humanities does indeed stand a decent chance of teaching students to think critically, to exercise their imaginations and to become better people (that is, certifiably politically *correct* people)—though George Steiner and Thomas Pynchon would remind us that a love for Rilke doesn't prevent a man from participating in genocide. (*Public Access*, 249)

This is a wonderfully dense and allusive passage that removes each assertion for the political value of cultural training just as Bérubé makes it. He continues:

From my perspective, it cannot but be a politically progressive act—in the radical democratic sense—to provide students and other readers with access to advanced literacy (that is criticism and interpretation), even though we cannot guarantee (how could we?) that they will use advanced literacy for certifiably "progressive," that is, leftist, social, and political ends. (*Public Access*, 249)

It cannot but be a politically progressive act, though—as Steiner and Pynchon remind us—it might well not be politically progressive at all. The progressive critic as the priest of advanced literacy seems rather unsure about what powers he is vested with and what the mysteries he communicates mean.

The one lesson Bérubé hasn't learned (because an intellectual cannot learn it and remain an intellectual) is the one that Andrew Ross prescribes for academic populists: "The business of contesting popular meanings without speaking from above." For if, as Ross continues, "what intellectuals stand to learn most from [popular discourses] . . . are lessons in self-criticism, especially with respect to their habitually recruitist or instructional postures in the field of popular correction" (Ross, 207), then either this lesson cannot be learned, or learning it makes no difference. Self-critical intellectuals must still pursue their habitual projects of recruitment and reform, persuasion and critique. They may become more circumspect, but the persistence of racism, homophobia, and other pathologies in American culture makes the project of correcting popular opinion an important, if increasingly difficult, project. Those who aspire to correct popular prejudices, however self-critical they may be, inevitably attempt to assume a position at least provisionally "above" the public they address. Effective recruitment for progressive causes may require an assumption of authority to argue, to contradict, and to persuade. The sources of that authority are various and sometimes far from clear. But the authority itself is indispensable, though it remains involved with institutional and political relations of power. For who will do the credentialing or certifying of the politically correct progressives we hope to (re)produce? Nearly a decade ago, Frank Lentricchia wrote that "the practice of a critical pedagogy must emerge from, be irritated into existence by, its own discomforting social ground."[25] The social ground of pedagogy remains the ground where power and empowerment, elitism and egalitarianism, knowledge and ignorance, have it out. These discomfiting precincts are the arena in which the intellectual works.

3

Community: Pragmatism as a Profession of Anxiety

Everyday life in dissensual communities

Critics of university intellectuals tend to echo Benda's *Treason of the Clerics* by accusing them, as he did, of yielding their proper preoccupation with the grand requirements of "truth" to the demands of politics in one petty form or another. Conservatives like Dinesh D'Souza and progressives like Todd Gitlin appear most worried about what goes on in the classroom, where they see a theoretically informed challenge to the "traditional" curriculum and to "traditional" understandings of culture undermining Western identity and values within the very institutions entrusted with reproducing them.[1] Yet I don't think canonical and curricular revision alone, which is the tradition in U.S. universities, accounts for the alarm.[2] Rather, the altered place of intellectuals and the changed nature of the community they both address and help to form occasion the uneasiness that keeps fueling these "debates."

Bill Readings, whose phrase "dissensual community" I have borrowed for the title of this section, sketches the history of the university in Europe and America as part of the nineteenth century's attempt to base national identity in national culture. In Readings's view, both this project and the nation itself no longer possess the force they once had:

> The notion that culture matters is ineluctably linked to the ascendancy of the nation-state as a political formation, and the decline of the nation-state means that the question of power is no longer structured in terms of the inclusion or exclusion of subjects from cultural participation. . . . This, then, is what it means for me to say that Cultural Studies arises as a quasi discipline once culture ceases to be the animating principle of the University and becomes instead one object of study among others. The problem of participation becomes most acutely the object of reflection when we no longer know what it would

mean to participate, when there is no longer any obvious citadel to be captured.[3]

Yet the fury of the endless attacks on cultural studies and the politics of inclusion from both right-wing and left-wing critics indicates that culture for many intellectuals is still something more than one object of study among others. Unlike most other disciplinary objects, this one seems attended by particular anxieties concerning identity and inclusion. Moreover, as Readings says, it is precisely because we no longer possess the illusion of clear grounds on which to decide what inclusion, participation, or identity mean for ourselves or for others that cultural studies has become a particularly vexed arena in the dissensual community Readings imagines the contemporary university to be. For though he suggests that "the university will have to become one place, among others, where the attempt is made to think the social bond without recourse to a unifying idea," I would suggest that such an idea is impossibly utopian (Readings, 190). In the real spaces of community, recourse is always made to a unifying idea. In the real spaces of dissensual communities, the fight is always over what that unifying idea should be and what it should include or exclude. Dissensus, like consensus, cannot end fundamental conflict. If cultural studies is, as Readings puts it, "the contemporary way to speculate on the question of what it means to be *in* the University" (118), then it is also a fair indication of what daily life in a dissensual community is like, especially for intellectuals whose task it is to reflect or speculate on what the community and their place within it might be. In heterogeneous and conflicted communities like our own, it can be difficult to decide which side is telling the truth, and which truth one had better believe. The problem is not that there are no truths or values but that the truths and values there are often conflict.

The problem of relativism emerges when conflicts occur within the space of communities that can no longer be imagined as homogeneous. If the West appears more diverse than it once did, then an authoritative referee to separate its true cultural legacy from foreign impostures might well be needed. Both D'Souza and Gitlin believe that intellectuals should do this job. It is one job intellectuals have long dreamed of doing. With notably different agendas, both D'Souza and Gitlin would like a crack at it.

But does this job actually exist? Is it necessary? Could anyone in the West do it? Whether or not one believes that the West is faced with hordes of others who threaten its traditions and institutions and who will change the nature of its community and the norms by which it operates, these questions remain. For if self-evidently objective truths and universal norms are unavailable—if they were available we would not have so many arguments and so much anxiety about them—then the implications of this situation are what we must address, and not only in dealings between communities but for the life that goes on within a community.

Cultural relativity, the belief that values are not universal but are rooted in the lives of various and varied communities, enjoys a good deal of prestige among many intellectuals today. "Community," as Zygmunt Bauman remarks, "has come to replace reason and universal truth, and the one method leading to both. It is in community, rather than in the universal progress of mankind, that the intellectuals of the West tend to seek the secure foundations of their professional role."[4] Yet how secure can such foundations in community be? Can intellectuals function as organic intellectuals of specific communities rather than as shills for universals?

Community, in fact, is one name for the intellectuals' problem, not its solution. As Bauman explains: "The erosion of the universal ascendancy of the setting within which the Western intellectual tradition developed and took shape exposed the previously invisible link between the pragmatic validity of such tradition and the commonality of the 'form of life' or the 'community of meanings.' The question is, however, how large is the community? Whom does it entail? Where should its boundaries be drawn?" (Legislators, 146).[5] Gitlin's and D'Souza's avowed longing for reason and universal truth is, I think, symptomatic of a longing for a moment when a community seemed to speak with a single voice, the voice of the intellectual. This was a moment when the boundaries between communities seemed clearer, a moment when East was East and West was West, and the twain never met. Each "community" seemed to keep its unique identity intact, and the boundaries or borders between them were easy to draw and easy for intellectuals to police. Whether such a moment ever existed outside the poetics of imperialism and the dreams of intellectuals is doubtful. It doesn't exist now.

This situation poses pressing pragmatic questions for intellectuals. These questions complicate one's sense of the place in which one works and the people for whom one speaks or writes. For, today, the most important boundaries we face are internal to, rather than outside of, the limits of the communities in which we live. In this light, Henry Louis Gates's comment that the "new scholars" that neoconservative defenders of the West deplore appear as the return of the repressed is uncannily apt.[6] For what returns with these scholars and their work is not something from beyond the boundaries of the West but something that has been Western all along—the question of difference itself. What has been repressed, and now returns, is not only the content and implications of difference but the fact that American or Western identity has been conflicted from the first. The most important thought repression denies is repression itself.

The repressed returning in the U.S. academy unsettles common certainties and dissolves whatever illusion of a univocal voice the community may once have had. The community is now, and in fact always has been, more various and more conflicted than we have wanted to remember. Gitlin himself tempers his appeal to common dreams with continuous avowals that the commonality of the past was mighty white, mighty male, mighty heterosexual. He does not want to admit, however, that today the road to community lies through conflict. This is not to abandon but to attempt to fulfill Western ideals. To recover the conflicts within the identity of the West has been one project, and a very old project, in the history of the West itself. But why then does it occasion so much anxiety among Western intellectuals?

TEGWAR: the game of disciplines and the pragmatics of communities

Among U.S. literary intellectuals, no one has written more or more persuasively about community, relativism, and professionalism than Stanley Fish. His work, when closely examined, reveals the problems that cause intellectuals to worry about community. Interestingly (and symptomatically), he has had little to say about anxiety since his earliest explorations in affective stylistics, where the uneasiness of the reader was often central to the argument.[7] In fact, his later work repeatedly denies that intellectuals should be anxious at all. For example, in an anthology of new historicist essays, Fish urges his younger colleagues to abandon their uneasiness about the meaning of their professional success and instead enjoy its rewards. He writes, "In the words of the old Alka-Seltzer commercial, 'try it, you'll like it.' "[8] In *Doing What Comes Naturally*, Fish also claims to offer speedy relief from anxiety. He attempts to explain worry away when he makes the distinction, crucial for his argument, between "thinking *with*" and "thinking *within*" a practice:

> To think *within* a practice is to have one's very perception and sense of possible and appropriate action issue "naturally"—without further reflection—from one's position as a deeply situated agent. Someone who looks with practice-informed eyes sees a field already organized in terms of perspicuous obligations, self-evidently authorized procedures, and obviously relevant pieces of evidence. To think *with* a practice—by self-consciously wielding some extrapolated model of its working—is to be ever calculating just what one's obligations are, what procedures are "really" legitimate, what evidence is in fact evidence, and so on.[9]

In the literary profession, for example, we think within the limits of our professional context. Therefore, Fish contends that the anxieties involved in thinking with the practice—calculations of obligations, procedures, and legitimacy—cannot be our problem. Yet Fish's antifoundationalism provokes more anxieties than it assuages. More interesting, his work manifests anxieties of its own. I do not think we can avoid such anxieties. English departments are much like the communities in which they are embedded. Distinguishing between thinking within and thinking with the practices in which we are embedded turns out to be very difficult to do.

Because English departments are frequently blamed for importing the foreign contagion of cultural relativism into the intellectual body of the U.S. university, let us consider the question of practice in the community of literary academics. In that community, practitioners often find themselves constrained to play a game in which playing with the rules appears to be the order of the day and the meaning of playing within the rules seems to be in question. What counts as the common interest of an English department at this moment? Literary appreciation, deconstruction, new historicism, Marxism, feminism, cultural studies? What counts as literature? The great books of Western civilization? What does that include? Women's literature? African diasporic literature? Philosophical texts? Postcolonial discourses? Film? Painting? Television? Folklore? Technology? Pamphlets on sexually transmitted diseases from the surgeon general's office? All of these may be methods for, or objects of, study among the diverse population of those who occupy the space assigned to the English department. They necessarily do not form a peaceful community, since each of these methods and objects has come into being through active antagonism to at least one other method of reading or constitution of the discipline. To practice within such a community constrains the players to be ever calculating and never certain of obligations, procedures, and legitimacy within the confines of their own professional context.

Many have celebrated the breakdown of disciplinarity these alterations in English and other humanities departments may portend.[10] Fish is not one of them. Whether we celebrate or decry this situation, the question remains, how can such a field be organized or ruled? This question calls for a moment of theoretical reflection, a moment when the intellectual guardian plays referee and rules some things in and some things out of the republic of letters. Fish, while claiming to eschew theory, has made his own theoretical pronouncements—for him, the only game that really counts is the game of literary interpretation. He argues this point with considerable verve in *Professional Correctness* (which we will consider at some length in the last chapter) and at the end of the introduction to *There's No Such*

Thing as Free Speech: "Those who conflate and confuse literary with political work end up doing neither well" (27). In *Doing What Comes Naturally* he insists that "philosophy [i.e., theory] is one thing, and literary criticism is another," even though the point gets obscured because he must admit that "philosophy has become something that literary critics also do or attempt to do" (334).[11] How can such obscurity and confusion be possible? Can it be avoided? Who is to say when a thing done is done well or merely attempted? And isn't the statement that theory and literary criticism are distinct activities a theoretical pronouncement?

These rhetorical questions are not meant to obscure or confuse Fish's point, with which I agree. Theoretical formulations of rules—E. D. Hirsch's claims for validity in interpretation based on respect for authorial intention, for example, or Kant's formulation of the categories of cognition, or Marx's theory of value—claim to exist on another plane from the practice of interpretation, of thinking, or of political economy that they explain and by explaining seek to control. This explanation cannot master or predict practice in the manner that these theorists claim because these theories are actually forms of practice. Like other forms of practice, their consequences are contingent on various and not wholly predictable situational factors. It is the contingency of practice, its rhetorical dimension as Fish describes it, its dependency on the vicissitudes of persuasion rather than the certainty of proof, that determines the inconsequentiality of theory, its inability to master practice. Theory has no consequences if the consequence you are expecting theory to have is the mastery, clarification, or explanation of practice. Fish makes clear that this does not render theoretical formulations meaningless or useless. It means, according to Fish, that Hirsch's theory, for example, is not a theory of interpretation but an interpretive act, that Kant's categories are not a theory of thinking but an act of thought, and that Marx's theory of value is not a theory about politics but a political argument. While there may be practical distinctions to be made between those practices recognized in specific contexts as "theoretical," what determines their significance is not their truth, accuracy, or explanatory power in some impossibly (implausibly?) unsituated general sense, but their contingent usefulness and power in a given context. What defines their force and their meaning in a given context is their relation to specific institutions—structural, political, cultural, "personal"— that constitute what Fish calls interpretive communities.[12]

In Fish's rhetoric, uncertainty and anxiety appear only as what Fish himself might call a "missing portion." This missing portion—and the force required to sustain its absence—are most in evidence in the chapter entitled "Withholding the Missing Portion," which is, not by chance, on

Freud and supplies, significantly, the end of *Doing What Comes Naturally*. Need I say that this missing portion is not simply missing and cannot in any simple way be supplied? Because it cannot be supplied, I suspect, Fish avoids confronting its absence and the implications of that absence for the practice he so powerfully describes. In considering the role anxiety plays in Fish's work, I am drawn to the remark he makes about winning the contest of telling theory's story, a contest in which *Doing What Comes Naturally* is a strong entrant. For winning any contest recalls the traditional project of metaphysics, the traditional goal of theory—to win the argument with argument, to rule out the distorting and anxiety-provoking force of rhetoric, to find indisputably certain grounds for thinking and acting—the end of which project, along with the end of theory, Fish at times attempts to declare though the declaration itself inevitably appears as one more move in the game.[13] Yet if "rhetorical" is Fish's master word, it must lead him eventually to confront mastery as an issue. What does winning an argument mean, pragmatically or theoretically, when the argument in question pits practice against theory?

In some practical matters, distinguishing winners from losers may be done more easily than in others. When Fish speaks of practice, he often draws examples from baseball. In baseball the rules are always in force, and they always rule the game the players play. As Fish says in *Doing What Comes Naturally*, baseball offers a perfect example of "what transpires between fully situated members of a community" (372). Here theory has nothing more to say because the rules are so implacably in place that no one can argue about them. Disputes are limited to the purely practical matters of missing a call and cheating. Even these arguments seldom progress beyond ad hominem attacks, since no matter of baseball principle is involved. The instituted rules of baseball define the game and sanction the members of its community, determining what "play" means, who is qualified to play, and what each player's action signifies toward the specific end of winning. In baseball, as Fish notes, the only thing one can say is "What did you expect?" Expectation remains an expression of what the rules have already defined. No one in baseball would consider questioning the significance or propriety of these expectations. To do so would be to question the rules that make baseball, as it is, possible, and no player in this game has the institutional ability or any stake in doing that.

Yet if this is so, it must be because in baseball, theory—understood in the strong sense Fish defines as rules that master practice—has such complete possession of the field it defines that it does precisely what theory and metaphysics since Plato have dreamed of doing. It renders all activities and meanings within the game so clear that fundamental disagreement about the rules of the game is ruled out of the game. Umpires, the institutionally appointed guardians of the game—empowered intellectuals entrusted with a legislative function—resolve all disputes according to their sanctioned judgment of how the rules apply and what they mean, the force of their judgment being itself legitimized by the rules they administer.

Rather than follow up the similarities between the world of baseball and Plato's *Republic*, I note how strikingly the discursive world of baseball, as narrated by Stanley Fish, differs from the discursive world of literary criticism or of community in the world at large. In these, no party to arguments in the public sphere occupies a position from which an uncontested winner could be declared; no one has incontrovertible authority to call the game of disputation because of darkness or mystification.

Fish imagines a world of practices, a world of academic disciplines and cultural communities, that divides into distinct fields with various games going on in each that must not be confused.[14] As he notes, playing baseball and explaining playing baseball are two distinct activities. "Philosophy," he adds, "is one thing, and literary criticism is another": "They are different games, and they remain different even when they are played by the same person" (*Doing What Comes Naturally*, 335). Each field constitutes in itself an interpretive community in which each local practice is simultaneously situated and judged. We are always, in Fish's account, situated in a context, a community, or a game as "agents fully committed to a practice."

Yet baseball and the humanities (as some still call those disciplines that interpret human culture) are different sorts of games. The very difference between them gives theoretical uncertainty a place in the play of critical studies and community politics that it cannot have in baseball. For no ballplayer can doubt that the game being played is baseball, yet Fish indicates that many and perhaps some of the best critics have thought that the game being played was literary interpretation when actually the game was philosophy or politics. Similar confusion seems to obtain in legal theory, prompting Fish to remark: "The law, however, is not philosophy; it is law, although, like everything else it can become the object of philosophical analysis, in which case it becomes something different from what it is on its own terms" (*Free Speech*, 177). This is odd, since as Fish argues elsewhere in *There's No Such Thing as Free Speech*, the amazing trick of the law is to disguise the fact that its values and discriminations emerge from extralegal contexts that give the law its sense of identity and purpose even as they undermine its identity with itself. The law cannot fulfill its wish "to be distinct, not something else"; the law cannot realize its wish to have a formal existence (141). Neither can literary studies. Other disciplines—history, sociology, and political science, for example—tend to reappear within the space of their exclusion, often when they are least acknowledged.

Sometimes the same person, as Fish says, confuses the issue by playing the wrong game: philosophy instead of law, literary theory instead of literary interpretation. Do they do this consciously? Who are the referees? Where are the guardians? Given the possibilities of such errors and the obscurity of the disciplinary boundaries and rules that make such errors possible, how could one know the relation between the game one plays and the rules in force? Can "the" rules simply be in force if the rules from one game call those from another into question and the question of how many and which games are being played is always and endlessly debatable? In what field could questioning like this be said to occur? Could it be in a field where contingency rules as it does in the field of rhetoric? And isn't it contingency that separates rhetoric and baseball as different kinds of games? There is no contingency in baseball. The rules—and the institutional guardians of the rules—ensure that once hit, a home run will fulfill the expectations with which it was hit. At least one run will score. But as Fish asserts in *Doing What Comes Naturally*, the same cannot be said of persuasion, where the only rules are rules of thumb (461). And persuasion, as Fish also points out, is what rules in communities that play the game of democracy.

Academic and political communities may not be like baseball, but they might be like the game TEGWAR in Mark Harris's baseball novel *Bang the Drum Slowly*. When not playing baseball, Harris's players pass the time with TEGWAR. It occupies and symbolizes their haphazard lives off the field. The letters stand for "the exciting game without any rules." What appears to be a regular card game is actually an improvised performance in which one plays at offering and taking cards. Winning in this game means manipulating a spectator's anxiety at being left out of the play so that he or she enters into and continues it. As Fish has often noted, there are always rules. Here the game consists in constructing the impression that the rules are actually in force, while the knowledge that that impression is a construction actually rules. Persuasion might be like TEGWAR if it were a deadly serious game in which the rules themselves were the cards being played and taken according to rules endlessly invoked and challenged, and if the anxiety that kept the game going were split between fearing to be taken in and worrying about being left out. The law may be like TEGWAR as well, if as Drucilla Cornell (approvingly quoted by Fish) suggests, "the rule itself is always in the process of reinterpretation as it is applied." [15] What is true of life within the vexed and divided interpretive communities of English departments is true of life in communities generally. Anxiety and interpretation are inextricably linked.

If there weren't uncertainty and anxiety about precisely the sorts of communities and interpretive rules that Fish claims are always in place, if the field of literary criticism and the space of everyday life were not so filled with fundamental disagreements about the rules in force, then books such as *Doing What Comes Naturally* and *Professional Correctness* would not only be unnecessary; they would be impossible. This follows, of course, from Fish's own formulations. These books are symptomatic of precisely the sorts of uncertainties and anxieties about which they finally have little to say.[16]

In the first chapter of *Doing What Comes Naturally*, Fish distinguishes between "styles of self-presentation and styles of knowing":

> Of course there are distinctions between the ways in which the objective knowledge that flows from one's beliefs might be urged on others, styles of self-presentation that are often thought of wrongly as styles of knowing. I might say to you, for example, "what you have just said is obviously false for the following indisputable reasons" (this is, in fact, my style), or I might say, "I see your point, and it is certainly an important one, but I wonder if we might make room for this other perspective," and, depending on your sense of decorum and on the conventions in place in the arena of our discussion, the conversation between us would unfold differently. But whichever style of discussion I adopt, that style will always be grounded firmly in the beliefs that ground me. (21)

Fish's rhetorical performances enact a style of self-presentation that does not, I think, flow easily from Fish's belief that the world is a rhetorical place. Fish's style of self-presentation involves the mastering of opponents through the overpowering force of argument. His ability to win these arguments—his ability to construct arguments as the sort of games one wins—depends on the certainty of his grounding in knowledge, beliefs, and principles. But if one of these beliefs is Fish's often expressed conviction that "we live in a rhetorical world" (25), a world in which rhetoric not only flows from but establishes and also displaces the beliefs that ground a subject, a world in which "whatever foundations there are (and there are always some) have been established by persuasion, that is, in the course of argument and counter argument on the basis of examples and evidence that are themselves cultural and contextual" (29), then how firm can this grounding ever be? In the light of this knowledge, what could the self-characterized firmness of Fish's style mean?

Fish's apparent certainties may have more to do with the opponents he constructs than with the firmness of his own grounding. Fish himself acknowledges something like this in the final paragraph of *Doing What Comes Naturally*'s introductory chapter:

> But why, one might ask, is there so little of that acknowledgment [of the "fractured, fissured, volatile condition" of embeddedness] in your

work? . . . The answer to this . . . is that everything in discourse depends on what I call the "angle of lean," the direction you are facing as you begin your discursive task. (32–33)

In other words, everything depends on your attitude, your lean, toward or on your opponents. Fish concludes this paragraph with the observation that "it is not my task" to "develop a finely tuned picture of the operations of belief (or community or practice) . . . and indeed it is a task which, if taken seriously (as it certainly should be), would prevent me from doing what I have tried to do" (33). Should we accept the apparent clarity of Fish's self-reflection and his refusal to confront or face the directions toward which the fractures, fissures, and volatility in his own embeddedness might cause him to lean, or should we subject Fish's attitude to analysis? When Fish insists that confronting in detail the picture of belief that he himself paints would render his portrait impossible, he may be indicating the depth of his resistance to, and the force of his anxiety about, the direction in which his argument nevertheless tends.

Fish believes that all utterances and all thinking are governed by pre-existing beliefs or principles. This may be true, but it remains a philosophical or theoretical observation until and unless it can be realized in or through practice. Self-reflection, as Fish effectively argues, can find no neutral position from which to make its measurements or discover its own grounds. Given the rhetorical nature of self-reflection, one most strongly experiences one's principles—the rules by which one believes oneself to be playing—through the intervention of another player to whom one's rhetoric of self-reflection appeals. Self-reflection thus involves an agonistic relationship with another contestant who can always call the nature of one's relationship to principles and beliefs into question as a move in the rhetorical game being played. In this context, to know that one has principles is to be forced to acknowledge that they are in question, sometimes by asserting with as much force as possible that they are unquestionable. One experiences one's relationship to principles not in the self-evident significance of one's statements but in their appeal to others, interior or exterior to the self, who accept or resist those principles. Without the question of the other (which is the question of rhetoric even if the other is another aspect of the self, and self-reflection a fancy name for self-persuasion), the project of philosophy as a search for grounding principles would have been neither necessary nor possible.

This was already apparent to C. S. Peirce, one of pragmatism's founders, who explains the origin of the real in terms of a conflictual idea of community:

And what do we mean by the real? It is a conception which we must first have had when we discovered that there was an unreal, an illusion; that is, when we first corrected ourselves. Now the distinction for which alone this fact logically called, was between an *ens* relative to private inward determinations, to the negations belonging to idiosyncrasy, and an *ens* such as would stand in the long run. The real, then, is that which, sooner or later, information and reasoning would finally result in, and which is therefore independent of the vagaries of me and you. Thus, the very origin of the conception of reality shows that this conception essentially involves the notion of a COMMUNITY, without definite limits, and capable of a definite increase of knowledge.[17]

For Peirce, the presence of the community at the origin of the real does not obviate the possibility of disagreement. Knowledge operates in terms of disagreement. Thinking is agonistic. One discovers reality—one discovers or creates one's individual being, or *ens*—when one is struck by the difference between one's sense of things and the way things "are" in the community's determinations of them. Reality emerges through the conflict between the inner *ens* that is realized and constituted as a "fact logically called for" by the resistance of the outer community. This derivation of the inner *ens* constitutes the self as being in question and subject to illusions. Moreover, the final determination of reality appears projected into some indefinite future, which leaves alive the question of how to make and judge interpretations of reality, of the self, and of the community in any given moment. This account of "reality," depending on appeals from and to the community, also renders self-reflection rhetorical and has implications for Fish's practice as well as his beliefs.

Fish's account of communities is not so different from Peirce's. In the first chapter of *Doing What Comes Naturally*, Fish describes embeddedness in conflictual terms: "Being embedded means just that, being embedded *always*, and one does not escape embeddedness by acknowledging, as I do, that it is itself a fractured, fissured, volatile condition" (32). But this description raises the question toward which Fish sometimes tends, even though he finally refuses to move there. How easily can one rest on such a bed? How firmly can one be grounded in such a belief about embeddedness? What does it mean to find oneself *always* in such a position? Given the fractured, fissured, volatile condition of all of our communities and the contending cultures that find themselves embedded in them, the rhetorical nature of our self-reflection means that we find ourselves embedded and uncertain, anxious and engaged, at the same time.

An example of such embeddedness might be found in a crucial passage from the introductory chapter of *Doing What Comes Naturally* in which Fish responds to Frank Lentricchia's critique of the new pragmatism. In "The Return of William James," Lentricchia argues that "expounding of the anti-theory position 'at this juncture cannot help but bring comfort, energy, and ideas to the enemies of change' " (quoted in Fish, 28–29). In essence, Lentricchia asks Fish, What did you expect in making such an argument? Fish, for his part, admits the force of Lentricchia's objection. "The point," Fish writes, "is a nice one and difficult to gainsay." Then he attempts gainsaying it much too easily:

> I feel uneasy at the suggestion that before putting an argument into the world we should calculate the effects of its falling into the wrong hands. Such calculations can certainly be made, but, given the infinite appropriability of what we say, it would seem that predicting in the direction of possible harm is no less foolhardy than predicting in the direction of possible good. (29) [18]

Lentricchia does not quite catch Fish on this point. Yet from a pragmatist's point of view, it is odd to argue that we need not be concerned with calculating the effects of our actions, since in pragmatism as in rhetoric, the significance of an action lies precisely in its effects. If, as A. O. Lovejoy noted in 1908, the pragmatic view of knowledge makes intellectual life "wholly . . . a system of deferred payments," then each pragmatic actor on the public stage must await the response by which his or her actions are appropriated to realize their value and significance (Lovejoy, 33).

Fish's denial that consequences should be calculated seems particularly odd, since the point of rhetoric as a practice is to calculate effects without forgetting contingency. Rhetoric responds to contingency by seeking to constrain or exploit the manner in which utterances are appropriated or understood. "One acts," as Fish asserts, "on the basis of calculations that have at least the probability associated with rules of thumb" (*Doing What Comes Naturally*, 461). Since Gorgias taught Athenians the knack, rhetoric has involved the art of calculating probabilities. To suggest that one needn't be concerned with the possible conflict between the appropriateness and the appropriability of words lets the rhetorician off the hook. It suggests that some other criteria (like the transparency of original intention to itself, a possibility of critical self-consciousness that Fish emphatically denies) different from the pragmatic might be invoked to explain significance. At such points in his argument, Fish (as Bruce Robbins has noted) tends to render the crucial categories of rhetoric and persuasion purely aesthetic and formal. Yet given the pragmatic nature of both, they can never be simply aestheticized or formalized; they can never be safely separated from the political world of consequential action in which they occur. And it is precisely at this point, the importance of which Fish wants to minimize, that anxiety plays its part. It is precisely our embeddedness as professional intellectuals in conflictual contexts that makes anxiety central to what we do.[19]

In his encounter with Lentricchia, Fish performs like the Minneapolis City Council whose confrontation with Catherine MacKinnon's testimony on the links between pornography and rape Fish describes. As Fish characterizes MacKinnon's strategy, "the council members are to be made uncomfortable in their support of views that have effects they have never confronted" (Doing What Comes Naturally, 17). They confront the unacknowledged effects of their actions and the beliefs they believe ground them in a polemical characterization of those actions and beliefs. They are asked, in effect, What did you expect when you allowed pornography to legitimize violence against women? MacKinnon's appropriation of the council members' action is meant to force an uneasy reflective reassessment of where their actions place them in relation to commonly held principles such as justice and freedom or political expediency and personal ambition. MacKinnon's strategy reads the inconsistency of these principles with the actions done in their name. The anxiety she provokes becomes, or is supposed to become, an agent in the alteration of some beliefs leveraged by common grounds in others. In his own discourse, Fish registers the uneasy realization of his own principles in Lentricchia's objections to his practice, a realization that these principles or his relationship to them might be different than he had supposed. That certain arguments or beliefs could aid or abet certain political agendas seems a legitimate reason to worry, if not an instantly compelling argument. But does Fish ever confront the consequences of this anxiety? Isn't it this anxiety, concerning the political appropriation of one's work, that Fish counseled his new historicist colleagues against? For those of us concerned with more than the merely formal or theoretical requirements of persuasion, anxieties about the political implications of what we "win" is very much a part of what we do.

Fish, as we have noted, often seeks to assuage anxiety (here his own), though anxiety is just what Fish's thinking appears to produce (here in himself). This seems inevitable. For if pragmatism claims that consequences are contingent rather than necessary, it also asserts that consequences are all that matter. Thus it is precisely the contingency of consequences that opens the conflictual space in which anxiety motivates theory as an attempt, like rhetoric, to master contingency. The attempt to master contingency through rhetoric is active in Fish's texts at the level of their form as well as in their content. It functions in Fish's refusal to confront ambivalence and uneasiness and in his insistence on construing arguments that ground themselves in the "indisputable" while championing a position that holds nothing to be beyond dispute. This attempt to ground arguments in the indisputable cannot succeed, as Fish knows, because if the indisputable were available, the argument would not be necessary, and the world would not be, as Fish says it is, a rhetorical place.

Fish does not deny, as we have seen, that communities can be volatile and fractured, and that their subjects might experience "inner conflict." Yet much as he did with his own uneasiness and with his younger colleagues' anxiety, he dismisses the force of this experience:

> [Inner conflict] makes perfect sense so long as constraints are not required to be monolithic. One is often "conflictually" constrained, that is, held in place by a sense of a situation as requiring negotiation between conflicting demands that seem equally legitimate. One may be constrained, for example, both by one's understanding of what it means to be an academic and one's understanding of what it means to be a feminist. But even here we must be careful not to overdramatize the conflict by speaking of it as creating a "split-consciousness." An academic who is also a feminist is not two persons, but one—an academic-who-is-also-a-feminist. (*Doing What Comes Naturally*, 31)

In this view of things, to be a person means, in any one moment, to be on some level single-minded. Although the various roles one plays may be externally in conflict with each other, they are not internally split or ambivalent. Each represents what is simply an alternative interiority. Yet when Fish argues that self-reflection can never be transparent to itself because it remains an interpretive and rhetorical act, he implies (though he does not make this explicit) that as in the psychoanalytic situation, this act requires the intervention of another. Self-reflection in Fish's account is not impossible, but it is, like everything else, rhetorical, a negotiation of appeal and demand.

Fish does not explicitly confront the implications of this staging of self-reflection for the splitting of the self *within* any of the roles it might play or imagine itself to be playing. On the contrary, Fish urges that the plight of "split consciousness" not be overdramatized. This is a strange urgency in a polemic that claims to reveal the rhetorical, dramatic, and agonistic nature of self-reflection. Perhaps it is, as Fish suggests, an aspect of the "lean" in these essays, which determines their content in the construction of their opponents. Yet perhaps these denials of split consciousness are defensive, symptomatic of anxieties related to a vision of self-knowing as agonistic performance that defines itself in leaning toward or on its opponents. Appropriately, these anxieties are most in evidence when the opponent Fish confronts or constructs is Freud. The antiformalist road that *Doing What Comes Naturally* begins by describing tends from the first toward the confrontation with Freud that is the subject of the book's last chapter. On the one hand, Fish refuses to overdramatize the splits within identities; on the other, he argues that self-reflection is a rhetorical contest. This split in Fish already evokes Freud by attempting to deny him.

Anxious subjects

Doing What Comes Naturally works throughout its long course toward the engagement with Freud that takes place in its final chapter. And yet, in my view, this final engagement between Fish and Freud fails to occur; and as one might expect, it fails to occur for reasons that both Freud and Fish might understand. There can be, as Freud remarks, no war between polar bears and seals; or as Fish repeatedly asserts, for there to be conflict there must first be common ground. In reading Freud and in reading others who have recently read Freud, Fish elides the critical view of self-mastery that is at the center of Freud's theory and practice of psychoanalysis and has recently been read back into Freud's texts. Fish's Freud fulfills the desire that possesses all rhetoricians, the desire to be in control of his own rhetoric, the dream of being master of the master word. Fish's reading of Freud excludes precisely the Freudian categories of transference and anxiety that call this dream of mastery of both self and other into question. Fish's reading of Freud is symptomatic of anxieties that the contents of Fish's essays deny, but the desire to prevail evident in their form repeatedly throws those anxieties into relief.

For Fish, Freud's text enacts the repeated "drama of Freud's rhetorical mastery," repeatedly staging "the story of a master rhetorician who hides from others and from himself the true nature of his activities" (*Doing What Comes Naturally*, 541, 540). The character of Fish's Freud is evident in his reading of the passage where the Wolf-Man "recollects," through Freud's intervention, his childhood seduction by his sister: "The real seduction in this chapter (which is accomplished at this moment and in a single blow) is the seduction not of the patient by his sister, but of both the patient and the reader by Freud, who will now be able to produce interpretive conclusions in the confidence that they will be accepted as the conclusions of an inevitable and independent logic" (536). After Lacan and others (many of whom Fish mentions), this observation carries little force except for the word "confidence." Where does this confidence that Fish attributes to Freud come from; where in Fish's scenario would it or could it ground itself? As Fish points out, the supports for Freud's interpretations are rhetorically established and depend on the enlisted support of his audience, his patients and readers. Yet how could any rhetorically established support ever be simply firm? How could Freud, of all people, know the appropriateness or predict the appropriation of his words in advance or even be confident about knowing his own intentions when uttering them? Freud, the theorist of parapraxis and of so much else, well knew the contingencies—"internal" as well as "external"—that bedevil actions. How could he ever believe himself possessed of an audience by which he could not be abandoned and to which he would not have to abandon himself? Can one assume that for Freud, who experienced so much resistance to his theories in the medical community at large and within the psychoanalytic community he founded, such contingencies evoked no uncertainty or anxiety concerning his role in the Wolf-Man case? How dramatic is the drama of Freud's rhetorical mastery, and how would one know if one was overdramatizing it?

Which raises once again the question of rhetoric. In his chapter "Rhetoric," Fish borrows from Richard Lanham's *Motives of Eloquence* two passages contrasting two assumptions about being in the world. *Homo seriosus*, according to Lanham, "possesses a central self, an irreducible identity. These selves combine into a single, homogeneously real society which constitutes a referent reality for the men living in it." *Homo rhetoricus*, by way of contrast, "is an actor; his reality public, dramatic. His sense of identity depends on the reassurance of daily histrionic reenactment. He is thus centered in time and concrete local event" (quoted in Fish, *Doing What Comes Naturally*, 482–83). Yet in view of this description, can *Homo rhetoricus*, dependent as his sense of himself is on histrionic reenactment and his appeal to an audience, be centered at any time or in any event? Or is this dramatic being always constituted and split by conflict and by the possibility of conflict in the agon of acting or action? When and where does he achieve his sense of identity? In his performance? In his audience's reception of him? In his perception of their reception? In these oscillations that confuse the temporal and spatial localizability or grounding of the self and of the world, something of the terror evoked by the antifoundationalist critique becomes explicable.

Fish is certainly not unaware of the terror evoked by the antifoundationalist position. He notes, at the beginning of his essay on Freud, the reaction to a statement by I. A. Richards at the 1958 Style in Language Conference. Richards declares that "questions of value and meaning, are finally rhetorical; it is a matter, he says, of the context of discourse and, as Isocrates observes, good discourse is discourse that works." The response to this statement at the conference was, Fish notes, "terror" (*Doing What Comes Naturally*, 525–26). What is there to fear in the statement that good discourse is discourse that works? Such pragmatism calls mastery itself into question. If discourse and the subject who utters it achieve definition only by pragmatic criteria, by "working" or failing to work, then they achieve significance only in the judgment of those to whom they address themselves and whose judgments can always be questioned in turn. The author can never be certain in advance—nor perhaps after the fact—where he stands. Terror is not a reaction against Richards's statement, but a realization of the uncertainty it implies. It is this terror of uncertainty that Fish's essay on Freud the rhetorician seeks to suppress. As I press this point, I once again hear Fish's urging not to overdramatize the plot of split consciousness. For Fish, rhetoric is dramatic, but not too dramatic. But just how dramatic is it?

Once Fish, once rhetoric, establishes the exteriority of the self to itself by deconstructing the transparency of self-reflection and putting it on the stage, interiority and simple coherence cannot be recuperated on any level whatsoever. Once the self is realized and split in its rhetorical self-dramatizations of and to itself, that split cannot be healed at any level of analysis. Each level of analysis represents the activity of this split subject and enacts, in its rhetorical appeals and denials, the drama of split consciousness again.

Fish's image of selves constituted and constrained within practices or communities by internally homogeneous and externally heterogeneous demands does not seem adequate to the view of things that the dramatization of self-reflection presents. The pressing question becomes the precariousness and anxiety of one's embeddedness. Membership in a community—the very existence of community—becomes arguable like everything else within institutional spaces that always need to be and always are being reenacted and redrawn.

The incoherence and splits within institutions as well as subjects are implied but never confronted in the antifoundationalism of Fish's position. In the world as a rhetorical place, conflict comes to the fore and becomes, in a sense, the only game there is. In this game, the rules are always in question and emerge only in and through conflict. Yet it is precisely the anxiety that attends conflict—the possibility one might lose or that winning might not be possible—that Fish repeatedly refuses to discuss. And here, once again, we encounter the issue of institutional constraints. Fish notes that the institutional difference between a text in a legal court and a text in literary practice is that the interpretive practice of law demands that there be "a single reading" whereas the practice of literary criticism exerts "pressure for multiple readings" (*Doing What Comes Naturally*, 54). In literary criticism, as Fish's practice makes clear, the various readings of a text are not all equal, nor do they always peacefully cohabit. In fact, the practice of literary interpretation is often constrained to be conflictual,[20] which also means that the principles of literary interpretation can never simply be in place. Within the realm of literary criticism, practice is most often a matter of polemic; and polemic, it seems, leads—as a moment in a polemical strategy—to moments of theoretical reflection in which principles are questioned and proposed. Literary criticism is a realm of contestations, a career of persuasion, a profession of anxiety.

Throughout his essays on rhetoric and force, Fish returns again and again to words like "contestable" and "precarious":

> To be sure, this does not solve our practical problems, since we are still faced with the difficulty of adjudicating between beliefs in the absence of a calculus that is not itself a function or extension of belief. It is a difficulty that cannot be removed, but the fact that it cannot be removed does not condemn us to uncertainty and paralysis, but to conflict, to acts of persuasion in which one party attempts to alter the beliefs of another by putting forward arguments that are weighty only in relation to still other beliefs. By definition the career of persuasion is unpredictable and theoretically interminable; there is no guarantee that either party will be victorious. . . . But when victory occurs, . . . it is always provisional; for since it has emerged from argument, from the forceful urging of some partisan point of view, it is always possible, and indeed likely, that what has apparently been settled will become unsettled, and argument will begin again. (*Doing What Comes Naturally*, 522)

How could uncertainty be ruled out of such a situation? How could uncertainty not be a necessary constituent of such a game? Would such uncertainty necessarily lead to paralysis? Indeed, uncertainty might be a precondition for the recognition of the necessity of action—physical or mental, theoretical or antitheoretical. Uncertainty might, indeed, be the nature of the field.

One of the crucial differences between the institutions of criticism and politics on the one hand, and the game of baseball on the other, is precisely the contestability of significance, the contestability of the rules themselves. There can be no question of ends in baseball. Critical games and political communities constitute themselves most often not in the space of play but along the lines of contention. These lines of contestation rule a place in which the rules can be in place and in question at the same time and where the question of the rules can always be opened. Intellectuals have a role to play here, but it is not as empowered guardians of the rules or as referees.

It is toward a view of communities as conflictual rather than common places that our current historical moment and the history of "our" profession as academic intellectuals within it tend. Fish's work, as it reflects on and dramatizes the fissured volatility of these "contexts," addresses and dramatizes some of the forces and conflicts that constrain the players "in" "the" "field." A reading of communities must be a reading of the anxieties evoked rather than assuaged by cultural conflicts, whether within the specific context of an academic specialization such as literary studies or the more general arena of political argument in a multicultural society. These anxieties, which seem to be the uneasy points on which conflict and persuasion turn, Fish's work both evokes and exemplifies, especially while denying that it is anxious at all.

Intellectuals and the power of a dream

But this last point opens onto another question. Both the champions and the critics of the common dream of a common culture share a fantasy of disciplinary power. In this dream, literary intellectuals occupy a discursive space that is adjacent to, and impinges on, the disciplinary mechanisms that enable society's—or to be more precise, and to remain faithful to D'Souza's and Gitlin's polemic, the nation's—reproduction. The power of this fantasy speaks when D'Souza claims a vanguard role for university intellectuals not only as mirrors of society but as "leading indicators and catalysts for change," custodians of the nation's future and guardians of the nation's truth. We need to analyze this dream if we are to understand some of the pressures that determine the interminableness of the present debate.

Despite D'Souza's claims, the flux of racially and culturally different immigrations represents nothing particularly new in U.S. history. I suspect, however, that what gives the current situation its particular force are tensions generated by the concurrent rapid and often violent transformation of the national economy, transformations that reflect an ongoing redefinition of the contemporary nation-state in the postindustrial global economy.[21] These global transformations have been and continue to be exacerbated by local policies in the United States that have favored entrepreneurial and finance capital at the expense of manufacturing and industrial enterprises with an attendant contraction in the labor market and a deepening decline in living standards for many U.S. citizens. These trends have been intensified by the deunionizing of the labor force, the continuing implosion of the long-neglected urban and industrial centers, and the nearly complete and perhaps irremediable atomization and isolation of segments of U.S. society into contending, hostile enclaves. This complex of interlinked and oft remarked crises forms the real background for the sense of crisis and hysteria manifested in many of the current appeals to reclaim a legacy in Western liberalism that would bring the society together and discipline it.

Such hysteria, in the form of denial, is evident in the work of other liberal

pragmatists, like Fish, who would deny the anxious basis of their speculations. This applies even (or particularly) to the reflections of as genial a
liberal as Richard Rorty. Although I agree with many of the points Rorty
makes in his analysis of the shortcomings of what he calls the "cultural
left," I am also struck by the feeling I always have when reading his work
that he inhabits a world starkly different from the one I know. In Rorty's
world, conflicts seem less central to the processes of thought, and the pronoun "we" (as in his favorite locution "we liberals") can be deployed without too many worries about what its referent, if any, might be. This is true,
for example, in Contingency, Irony, Solidarity, where he writes of the figure
of the "liberal ironist," the ideal intellectual for the ideal "liberal utopia"
that he is attempting to sketch: "Liberal ironists," he writes, "are people
who include among these ungroundable desires their own hope that suffering will be diminished, that the humiliation of human beings by other
human beings may cease."[22] One puzzling aspect of Rorty's argument is
his tendency not to consider the obvious problems with this definition of
liberalism—those who believe there is nothing worse than suffering and
humiliation—when it comes to the pragmatics of its application.

No one could claim that Rorty is not aware of these problems; he lists
some of them in the very next paragraph of his introduction:

> For liberal ironists, there is no answer to the question "Why not be
> cruel?"—no noncircular theoretical backup for the belief that cruelty
> is horrible. Nor is there an answer to the question "How do you decide
> when to struggle against injustice and when to devote yourself to pri-
> vate projects of self-creation?" This question strikes liberal ironists as
> just as hopeless as the questions "Is it right to deliver n innocents over
> to be tortured to save the lives of m × n other innocents? If so, what are
> the correct values of n and m?" or the question "When may one favor
> members of one's family, or one's community, over other, randomly
> chosen, human beings?" (Rorty, Contingency, xv)

Now, I agree with Rorty that there are no theoretical answers to such questions, no abstractable algorithmic procedures to predecide the issues. But
that is because these are not theoretical questions but pragmatic problems.
And they are the very problems that Rorty himself, liberal pragmatist as he
claims to be, purports to address.

There are, in fact, many reasons to be cruel, and redistributive justice,
which Rorty enthusiastically supports, is a form of cruelty practiced in
which those who have a lot (though not always by their own account)
must be made to suffer (as they often see it) in order to benefit those who
have less. Republicans tend to see such redistributions of wealth as unjust and as inflicting cruel punishment and even humiliation where it is

unwarranted. Similarly, they purport to see those who have less as being themselves to blame. Therefore their suffering appears to conservatives to be merited and thus not cruel at all. Rorty's position on these issues is clear (he favors redistributions of wealth and believes that the rich cheat the poor), but he seems unimpressed with the necessity of offering arguments that support those positions especially with regard to those who clearly do not agree—and most political indicators suggest that many Americans do not. Such arguments might require recourse to some theoretical-sounding propositions involving, for instance, appeals to locally transcendent values such as fairness, justice, and compassion. Rorty's tendency is to treat such issues as test cases for separating liberal sheep from conservative goats.

Even more vexed these days is the issue to which Rorty's last theoretical example alludes: when may one favor one's own family or community over other human beings? This question pertains to the problem of immigration, a problem that requires us to rethink the limits of community and the nature of national identity. Rorty, again, is not unaware of this problem; he just has little to say about it. In his most recent book, *Achieving Our Country*, Rorty narrates an event that occurred at the "Teach-In for Labor" held at Columbia University in 1996:

> Orlando Patterson, the eminent historian of slavery, argued that the border with Mexico would sooner or later have to be closed to protect American workers. He was heckled by people shouting, "What about the workers in the Third World?" Black scholars do not often get booed by predominately white and leftist audiences, but it happened this time. I suspect that the issue Patterson raised will be the most deeply divisive that the American Left will face in the twenty-first century. I wish that I had some good ideas about how the dilemma might be resolved, but I do not.[23]

I am disappointed that Rorty has nothing to offer, no good ideas at all, on this pressing issue because it involves so many of the issues in which he claims an interest: national pride, liberal community, and practical politics, not to mention human suffering and humiliation as well as redistributive justice. Leaving aside the obvious objection to Patterson's position — that restricting the movement of Mexicans across the border may in fact be impossible and is unlikely to benefit American workers, since it is the low wage paid to workers in Mexico and elsewhere that most threatens the wages of North American workers and human dignity here and abroad — let us merely consider the more "theoretical" issues involved.[24]

I don't mean to play the mean-spirited game of attempting to catch Rorty out here. I admire him and respect his work. But I do mean to attempt an account of why I find that work troubling and unsatisfying. The instance I cite is not a solecism or slip but rather a symptom of a character-istic inability or unwillingness on Rorty's part to actually engage the issues to which he refers. To engage them would constrain him to adopt a much more tortured and conflicted sense of the liberal utopia and the American nation than he wants to project.

This returns us, for a moment, to Rorty's suspicious lack of suspicion about the pronoun "we." In *Contingency, Irony, Solidarity* he offers, with his characteristically bald frankness, precisely this point to separate him from Foucault, and by implication from the entire cultural Left that Rorty claims Foucault has influenced: "I disagree with Foucault about whether in fact it is necessary to form a new 'we.' My principal disagreement with him is precisely over whether 'we liberals' is or is not good enough" (64). For Rorty, who deploys the term with a purposely provocative equanimity, "we liberals" is meant to seem good enough.

But I find myself wondering why that should be. If the liberal utopia Rorty imagines is to be led by liberal ironists, then what becomes of the ironist's characteristic anxiety as Rorty himself describes it? In a chapter called "Private Irony and Liberal Hope," Rorty describes "the ironist" as "a nominalist and a historicist" and goes on to say:

> The ironist spends her time worrying about the possibility that she has been initiated into the wrong tribe, taught to play the wrong language game. She worries that the process of socialization which turned her into a human being by giving her a language may have given her the wrong language, and so turned her into the wrong kind of human being. (*Contingency*, 75)

If this is how the liberal ironist spends her time, then one wonders why Rorty does not spend more of his time worrying about precisely these issues.

His lack of worry and his own ruthless tendency to theoretical abstract-ness emerges most clearly when he seems to approach these issues most directly. For example, the penultimate paragraph and peroration at the end of *Contingency, Irony, Solidarity* offers the reader the following gloss on the relationship of liberals to ethnocentrism:

> *We* have to start from where *we* are—that is part of the force of Sellar's claim that we are under no obligations other than the "we-intentions" of the communities with which we identify. What takes the curse off this ethnocentrism is not that the largest such group is "humanity" or "all rational beings"—no one, I have been claiming, *can* make *that* identification—but, rather, that it is the ethnocentrism of a "we" ("we liberals") which is dedicated to enlarging itself, to creating an ever

larger and more variegated *ethnos*. It is the "we" of the people who have been brought up to distrust ethnocentrism. (198)

This, I am tempted to say, sounds all very well in theory, but what does it mean in practice? Pragmatically, where does the limit of our *ethnos*, our border of distrust, occur? Apparently, for Rorty, it might occur at the border with Mexico. But for a historicist like Rorty, that border—given the history of violent colonization and appropriation that characterized "our" acquisition of Mexican territory—should be particularly vexatious to police. Especially so in that if you accept the artificial border of the nation-state (the Rio Grande, let's say) as defining the natural border of our ethnos, then that community contains within it a large number of citizens who find the validity of the border questionable. What if the "we" of our community already contains the other within it? How do we negotiate that? This is not a question particular only to Mexico, Mexicans, Chicano/a citizens, or the Southwest. In one way or another, it defines the question that "achieving our country," to borrow another phrase from Rorty, entails.

In the face of rapid and ongoing redefinitions of economic and social life, in the face of shifts in the nature and limits of nation-states, in the face of alterations in the means by which power perpetuates and reproduces itself in postindustrial and postnational economies, and in the face of power relations that construct and maintain themselves less by ideological reproduction than by commodity circulation, literary intellectuals in the university must confront the fact that their links to, and leverage on, the politics of their societies are tenuous at best.[25]

This does not mean that the links between ideology and discipline, academia and the world, are nonexistent. It does mean that the fantasy of intellectuals as a vanguard for, or a bulwark against, cultural change, as guardians or betrayers of transcendent truths, needs to be questioned. This shifting in the intellectual's place and power—from a site where the nation's ideological power to reproduce itself once seemed to originate, to one where the nature of the nation reproduced remains an open question— produces one real pressure that drives the endless debate about a common culture. Academic intellectuals are in no position to undertake the task of imposing culture as discipline that critics like D'Souza and Gitlin call on them to perform.

Both those who champion the "traditional" curriculum and those who challenge it share a common assumption, which is itself an unexamined legacy of the Enlightenment. This legacy from the moment when the word "ideology," the idea of the intellectual, and the lineaments of the bourgeois state emerged assumes a certain vanguard role for intellectuals in the nation as cultural experts, guarantors of tradition, and projectors of moral improvement ensuring the progress of enlightenment and the solid grounding of the nation's social life. Neither those who would shore up an older consensus about the origins and trajectory of Western civilization from the heroism of the Greeks to the triumph of market capitalism nor those who would reconstruct the meaning of community by making difference the curriculum have much considered the limited leverage afforded to intellectuals in a regime where the marketplace reproduces citizens as consumers.

I am suggesting not that those of us located in the university should despair but only the obvious and even banal point that any political assessment of traditional or innovative curriculum—and such assessments remain a crucial part of the work we do—must also assess the opportunities and limitations of our positioning as intellectuals among the differences and disputes of our common lives. Although for many this may belabor the obvious, it is because the question of the intellectual's place and the nature of community has not been articulated as part of most battles in the culture wars that this improbable debate about literary intellectuals and cultural community has assumed the often fantastic and repetitive form that has distinguished it so far.

4

Culture: Western Traditions and Intellectual Treason

Heroes of the West: cultural relativism and
the challenge to cultural studies

Fredric Jameson, in a long review article on cultural studies, notes that "it does not seem wise to go on thinking of academic politics, and the politics of intellectuals, as a particularly 'academic' matter." [1] This seems especially true of the politics of culture, one of the most important objects of cultural studies as an academic discipline. On a global as well as on a local level, intellectuals within and outside of the academy often assume that culture grounds community and explains conflict. Recent work by conservative political theorist Samuel P. Huntington—director of the John M. Olin Institute for Strategic Studies at Harvard, chairman of that university's Academy for International and Area Studies, former director for Security Planning in the National Security Council during the Carter administration, and a significant voice among foreign policy strategists today—makes this starkly clear.[2] In an influential article and book, Huntington argues that in the post–Cold War new world order, "The clash of civilizations will dominate global politics. The fault lines between civilizations will be the battle lines of the future" ("Clash of Civilizations," 24–49).[3] Most important for my purposes, Huntington's views are rigorously relativistic. The West, or an ideological fantasy of the West that Huntington represents, must prepare to defend its own parochial culture and beliefs against other civilizations, strengthening its ties to its own cultural identity, containing or subverting other civilizations, especially Islam, wherever possible, not because the West is "better" (since Huntington admits no objective criteria by which to judge such merits), but because it is different.

It may seem that cultural intellectuals have no license to pursue the arguments of a political scientist. But when a political scientist such as Huntington makes policy recommendations that ground themselves in appeals to culture, he may be the one who is poaching. Culture has long been the preserve of intellectuals in disciplines like literature, history, and cultural studies where political scientists seldom trespass. Yet culture and politics seem these days to have become increasingly confused.

Cultural relativism has been one name for that confusion. Conservative and progressive critics sometimes agree, as we have seen, that cultural relativism is a basic flaw of cultural studies and multiculturalism that blunts whatever political point they might have. Relativism, they believe, is antipathetic to Western traditions, which they understand to be grounded in universality and objectivity; relativism disables the ethical sense, making firm political judgments and actions impossible to justify. Yet Huntington's recent attempt to ground a neoimperialist politics in a relativistic view of cultural specificity gives the lie to those who claim that cultural relativism disables political commitment. Huntington's position exemplifies what Andrew Ross has called a "conservative, even racist multiculturalism" that "appeals cynically to the alleged virtues of cultural difference."[4] In Huntington, however, the cynical appeal to difference legitimates not segregation but war. Conservatives may be surprised that relativism, usually identified with the weak liberal PC enemy, can be so effectively made to legitimate an unapologetic hostility toward other cultures as the principle for maintaining the preeminence of the United States in the new world order. Progressive critics, who often have reason to oppose the irresponsibilities and abuses of the United States as a neocolonial power, will find Huntington's recommendations less congenial, though they may not be so surprised. In fact, Huntington's argument seems to offer satisfying proof that relativism (which leftists sometimes see as a particularly vicious brand of bourgeois idealism vitiating possibilities for effective oppositional coalition building) offers no ethical or political leverage against the ideological impositions of power and is therefore inherently complicit in power's abuses.[5]

Both these reactions, the conservative's surprise and the progressive's satisfaction, are ill founded. If cultural relativism can lend credence to imperialist postures, it can also legitimate opposition to imperialism's claims. To champion local customs and traditions, in certain contexts, functions as resistance to a colonizing West that has often masked the violence and brutality of its impositions by invoking the universal value of its own institutions. In other contexts, the insistence on cultural specificity can support aggressive posturing and provide ideological cover for renewed commitments to imperialistic manipulation. Huntington provides an example of this. Relativism, in itself and in the absence of other values, has no particular political tendency at all.

In practice, however, relativism never functions in the absence of other values. Relativists believe that our values and choices emerge from, and are structured by, the contexts and situations that define us and our view of the world. This should pose problems for Huntington's position as a cultural relativist committed to Western civilization defined, as he says, by its commitments to secularism, the rule of law, social pluralism, and representative government (see *Clash of Civilizations*, 69–72). If a cultural relativist argues for, and in defense of, the West's cultural specificity, its Enlightenment traditions, ideals, and values, then those particular political principles and ideological commitments must be among the criteria by which the argument's effectiveness gets evaluated. Is the argument faithful to, or does it betray, the traditions and identity it purports to defend? Huntington, who tends to accept a common and uncritical equation between the West and the United States, argues that the "survival of the West depends on Americans reaffirming their Western identity and Westerners accepting their civilization as unique, not universal, and uniting to renew and preserve it against challenges from non-Western societies" (20–21). But the very Western or American identity and culture for which Huntington claims to speak renders his tendentious mapping of the world in terms of cultural conflict and his neoimperialist recommendations for the exercise of U.S. power extremely problematic. Richard Rorty, like Huntington a cultural relativist and an unapologetic defender of the West, says of its traditions: "Its sense of its own moral worth is founded on its tolerance of diversity. The heroes it apotheosizes include those who have enlarged its capacity for sympathy and tolerance." [6] By this measure, Huntington is no Western hero. His lack of tolerance for diversity among cultures and his insensitivity to the moral tenor of the tradition he champions is a fatal flaw in his argument for those who take culture seriously.

Cultural studies, of course, takes culture seriously. It has taken the relationship between culture and politics to be its most characteristic concern, especially the cultural politics of diversity, or multiculturalism. For his part, Huntington calls multiculturalism a "siren song" leading the West to its ruin (*Clash of Civilizations*, 307). Fredric Jameson, like Huntington an academic intellectual with political interests, is a progressive critic who has an ambivalent relationship to cultural studies. His critical distance makes his review essay "On 'Cultural Studies,'" a useful guide to the field. He identifies its tendencies, as distinct from the more universal programs and totalizing philosophy of the Western Left, with the politics of identity-based movements such as "antiracism, antisexism, antihomophobia, and so forth" (17). The list should certainly be expanded to include anti-imperialism. All of these usually ground themselves in a profound skepticism concerning the universalizing claims attached to the values and worldview of the West. Although Jameson has little patience with this characteristic antipathy toward "totalization," his work (like work in cultural studies generally) constitutes a viable continuation of what is best in the West. Thus, paradoxically, cultural studies remains faithful to "Western" traditions it frequently seems to deplore, especially progressive traditions of tolerance and justice, whereas Huntington betrays the traditions he pretends to defend.

Huntington's and Jameson's essays represent opposed positions on the relation of culture to politics—one conservative and instrumental, the other progressive and critical. In different ways, they each speak for what might be imagined as traditions of the West, though it is Jameson's work, and other work like it, that represents the best of the West.

In a strange sense, Huntington, whose position has been called "warmed over Cold War pie," seems to be doing a sort of cultural studies.[7] He urges U.S. policy makers to consider topics and relations that cultural critics often claim as their special area of expertise, especially the relations between culture and group identity and the linking of both to perceived interests within "civilizations" in a conflicted global arena. He touches on the problematics of communication and of the translation of values across cultures in an increasingly mixed world. Moreover, the spatialized logic of his model and its abstraction from history chime with similar tendencies in contemporary critical thought among certain academic leftists about which Jameson, in particular, has been especially critical.[8] The uncanny resemblance between Huntington's work and cultural studies should mute whatever simplistic, "triumphalist" note there may be in celebrations of the latter field by its own practitioners.[9]

Jameson, as a critic of cultural studies, provides an effective foil for Huntington. Both are quintessentially Western and essentially academic intellectuals, and both ask their colleagues to think conflict, politics, and culture on a global scale. Yet each has radically different goals and generates radically different narratives about the world he surveys. Whereas history is largely absent from Huntington's attempt to spatialize cultural conflict, it is for Jameson one form of narrative that intellectuals and leftists cannot do without. Thus, ironically, Huntington's theory may be a symptom of the "loss of historicity" that Jameson has repeatedly diagnosed as postmodernism's peculiar pathology, one to which cultural studies as a progressive project seems dangerously susceptible.[10]

"On 'Cultural Studies,' " in which Jameson confronts the field, touches on issues crucial to Huntington's argument as well. Jameson sees cultural studies interrogating "groups, articulation, and space" and undertaking a sort of cognitive mapping on a global scale. He notes "a new requirement of geographic reflexivity or geopolitical self-consciousness."[11] Moreover, Jameson offers no easy version of a globalized cultural pluralism. For him, as for Huntington, relations between cultures are essentially agonistic: culture is "the space of the symbolic moves of groups in agonistic relation to each other." That conflicted relativity, as he says, is its "hidden inner meaning" ("On 'Cultural Studies,'" 38–39). It seems that the strongly opposed positions of Huntington and Jameson, like the opposed positions of Huntington and cultural studies, have considerable areas of overlap. One looks to cultural difference to rationalize a neoimperialist foreign policy; the other searches for a way to analyze culture and conflict to further decolonization. Could the difference between these views of culture itself be a cultural difference? What would such a difference among cultural representatives of the West mean? Faced with this difference, can a relativist do more than shrug? Or is this a struggle where criteria of judgment may be found within the arguments of the antagonists themselves? In what terms might the dispute between cultural warriors and cultural scholars that I have constructed here be adjudicated?

Dueling totalizations

On a general level of analysis, many critics who "do" cultural studies might criticize both Jameson and Huntington for a similar penchant for "grand theories" or totalizations. As Jameson notes, "Cultural Studies does not do Grand Theory anymore," and totalization is "the hoariest of all negative buzzwords" ("On 'Cultural Studies,'" 28, 30). The attempt to abandon grand theories and totalizations is part of what Jameson calls cultural studies' desire to elaborate "a whole new politics of intellectuals as such" (23): less elitist, less authoritarian, and more immediate than intellectual politics has traditionally been. Those who do cultural studies characteristically refuse to judge, rejecting the legislative function of intellectuals as cultural elites, eschewing both abstraction and totalization in favor of a populist turn toward identification with their objects of study.

Yet as Jameson is quick to remark, even when the object is domestic popular culture, the intellectual's disappearance into identification is an illusion: "The intellectual is necessarily and constitutively at a distance, not merely from her or his own class of origin, but also from the class of chosen affiliation. . . . she is also necessarily at a distance from the social groups as well" ("On 'Cultural Studies,'" 40). This constitutive distance means that populism cannot solve the problems of representation, distortion, and power inherent in the intellectual's work. Therefore, criticisms of Huntington and others like him that simply decry their ethnocentrism or their totalizing will to power are not likely to be terribly effective. Such accusations, as Bruce Robbins has noted, can always be reversed.[12] The problems of representation and abstraction they bespeak are a troublesome feature of all intellectual work. Intellectuals cannot escape the equation of knowledge and power, but this does not mean that all the effects of knowledge and power are equivalent. Similarly, intellectuals cannot escape the mark of totalization in their representations of the world, but not all totalizations are the same.

In these terms, Jameson mounts a telling critique of the populist pretensions frequently evident among those who work in cultural studies. As he puts it, "The negative symptom of populism is very precisely the hatred and loathing of intellectuals as such (or, today, of the academy that has seemed to become synonymous with them)" ("On 'Cultural Studies,' " 40–41). Only part of an adequate critique of this populism consists in noting, as Jameson does, that "populism is itself very precisely an ideology of intellectuals (the 'people' are not 'populist'), and represents a desperate attempt on their part to repress their condition and to deny and negate its facts of life" (41). The other part must consist in analyzing, as Jameson begins to do later in his essay, the ways in which representations—tinged as they always are with totalizing distortions, ethnocentrisms, and the will to power—are inevitably part of any group's identity and therefore of any politics related to identity.

If cultural studies finds its political orientation in questions of identity, it finds its political will in the desire Jameson notes as everywhere evident in the essays he reviews—a desire to be an organic intellectual working on behalf of an emerging or oppressed class, one whose labors are in the interests of justice and right by virtue of being in the interests of that group ("On 'Cultural Studies,' " 24). This is where the political grounds of cultural studies should be sought, not in theories of cultural relativism or in critiques of totalization but in the political and moral choice of solidarity with specific groups or values. In this choice, and not in any preexistent, formal theory—for or against totalization or populism—Jameson bases his own work. Because of this choice, the difference between his view of the world and Huntington's can never really be confused, even though both share a view of cultural relativism and a tendency toward totalization. Huntington chooses to work in the interests of the continued domination of the West; Jameson chooses to work in the interests of the oppressed.

As Jameson suggests, many have found this answer to the problem of the intellectual's role to be "scandalous." It is scandalous to suggest that our political positions precede and ground our theories, that our theories do not offer a solid, scientific (as Marx hoped) basis for our political choices. Yet Jameson does not shrink from scandal: "Social solidarity," he writes in an essay on postmodernism, "must precede the ethicopolitical choice and cannot be deduced from it." [13] This suggests that the grounds of Jameson's political positions are not to be found in the Marxist theories and historical narratives he constructs—Marxism is, in fact, the name of the ethico-political choice he has made to speak for the oppressed and against the impositions of the powerful. Moreover, I would add that the grounds of his Marxism, the grounds of his ethico-political choice, may be found in the traditions of the West, the Enlightenment traditions from which we, like Marx, derive the ethico-political language and values in which we understand the nature of the choices we must make. Ironically, these are the same Enlightenment traditions for which Huntington purports to speak. That such different political positions can find roots in the Western Enlightenment does not obviate the need to choose between them, though it does offer a means to focus the terms in which that choice presents itself.

Among other things, I am suggesting that totalization is not the problem. Choosing between totalizations is. Jameson, like Huntington, defends both his totalizing impulse and the tendency toward abstraction in his work. However scandalous these may seem, he notes, they are an important part of intellectual work. In a section of *Postmodernism, or, The Cultural Logic of Late Capitalism* entitled "How to Map a Totality," he writes:

> The interesting question today is then not why I adopt this ["totalizing"] perspective, but why so many people are scandalized (or have learned to be scandalized) by it. In the old days, abstraction was surely one of the strategic ways in which phenomena, particularly historical phenomena, could be estranged and defamiliarized. . . . Historical reconstruction . . . , the positing of global characterizations and hypotheses, the abstraction from the "blooming, buzzing confusion" of immediacy, was always a radical intervention in the here and now and the promise of resistance to its blind fatalities. (400)

Jameson ends this passage by noting that "one must acknowledge the representational problem," though he also notes that acknowledging it does not entitle one to believe that one has in any way avoided it. Huntington, for his part, begins *The Clash of Civilizations* with a similar defense of representational abstraction in ordering a view of the world and an orientation for foreign policy (29–39). He claims that his model of a multiplicity of clashing world cultures better represents the world than the older bipolar and statist models that previously directed strategic planning. Each model, he admits, requires a certain amount of forgetting. "Realism" and detail must be sacrificed for clarity and utility, the ability to effectively (given a political and ideological understanding of what is effective) structure decision making and planning (36). Totalizing abstraction offers Huntington the hope of resisting the blind fatalities of the here and now. Yet again, some totalizations are better than others.[14]

What assumptions structure Huntington's map? One might describe his work as a neo-Weberian interpretation of the post–Cold War world.

It depends, that is to say, on what the sociologist Anthony Giddens has called the "orthodox consensus" in modern sociology. Zygmunt Bauman describes the orthodox consensus as follows:

> Constantly lurking behind the scene in the orthodox visions of social reality was the powerful image of the social system—this synonym of an ordered, structured space of interaction, in which probable actions had been, so to speak, pre-selected by the mechanisms of domination or value sharing. . . . The orthodox consensus focused accordingly on mechanisms which trimmed or eliminated the randomness and multidirectionality of human action and thus imposed co-ordination upon otherwise centrifugal forces; order upon chaos.[15]

Huntington's model, his attempt to bring order out of chaos, assumes determinate links between cultural forms and social agency. He has no trouble accepting the specificity of culture and the absence of universals. For him, however, relativism becomes the basis for an essentially Hobbesian construction of a global civil society in which a war of each culture against all others is the rule. The apparent contradiction in his model between a rational and constricting coherent order within each society and an irrational and chaotic conflict among all societies requires some analysis, though it also has a Weberian cast. Like Weber, Huntington attempts to establish the grounds of Western self-identity on the one hand in the supposedly religious roots of its "Judeo-Christian" culture, and on the other hand in the Enlightenment, which Weber called Protestantism's "laughing heir."[16] Cultures, for Weber and for Huntington, form coherent totalities in which the dominant order grows from roots in fundamental religious beliefs.[17] Huntington takes his cue from Weber. For him what separates the West from Islamic, from Hindu, from Buddhist, and from Orthodox Christian cultures is a similar orientation of the cultural dominant through or in religion. Whereas Huntington celebrates, and Weber implicitly satirizes, the ethos each describes, the differences between them are not fundamental and may be attributed to the differing historical perspectives that result from surveying the world from a vantage at the point of the West's triumphant domination or in the midst of its feared decline.

The fear of the West's decline is everywhere evident in Huntington's view of the world. The program he proposes is depressingly familiar:

> It is clearly in the interest of the West to promote greater cooperation and unity within its own civilization, particularly between its European and North American components; to incorporate into the West societies in Eastern Europe and Latin America whose cultures are close to those of the West; . . . to limit the expansion of the military

strength of Confucian and Islamic states; to moderate the reduction of Western military capabilities and maintain military superiority in East and Southwest Asia; to exploit differences and conflicts among Confucian and Islamic states; to support in other civilizations groups sympathetic to Western values and interests; to strengthen international institutions that reflect and legitimate Western interests and values and to promote the involvement of non-Western states in those institutions. ("Clash of Civilizations," 49)

Division of the world, containment of the enemy, subversion and co-optation—this is indeed an attempt to rewarm the Cold War using culture instead of ideology or economics to provide the heat. Yet the model on which it is based totalizes a world in which too much "reality" is left out of the final representation.

Huntington attempts to support his position by constructing "civilizations" or cultures as internally coherent and externally opposed. This, as has frequently been the case in colonialist discourse, involves a mutually constitutive opposition between the "domestic" and the "foreign." Both terms of Huntington's analysis, "the West and the rest," as he puts it, are easily seen in concrete demographic, political, and cultural terms to be far too simple. As Fouad Ajami puts it, the "West itself is unexamined in Huntington's essay. No fissures run through it. No multiculturalists are heard from. It is orderly within its ramparts."[18] No multiculturalists are heard from because Huntington is intent on silencing them. Given the remarkable and increasing heterogeneity of world populations in the "West," Huntington's uncritical deployment of the term "us" as synonymous with what he unreflectingly calls "Western" culture is far from innocent. It serves as the foreign policy rationale for a domestic policy of cultural purgation and repression. The many well-orchestrated and well-financed attacks on multicultural initiatives in U.S. education find their real political justification in Huntington's argument. If Huntington's goal is to protect the purportedly Western value of democracy, this is a strange way to do it.

Equally important, Huntington's decontextualized and ahistorical characterizations of cultural politics in general and Islam in particular must also be subjected to rigorous critique, and his many evasions, inconsistencies, and half-truths exposed. Attention to the remarkable variety of voices and experiences, narratives and critiques, emerging from within the "Islamic world" and constituting a significant portion of the literatures of North Africa and the Middle East indicates that there are other, more compelling ways to model phenomena like Islamic fundamentalism. As Ajami suggests, "traditions are most insistent and loud when they rupture. . . .

The phenomenon we have dubbed as Islamic fundamentalism is less a sign of resurgence than of panic and bewilderment and guilt that the border with 'the other' has been crossed" (Ajami, 2). No model of the world that fails to represent what Ajami calls the "complicities and ambiguities between civilizations, especially the West and Islam," can provide a reliable guide for a just policy (2).[19] But justice, or equity, is not Huntington's goal. His politico-ethical commitment is to the continued dominance of the West in the world. It is that political commitment, that ethico-political choice, that "value," which ultimately rules his map and shapes his theory.

Here, because value is a cultural construct, I want to take up one of Huntington's more serious challenges to contemporary cultural studies, one that emerges when he sounds most like a practitioner of a certain sort of cultural studies himself. This is the most uncanny moment in this confrontation. It is the crucial moment when Huntington argues for cultural relativism and claims that "Western concepts differ fundamentally from those prevalent in other civilizations. Western ideas of individualism, liberalism, constitutionalism, human rights, equality, liberty, the rule of law, democracy, free markets, the separation of church and state, often have little resonance in Islamic, Confucian, Japanese, Hindu, Buddhist or Orthodox cultures" ("Clash of Civilizations," 40). What is uncanny here, of course, is that these claims for the cultural particularity of terms imposed as universals have been the fundamental theoretical underpinning of much work in critical theory, cultural studies, and postcolonial critique. Yet Huntington uses this critique of the Enlightenment to furnish the theoretical grounding for neoimperialism. If these values—human rights, equality, liberty—have little resonance in other cultures, then we need have no compunction about following policies that violate the rights or exploit the populations of these other groups.

Huntington's map of the world depends on a model of cultures that is static and monological. Cultures remain impermeable to each other. Such a view of culture is inadequate to the exchanges that have characterized the history of colonialism itself and continue to characterize its aftermath. This does not mean merely that cultures that have been in contact with the West for centuries have inevitably been infected with its values. The relationship has neither been so passive nor so univocal. In fact, the opposition between the "West" and the rest on which Huntington bases his argument and on which many who adopt (or attempt to) a position of relativism with regard to Islamic fundamentalism, for instance, is neither so stark nor so simple as it first appears.

Thinking of cultural differences, Richard Rorty reminds us that we should not assume that "untranslatable" means "unlearnable," for the "notion of a language untranslatable into ours makes no sense."

If I can learn a native language, then even if I cannot neatly pair off sentences in that language with sentences in English, I can certainly offer plausible explanations in English of why the natives are saying each of the funny-sounding things they say. I can provide the same sort of gloss on their utterances which a literary critic offers on poems written in a new idiom or a historian of the "barbarism" of our ancestors. Cultural differences are not different in kind from differences between old and ("revolutionary") new theories propounded within a single culture.[20]

Differences are never unbridgeable, though bridging them requires interpretive representation, the work of cultural intellectuals with all the problems that entails. Yet this is a preferable and more persuasive model of difference than the one Huntington offers. The difference between the West and the rest of the world can be made as stark as his model requires only by repressing history, forgetting the actual composition of contemporary societies, and misrepresenting the nature of difference itself.

For example, Michael Ignatieff has argued that to examine closely a conflict like the one in the Balkans between Serbians and Croats is to find that their differences from each other and from us are not so pronounced as they at first appear. Huntington specifies this conflict as an example of a clash between mutually exclusive cultures, different from each other and different from the West. Ignatieff, however, argues that "all of the delusions that have turned neighbors into enemies are imports of Western European origin."

> Modern Serbian nationalism dates back to an impeccably Byronic style of national uprising against the Turks. Likewise, the nineteenth-century Croatian nationalist ideologue Ante Starcevic derived the idea of an ethnically pure Croatian state indirectly from the German Romantics. The misery of the Balkans stems in part from a pathetic longing to be good Europeans—that is to import the West's murderous ideological fashions. These fashions proved fatal in the Balkans because national unification could be realized only by ripping apart the plural fabric of Balkan village life in the name of the violent dream of ethnic purity.[21]

As the Yugoslav partisan leader and early theorist of the new class Djilas reminds us, nationalism is not "an intrinsic folk emotion, but . . . an alien virus, the work of city intellectuals" (quoted in Ignatieff, *Blood and Belonging*, 52). The present situation in the Balkans would then appear to be the result not of strange civilizations in local conflict but of familiar European ideologies, confusions, and abdications (53).

Closer to home, according to Huntington, the clash of global cultures implicates the clash of cultures within U.S. national borders. In his review of *The Clash of Civilizations*, Ignatieff points out that Huntington "never clearly specifies when the right to cultural difference—which is what the United States is surely all about—shades into moral decline."[22] But in Huntington's imagination, cultural difference and moral decline are clearly linked:

> Some Americans have promoted multiculturalism at home; some have promoted universalism abroad; and some have done both. Multiculturalism at home threatens the United States and the West; universalism abroad threatens the West and the world. Both deny the uniqueness of Western culture. . . . A multicultural America is impossible because a non-Western America is not American. A multicultural world is unavoidable because global empire is impossible. The preservation of the United States and the West requires the renewal of Western Identity. The security of the world requires acceptance of global multiculturalism. (*Clash of Civilizations*, 318)

Is the United States simply the same as the West, or are both entities more complicated than Huntington supposes? Is cultural difference what the United States is all about? Or is a multicultural America not American? Contending totalizations of U.S. national identity meet here; how is one to choose between them?

In terms of democratic equity, a value of both the West and the United States, Ignatieff's model is far better. In Huntington, the argument for contending against, or at least containing, certain foreign cultures slides over into an argument for disciplining or containing domestic populations. The dynamic is familiar from the repressive machinations of U.S. domestic policy during the Cold War. Huntington, one should remember, once argued during the Cold War that democratic societies sometimes need to be less democratic and less tolerant of dissent. Must we once again have an Un-American Activities Committee for Culture? To me that prospect seems un-American.

Once again, the problem is not totalization itself. Both Ignatieff and Huntington totalize U.S. identity, but they do it differently. Similarly, when Jameson maps a totalizing perspective based on a Marxist analysis of global capital and multinational corporations, the ethico-political choice he has made to respect other cultures and to argue against the inequities of the powerful generates a narrative construction of history, economics, and identity that proffers a totality more compelling, more politically efficacious, and more intellectually sound than Huntington's attempt to map the globe based on a brutally simple model of cultures in conflict. Jameson might have had aparchiks like Huntington in mind when he wrote that "cognitive mapping cannot (at least in our time) involve anything so easy as a map" (*Postmodernism*, 409).

If on Jameson's map constructions of culture also assume the centrality of conflict, for him most crucial conflicts are interior to a given cultural space. This is also true of cultural studies, which offers a salutary correction for the oversimplifications of Huntington's model. As Jameson puts it, "this particular space called Cultural Studies is not terribly receptive to unmixed identities as such, but seems on the contrary to welcome the celebration (but also the analysis) of the mixed, per se, of new kinds of structural complexity" ("On 'Cultural Studies,' " 26). If the dual memberships, split identities, and heterogeneity that ground cultural studies today produce tensions within and between the discourses of identity and non-identity in the field, then as Jameson (citing Stuart Hall) remarks, those are precisely the tensions with which we have to live and of which we need to gain some understanding. The alternative would be "that isolationist conception of group identity [that] would at best open up a space for Cultural Studies in which each of the groups said its piece, in a kind of United Nations plenary session, and was given a respectful (and 'politically correct') hearing by all the others: neither a stimulating nor a very productive exercise, one would think" (27). Not very productive, because such a dehistoricized and isolationist view of cultures falsifies the dynamics within and between cultures. Such a view lends itself to the self-serving formulations concerning the cultural specificity of human rights, for instance, that Huntington offers to legitimate the Kulturkampf he proposes. Such an isolationist view does not escape the problem of totalization; it lends itself quite easily to totalizations like Huntington's in which the principle of cultural relativity becomes a legitimation for cultural warfare. For Jameson, by contrast, a different totalization of capital's depredations of the life world, one that bespeaks a different ethico-political commitment, allows one to hope for the construction of common understandings and of common causes, translations and representations that mark and cross the boundaries of cultural difference, coalitions against the inequities of power and wealth in the world. Such coalition building is one use to which an intellectual might put a cognitive map of global conflicts.

Representation and representativeness: culture as
an inorganic formation

I have been arguing that the existence of policy initiatives legitimated by appeals to Western ideology from traditional intellectuals like Huntington requires a response from organic intellectuals speaking for an increasingly beleaguered tradition that originates in the Enlightenment. Yet the organic cultural intellectual seems an uncannily inorganic construct. For Jameson, who has been my model of such an organic intellectual, as much as for Huntington, culture is realized as conflict. Echoing Franz Fanon, Jameson describes culture as "the ensemble of stigmata one group bears in the eyes of the other group (and vice versa)" ("On 'Cultural Studies,' " 33). Thus no cultural intellectual can emerge organically from within the group or subgroup whose culture he undertakes to consider or for which he undertakes to speak, for culture itself is inorganic: "Culture must thus always be seen as a vehicle or a medium whereby the relationship between groups is transacted. If it is not always vigilantly unmasked as an idea of the Other (even when I reassume it for myself), it perpetuates the optical illusions and the false objectivism of this complex historical relationship. . . . For the relationship between groups is, so to speak, unnatural and conflictual, entailing extremes of envy or loathing" (34). The dynamics of envy and loathing leave us no room for neutral identification (an oxymoron in any case) or populist abdications. Moreover, there can be no construction of culture that is not multicultural and symptomatic of relationship. There can be no West that is simply itself and no rest to which it can be unproblematically opposed. Any model or map of a totalization that forgets this forgets too much.

To make his model work, Huntington needs to homogenize the populations of his civilizations and link them to specific geopolitical constructs. This, despite the Weberian orthodox consensus among social theorists, does not adequately describe the intractable heterogeneity of either the "West" or the "Rest" of the world. With remarkable violence, Huntington makes whole populations disappear and performs a conceptual and intellectual ethnic cleansing far exceeding any nationalist's dreams.

Huntington's attempt to translate the urgency and terror of Cold War paranoia to the so-called new world order leads to dangerous distortions and blindnesses. If non-Western civilizations are merely "our" others, then attempts to understand these cultures in their own terms and ourselves in relation to them are subordinated to the presumed antagonism among them. This is the reinvention of the imperialist imagination in the postcolonial environment. It begs the truly painful and interesting question of who *we* are, the question multiculturalism attempts to ask. Conceptually and materially, our commonality contains these others within it. For Huntington, this knowledge is subordinated to our perceived need to police and purify our interiors of agents and identities too simply circumscribed as "other" or foreign.

Huntington does his best to re-create the terrified paranoia of the Cold War, yet his apocalyptic rhetoric is strangely hollow.[23] He whips himself up to write that "rejection of the Creed and of Western civilization means the end of the United States of America as we have known it. It also means effectively the end of Western civilization. . . . The futures of the United States and of the West depend upon Americans reaffirming their commitment to Western Civilization. Domestically this means rejecting the divisive siren call of multiculturalism. . . . When Americans look for their cultural roots, they find them in Europe" (Clash of Civilizations, 306–7).

Many Americans have cultural roots in Asia, in Africa, and in Latin America and the Middle East as well. An awareness of such diversity is more and more a commonplace of school curricula and political rhetoric. In this limited sense, one might claim that the battle for multiculturalism has already been won. For the West and for the United States, no catastrophe has followed. I agree with James Shapiro in his review of The Dictionary of Global Culture, edited by Kwame Anthony Appiah and Henry Louis Gates Jr.: "There is no going back, no retreat to a time when Western cultural achievements could be artificially severed from non-Western." [24] This is so, I would add, not because the West has been undermined or subverted but because its best, most enlightened traditions are finally being realized in multiculturalism; severing the West from the Rest was always artificial. This means that those like Huntington who understand little of U.S. history and even less about Western traditions have had their errors and distortions exposed. It does not mean that those errors will not persist.[25]

In North America, despite what both conservatives and leftists claim about recent immigration patterns and problems of assimilation, conflicts between heterogeneous groups in a diverse population have a long history. Of the colonial era in British North America, for example, Michael Kamen observes in Mystic Chords of Memory that the emergent Whig consensus regarding the legitimate origins of political power in the people's will merely pointed up an ongoing and intractable crisis in the nature and roots of North American society and government. There is "an awkward anomaly in American thought," a tendency to gesture back to an earlier era of greater homogeneity and more perfect harmony that never, in fact, existed:

> Americans have sought to validate their own aspirations by invoking the innovations and standards of our hallowed pantheon as unchanging verities. This nostalgic view of the Golden Age actually conjures up an era when values were unclearly defined, when instability often seemed beyond control, when public rancor and private vituperation were rampant, and institutions frail and unformed. (Kamen, Mystic Chords, 56)

The earlier period, that is to say, was much like the present moment of "crisis." Which is not to say that that crisis was not real or that the present crisis is merely the result of foreshortened perspective and will lose urgency if one takes a longer view. The nature of the urgency may be less confused, however, if we glimpse into this distant mirror of the not so distant past.

At the root of the American crisis during the colonial and revolutionary periods and, according to Kamen, at the origins of the American civilization and character is the "unstable pluralism" of North American societies, an instability rooted in the constantly changing nature and frequently anti-authoritarian disposition of the varied and heterogeneous groups that have come to people the nation (*Mystic Chords*, 60). Thus, for all the recent furor over altered patterns of immigration to the United States, the structure of the problem and the rhetoric surrounding it have not changed that much since the settling of the Massachusetts Bay. In this light, multiculturalism appears to be very much a part of, and not apart from, the American grain.

The war over culture, of which Huntington's book is more a symptom than an analysis, is importantly a war of representations. Huntington himself seems to acknowledge the crucial importance of representational systems to cultures and to cultural identity when he says that "the central elements of any culture or civilization are language and religion" (*Clash of Civilizations*, 59). Cultures understand themselves, and individuals understand their relationship to culture, within the structures and strictures of representational systems. These, as both Jameson and Huntington note, are frequently agonistic constructs, constituted by differentiations and distinctions. As Huntington puts it, "People define their identity by what they are not" (67). Intellectuals, then, those secular or ecclesiastical clerics who accrue to themselves the work of forging and communicating representations of both the cultures they inhabit and the cultures they perceive, have a peculiarly important role to play. Representation is a crucial component in any world where competing or contending cultures, identities, or groups must realize themselves in their relationship to each other.

In this light, Huntington's attempt to represent and defend the West is paradoxical. The paradox resides in his betrayal of the Western traditions he pretends to defend. The West without universalism, however ungrounded, cannot be the West at all or can only be a West given over to its own worst tendencies toward domination, disrespect, and violence. Huntington, I think, is wrong when he claims that the "West was the West long before it was modern" (*Clash of Civilizations*, 69), since peoples living in Northern Europe before modernity, before global capitalism, before colonialism brought them in contact and conflict with the rest of the world, had no need for such a concept and no sense of such an identity. Multiculturalism, on the other hand, poses its own paradoxes. It may be understood as the ultimate realization rather than the final negation of the quintessentially but not exclusively Western project of Enlightenment. It is undergirded by the rational adherence to values such as justice, equality, and freedom from domination. Multiculturalists seek, I think, to make the West more perfectly itself.

The painful questions that intellectuals who wish to preserve the best of the West must confront derive from the paradox that the universal pretensions of Enlightenment commitments to abstract values, while they remain politically and culturally indispensable, are ungrounded and ungroundable. They are neither self-evidently true, nor nature's law, nor the exclusive property of the West, nor the West's only tradition. Fascism, racism, and exploitation are equally if not uniquely Western. Nonetheless, the values of the Enlightenment are, as Jameson suggests, an existential commitment, a historically emergent and still vital commitment that may well represent the best of the "West." They are, and I would argue that they remain a historical necessity. Yet they are not universally acknowledged—especially in the West—or simply transcendent, or reliably triumphant. They must be struggled over and fought for.

In most forms, multiculturalism is a struggle for, rather than an attack on, the values of the West. Some of those values are tolerance, justice, and equality. Attacks on multiculturalism, however well-intentioned some may be, reveal that the most profound threat to Western values and their intrinsic cosmopolitanism remains where it has always been, internal to the societies and cultures of Europe and North America, lodged in the violence of appeals to racial or cultural homogeneity. These, and not the clash of cultures, which are never simply external to a Western identity that can never simply be purified, are the real threat.[26]

The appeal of an American identity has been the special dream of U.S. intellectuals. It is a dream that often fascinates for the best or most laudable of reasons, because it promises the realization of a people created in the image of that other persisting and perhaps indispensable dream of intellectuals, the Enlightenment. And yet it is precisely because of its origins in Enlightenment ideals and ideas of justice, equality, freedom, and democracy that the dream of American identity has so often confronted the nightmarish reality of its own failure, its own betrayal of those principles. This ideal, this tradition of the West, can be turned against those like Huntington who would turn against it, betraying the West even as they claim to defend its culture. Adequately representing these traditions and choices is a more fundamental and more intractable problem than the problem of totalization or the problem of elitism. A totalization that enchains both the reality of differences and the necessity of coalition is precisely what we need. The survival of the "West" requires struggle not with other civilizations but within our own.

Such a totalization of relational and conflicted entities within cultures is precisely what Jameson attempts to map. In his map, the key is not unicity of culture but the contradictions of global capitalism and the conflicts within and among the cultures it produces. Jameson's view posits an equivalence in the flow of capital that shapes and defines the conflicted relations characteristic of communities on local, regional, and global levels. His map charts conflict as a decentering principle from which we cannot escape. There is, for Jameson, no homogeneous civilizational space, no cultural club with restricted membership, where the conflicts of our present situation are not an issue.[27] Therefore, paradoxically, his model, which recognizes and respects difference, also proffers the hope, the utopian aspiration, that commonalities of experience and interest might also be made to emerge and effective coalitions in opposition to the abuses of power might also be formed:

> I take such spatial peculiarities of postmodernism as symptoms and expressions of a new and historically original dilemma, one that involves our insertion as individual subjects into a multidimensional set of radically discontinuous realities, whose frames range from the still surviving spaces of bourgeois private life all the way to the unimaginable decentering of global capital itself. Not even Einsteinian relativity, or the multiple subjective worlds of the older modernists, is capable of giving any kind of adequate figuration to this process, which in lived experience makes itself felt by the so-called death of the subject, or, more exactly, the fragmented and schizophrenic decentering and dispersion of this last (which can no longer even serve the function of the Jamesian reverberator or "point of view"). But what is involved here is in reality practical politics: since the crisis of social internationalism, and the enormous struggle and tactical difficulties of coordinating local and grassroots or neighborhood political actions with national or international ones, such urgent political dilemmas are all immediately functions of the enormously complex new international space in question. (Jameson, *Postmodernism*, 413)

A space centered on the decentering power of capital and structured by gaps on all levels between lived experience and ideological narratives, by conflict within as well as between its subjects, cannot be mapped in any simple representation of the globe or of the nations and cultures that populate it. Unlike Huntington's attempt to represent a beset fortress America legitimating violent foreign policies and domestic repressions, Jameson's cognitive map and the community he seeks to represent remain open to the world on every level, representing the struggle of the world in each of its gaps. This sort of totalization rests on heterogeneous and therefore shaky foundations. Paradoxically, viewed in terms of the ideological values of an

Enlightenment that should not too hastily be claimed as uniquely Western, this is its greatest strength. It is an enlightened totalization.

This totalization centers on the decentering realization that no political orientation or practical coalition can be made to flow naturally or organically from the totality constructed. Constructing totalities and representing coalitions, we intellectuals make an ethico-political choice. This, not relativism and not totalization itself, is the problem of intellectual work. Unapologetically, I would say that intellectuals should choose the "West" and represent a West that coincides with traditions of critical opposition, of political equity, of cultural tolerance, of mutual respect, and of the resistance to domination. This is a West that Huntington—with his uncritical view of civilization, his iniquitous characterization of other cultures, his intolerance for difference at home, his lack of respect for historical determinations abroad, and his willingness to play at a divisive global realpolitik—betrays at the very moment he pretends to undertake its defense.

Cultural relativism is not really the problem, and resistance to totalization is not really an answer. Nor is survival of the West in the face of a brown or black or yellow peril really an issue. The betrayal of the West by those, like Huntington, who pretend to preserve and protect it is. The task for intellectuals is not to preserve the West but to adequately represent its identities, complexities, contradictions, conflicts, and ideals. The "West" that Huntington represents in the clash of civilizations is not worth saving.

PART

Projected Identities, Universal Illusions, and Democratic Discourse

TWO

5

The Critic: Cultural Studies and Adorno's Ghost

Legacies of the Frankfurt School

We have seen that neither cultural relativism nor critical totalization in itself determines political tendencies. Yet the rhetoric of culture and criticism has long figured prominently in political arguments among intellectuals. This rhetoric has been used to project dreams of political resistance and nightmares of social control. For contemporary critics, the predisposition to link culture and politics (which I share) is one critical legacy of the Frankfurt School for Social Research with which the term "critical theory" itself originates. Cultural studies in particular has consolidated itself around a certain continuation of, and a specific resistance to, classical critical theory. Peter Hohendahl is no doubt right to note that Adorno has become a "classic" and that "discussion has increasingly been concerned with the process of appropriating . . . his legacy for the present."[1] Adorno's influence on those who have actively sought to appropriate his work is less interesting than his legacy when discerned in the work of those, especially in cultural studies, who have most consciously sought to resist his example.

If the influence of the Frankfurt School today seems ubiquitous, many critics still do their best not to acknowledge it. Few in cultural studies seem to have followed Jameson's suggestion that a return to Adorno may be just what is needed for the fin de siècle.[2] Most critics involved in the study of culture today get along quite well without the single-minded assault on the culture industry in *Dialectic of Enlightenment* or the muscle-bound theoretical peregrinations on nonidentity in *Negative Dialectics*. But we cannot simply escape the Frankfurt School, or at least we cannot escape the problems it represents; these continue to haunt intellectuals, especially those critics who believe they have laid Adorno's ghost to rest.

This is only in part because the topics that currently energize cultural studies—interdisciplinarity, bureaucratization, culture, politics, capitalism, modernity, tradition, power, and enlightenment—are issues with which Adorno and others in the school wrestled. They are part of the nexus of topics many intellectuals confronted in the first half of this century, and they remain of considerable interest to a variety of writers in a variety of traditions today. The specific positions represented in *Dialectic of Enlightenment* and in Adorno's critique of identity logic approximate thematics in poststructuralist and postmodernist modes of thought. But to believe that such issues must be rethought in terms of Adorno and his colleagues is to accord their work a privilege it would be difficult to defend.[3] Certainly there are many other legacies in the history of criticism and philosophy relevant to these topics. Nonetheless, I believe that the thought of the Frankfurt School confronts us everywhere in cultural studies with real urgency. Moreover, I believe that this is primarily because the Frankfurt School and its mode of thinking are precisely what many in cultural studies feel they must resist to consolidate their project. What they resist is not merely a set of positions characterizable as elitist or a series of propositions termed traditional or a discourse limited to high, as opposed to popular, cultural forms.[4] What many in cultural studies feel they must reject is a certain model of intellectual work, a certain mode of critical commentary, for which Adorno has become the preferred example.[5]

This model of intellectual work (the special insight and knowledge that the critical theorist claims, the power and elitism inherent in his or her interpretations of cultural phenomena, the projection of preferences particular to intellectuals as universal values) is not as easily rejected as many critics in cultural studies, especially the most avowedly populist, have imagined it would be. Today's cultural intellectuals prefer to masquerade as fans, but if you were to look at them closely, you might find them more proximate to Adorno than either they or he would find it comfortable to admit, as if the ghost of Adorno had materialized beside them, a balding, portly, middle-aged, middle-class, Middle European mandarin with pierced nipples and an electric bass. The Frankfurt School's ghostly presence, the figure of the critical intellectual with all its problems, is not easy to escape.

The Frankfurt School's most haunting legacy may be its assumption of the critic's autonomous position, a position from which the mystifications of contemporary culture could be disenchanted and its dupes and victims set free. For Horkheimer, Adorno, and Marcuse, this was the meaning of theory. As Rolf Wiggershaus puts it, "Despite their differences, after the Second World War Horkheimer, Adorno and Marcuse shared the conviction that, in the tradition of Marx's critique of the fetish character of capitalist social reproduction, the theory had to be both rational and, at the same time, had to offer the right word, the word which would break the spell under which everything—human beings, objects, and the relation between them—lay" (6). Belief in critical theory, belief that it offered the intellectual a magic word that might break the spell of suffering, allowed the intellectual to imagine setting at least art, criticism, and reason free from the distortions and manipulations of the wholly commodified and totally administered capitalist world.

Today, neither this view of art and critique nor this model of the culture industry retains much persuasive force. As Umberto Eco tells it:

> Once upon a time there were the mass media, and they were wicked, of course, and there was a guilty party. Then there were the virtuous voices that accused the criminals. And Art (ah, what luck!) offered alternatives, for those who were not the prisoners of the mass media. Well, it's all over. We have to start again from the beginning, asking one another what's going on.[6]

Few still believe this fairy-tale romance. Not only do we know that no critical prince will come to break the spell of the culture industry with the kiss of reason, but we also suspect that the critical prince might really be a large, ungainly toad. More important, the culture industry no longer seems such a powerful sorcerer; nor does the audience appear to be a helpless and entranced heroine in need of rescue and protection. Not least do we resist the ways in which this narrative has always embodied and enacted traditional gender relations, since the critical heroes tend to be men and the audiences in distress tend to be women. All this is rather obvious, and we do not need a magic word to explain what's going on.

Having outgrown the fairy tale of the critical prince in the wicked world of media enchantment, cultural studies has made what's going on in mass culture its characteristic concern. What's going on seems to be a far more diversified and decentered panoply of cultural products and subcultural consumers working within the dominant and sometimes subverting it, however that dominant might be defined.[7] We now know that the culture industry is, as Andrew Ross puts it, "far from monolithic." It helps construct subjectivities, but it cannot control them. People and groups use cultural products in ways their producers never intended. There are no cultural dupes, and no one languishes passively under any spell, except perhaps those few mystified intellectuals who still believe that theorists possess the magic word of disenchantment—and they are the problem, not the solution to it. As Ross puts it: "The responsibility of the universal intellectuals to speak paternalistically in the name of the popular has been contested and displaced. But the exercise of cultural taste, wherever it is applied today, remains one of the most efficient guarantors of anti-democratic power relations, and, when augmented by the newly stratified privileges of a knowledge society, gives rise to new kinds of subordination."[8] Intellectuals, as elitists and as autocrats of taste, become demonic representatives of new class power and privilege. They project their tastes out into, and impose their values on, the world. By demystifying the illusion of theory's magic word, cultural studies seeks primarily to break the spell that intellectuals have attempted to cast.

Simon During explains that cultural studies may be understood as a critical appropriation of critical theory, one in which the culture industry no longer appears as an oppressive monolith. Instead, mass culture, "while in the service of organized capital, also provides the opportunities for all kinds of individual and collective creativity and decoding." Similarly, the critic in cultural studies frequently rejects the shamanistic detachment of the demystifying theorist in favor of a more populist or organic conception of the intellectual's work, one that "does not want the voice of the academic theorist to drown out other less often heard voices."[9] Thus the uses of culture, the activity of consumption, the multiplicity of meanings, the multifariousness of points of resistance, furnish topics for most work in cultural studies. That work decodes the messages of mass culture without imposing on them the meanings of the theorist or the values of the critic. This is, or would be, a good trick. I don't, however, believe it to be possible, as an examination of a few representative positions in cultural studies makes clear.

Jim Collins, for example, compares the model of culture figured by the Frankfurt School to a "Grand Hotel." He makes it clear that the structure needs remodeling, and that intellectuals need to change their conception of what they should be doing. British cultural studies, with its emphasis on subversive subcultural decoding, merely redesigns "the interior" but leaves its "structure" as an oppressive monolith guarded by intellectual house dicks "basically intact." Such a renovation still gives intellectuals too much univocal power. In the more radically populist project he envisions, this would be different: "Instead of redesigning the interior, theorists must reconceive culture not as one Grand Hotel that has fixed ontological status transcending its representations, but rather as a series of hotels, the style changing according to the way it is imagined by the discourses that represent it" (Collins, 26–27). Those discourses belong to the people who live in the rooms, not to the intellectuals who patrol the halls. If, as Collins argues, "culture does not have one center or no center, but multiple, simultaneous centers" (27) that are frequently in conflict, then what are we, as intellectuals, doing—what should we be doing? How can we know what's going on?

Collins imagines a series of positions whose significance alters according to the imagination of those who represent them. This does not seem so much to solve the problem of the intellectual that the Frankfurt School poses as it does to restate it. For if representation plays a determining function in the structure and self-understanding of subcultures and subjectivities, then intellectuals, with all the problems they bring, are and must be on the scene. In the process of constructing representations, they cannot simply rent a space like all the others, even when they appear to live where they work. Shifting metaphors (at last), intellectuals, even when they purport to speak from within a community, may not be able to keep from drowning out those for whom they claim to speak. Moreover, there may be no way out of this problem via either Gramsci or Foucault. The dream of an organic intellectual who would speak in and for the authentic voice and views of his or her community and the dream of the universal intellectual's demise are identical illusions. Each of them masks the persistence of the intellectual's presence in the work of representation as a necessary and necessarily problematic visitation by a spirit that continues, uncannily, to resemble Adorno.

Simon Frith makes an apt comment reported in the Grossberg, Nelson, and Treichler collection, *Cultural Studies*. Discussing the various myths that structure representations of pop music subcultures by social anthropologists on the one hand and cultural studies types on the other, Frith remarks that for the first, these subcultures are "a particularly *ordered* kind of social and symbolic structure," whereas for the second they are "a particularly *disruptive* kind of myth, a myth of resistance through rituals, the politics of style, etc. etc." Arguing that the first perspective is more positivistically accurate while the second, more mythic construction contains "much more powerful and much more materially effective truth," he goes on to offer a construction of his own:

> The point, though. . . . is that from my sociological perspective, popular music is a solution, a ritualized resistance, not to the problems of being young and poor and proletarian but to the problems of being an intellectual. And the paradox is that in making pop music a site for the play of their fantasies and anxieties, intellectuals (and I think this process has a rather longer history than that of cultural studies) have enriched this site for everyone else too. To take a simple example: the meaning of punk in Britain was, for all its participants, whether they knew it or not, made more exciting by Dick Hebdige's transformation of a disparate, noisy set of people and events into the fantastic theoretical narrative of *Subculture*.[10]

Frith's comment is bracingly honest and fearlessly clear-sighted. In other words, I am largely in agreement with his observation and want to follow its implications.

I like his reference to Dick Hebdige as a mythographer. The theoretical materials from which Hebdige created his seminal analysis of punk were not themselves popular; they were the professional tools of a cultural intellectual: Roland Barthes, Louis Althusser, Marx, Gramsci, Genet, Volosinov, and Hall.[11] As Frith points out, intellectuals tend to construct their objects according to the conventions and programs of their respective disciplines. Social anthropologists find patterns and structures of significance; cultural studies critics find chaotic moments of resistance: each finds what he or she is predisposed to find. Which view is more accurate is the least interesting question, since there is no way to answer it authoritatively across these disciplines. Each answer in its disciplinary context accomplishes significant work. Perhaps because the illusion of the organic intellectual still holds sway, there has been at least one baleful effect of Hebdige's brilliant study, an effect that Judith Williamson has described as "left-wing academics . . . picking out strands of 'subversion' in every piece of pop culture from Street Style to Soap Opera." As Meaghan Morris has argued, in "this kind of analysis of everyday life, it seems to be *criticism* that actively strives to achieve 'banality.' "[12] But the banality criticism longs for finally eludes it, because it cannot escape into a zero degree of insignificance that would obviate the problems of representation, power, and imposition.

Many in cultural studies would not welcome the power Frith grants to the work of representation or mythmaking that intellectuals do. Nor would they want to admit the degree to which they appropriate the phenomena they describe, decoding them in ways that further their own agendas. Popular music, for Frith, becomes something he as an intellectual can use to solve his own problems, among them a fear of his own irrelevancy. I think his point is undeniable. Intellectuals make representations, and those representations alter what they describe, sometimes even for those who are being represented. The direct effects of academic intellectuals on popular phenomena are most often negligible (I think Frith overstates his case when he claims that Hebdige enriched the experiences of punk rock for punk rockers, but he might have). The point is moot. Intellectuals, whether they are members of, or strangers to, the subgroups or cultural products they describe, make representations of which the best questions concern not their authenticity but their persuasive power. If the voice of the intellectual inevitably constructs the voices of the subjects it asks us to hear so that they frequently end up sounding a lot like intellectuals, if the decoding of intellectuals involves the projection of meanings, we can still ask to what ends and how effectively this may be done. In cultural studies and the communities it imagines, the figure of the intellectual, the specter of Adorno, is never wholly absent.

The academic fan's decoder ring
as magic projector

If intellectuals are in disrepute in certain sectors of cultural studies, theory, one important sort of work intellectuals do, has become especially suspect because of its inevitable tendency to appropriate, abstract from, and alter the phenomena it describes. The desire to avoid these pitfalls, which are often understood in moralized and political terms, frequently leads writers to attempt a positivistic empiricism in the form of ethnographic descriptions based on participant observation that attempt to eschew the work of decoding or interpretation altogether. In "Wanted: Audiences," Ien Ang, in response to David Morley's work on audiences and reception, attempts to balance the demands of interpretation with the requirements of ethnographic reportage. Inevitably, the question of the deformation of empirical data by interpretive frameworks (formalized theories or informal assumptions) comes up:

> Because interpretations always inevitably involve the construction of certain representations of reality (and not others), they can never be "neutral" and merely "descriptive." After all, the "empirical," captured in either quantitative or qualitative form, does not yield self-evident meanings; it is only through the interpretative framework constructed by the researcher that understandings of the "empirical" come about.[13]

However, if one were to recognize this, it would obviate the hopes that Ang wants by the essay's conclusion to lodge in empirical research. These hopes, in particular the hope that empiricism can protect intellectuals from the abstract impositions of theory by keeping them "sensitive to concrete specificities" and "unexpected history," are groundless (Ang, "Wanted: Audiences," 110). If empirical data are captured only within interpretive frameworks that cannot themselves be made specific and still be frameworks, and if understandings of those data are always therefore predetermined, as Ang suggests, then recognizing this means recognizing that there can be no contestatory relation between empiricism and theorizing, dialectical or otherwise. Empiricism, which is itself a theoretical construct, cannot resolve the issue of theory or the problem of being an intellectual, nor can it fulfill the intellectual's desire to let other voices besides the voice of the intellectual be heard.

Yet in work on fan culture, such hopes for empiricism continue to flourish. Such hopes motivate Janice A. Radway's influential account of romance readers in *Reading the Romance*.[14] Although she readily admits at the beginning of her study that it "is essential to point out here that in formulating a hypothesis about the significance of romance reading as an act, that hypothesis inevitably will be a critic's construction of the import of her reading behavior" (9), Radway still hopes to base her work on an empirical investigation of what "real readers" do with popular texts. Of course, what these readers do turns out to have progressive potential. Tania Modleski, in a critique of Radway's book that also refers to Ang's work on television, offers the following commentary on the narcissism that audience-oriented studies of popular culture often involve. Modleski describes these studies as "a criticism which, although claiming a certain objective validity by appealing to the pleasures and tastes of others, often seems to be based on an unspoken syllogism that goes something like this: 'I like *Dallas*; I am a feminist; *Dallas* must have progressive potential.'"[15] Modleski argues (and I agree) that the audience researcher's pose of disinterested scientific neutrality or participant observational objectivity often masks mechanisms of narcissistic projection and identification that shape the intellectual's representation of her objects. But I emphasize this not, as Modleski does, to attempt to correct it in favor of a clearer critical vision. Rather, I want to demonstrate that such projections and identifications are not to be avoided, no matter how critically self-conscious we try to be. They may, in fact, be one definition of the intellectual's work. Doing that work may entail a certain narcissism, a certain projection, and even a certain conceptual or rhetorical violence.

If the ghost of Adorno were to return and survey the activities of his legatees, he would no doubt be most puzzled by the work of John Fiske. Borrowing from traditional critical theory as well as Barthes, de Certeau, Baudrillard, Bourdieu, and others in the traditions of semiotics and poststructuralism, Fiske has construed some of the most unlikely aspects of popular pleasure as examples of popular resistance. Popular culture, for Fiske, is made from what mass culture offers to the people. It is a process of "making do." These offerings are refashioned in the use oppressed groups make of them in order "to make social meanings that are in the interests of the subordinate and that are not those preferred by the dominant ideology."[16] Thus homeless white males watching a videotape of *Die Hard* in a shelter cheer the murder of a CEO by the villains and thereby, Fiske says, express their disaffection from "the social order which, in their view, has decisively rejected them."[17] Similarly, women and teenagers who use shopping malls to hunt for bargains, to window-shop, or to socialize, in Fiske's view, exercise control of the commodities that seem—in a more traditional view—to control them. "Shopping" as he puts it, "is seen as an oppositional, competitive act, and as such as a source of achievement, self-esteem, and power" (*Reading the Popular*, 19). In this light, abusing shop assistants also counts as subversion (26).

As brilliant as Fiske's readings often are, they are frequently remarkable for the way in which they betray unsavory aspects of the popular activities he celebrates. For example, the white homeless men cheering the murder of the CEO seem less simply resistant to the masking of power relations in contemporary society when Fiske mentions that the murdered CEO is Asian. That Fiske himself describes the character's face as "impassive" (Power Plays, 4) indicates that the critic may not be immune to the manipulative deployment of racial stereotypes to deflect popular resentments into more easily managed channels. Fiske does not ask why the filmmakers chose to make the CEO Asian (certainly not typically representative despite determined attempts in the media to blame domestic financial problems on "foreign" influence and competition) or whether the men would have reacted as enthusiastically had the victim been white like them. Similarly, the shoppers who vex the sales force seem less sympathetically subversive when Fiske finally mentions that the shopper in question is "traditionally middle-class" and probably feels entitled to abuse the "mistress-servant relationship" (Reading the Popular, 26). Fiske mentions this fact but does nothing with it because such unattractive details are difficult to accommodate within the sanitized picture of popular pleasures he wants to present.

In States of Injury, Wendy Brown offers the following critique of the manner in which the term "resistance" often works—or fails to work—in contemporary cultural studies. In writing this, she may well have had Fiske himself in mind:

> For some, fueled by opprobrium toward regulatory norms or other modalities of domination, the language of "resistance" has taken up the ground vacated by a more expansive practice of freedom. . . . Yet as many have noted, in so far as resistance is an effect of the regime it opposes on the one hand, and in so far as its practitioners often seek to void it of normativity to differentiate it from the (regulatory) nature of what it opposes on the other, it is at best politically rebellious; at worst, politically amorphous. . . . it is neutral with regard to possible political direction.[18]

The point I would add to Brown's observation is that despite the attempts to differentiate resistance from regulatory norms, there is very often an unacknowledged tendency (both normative and regulatory) on the ethnographer's part to project his or her own image—the image of an intellectual with the intellectual's traditional attributes—into the portrait of the resisters he or she attempts to paint. Appeals to resistance, then, often entail a sort of magic trick in which the intellectual makes himself disappear only to project his own most flattering self-image onto the screen of the other.[19] Moments of "understanding," moments of identification, are also mo-

ments of projection. If we keep in mind the irreducible ambiguity of identification in which recognition and misrecognition always intertwine, then
we may also remember that this sort of problematic understanding may
not be merely a problem but also an opportunity. At least, one may as well
attach some hope to this prospect because the process itself seems wholly
inevitable.

It is inevitable not only psychodynamically but ideologically. Most intellectuals do consider the attributes valued by intellectuals—critical, even
skeptical, insight; fundamental, even visceral, attachment to some greater
"good"; masterful possession of some special knowledge—to be, in fact,
valuable. These are the attributes we like to find among those we speak to
and for; these are the values on which we would like to see a social order
founded. These represent both the terms in, and the goals toward, which
we work. For this reason, it seems silly to reduce them to props in a too
transparent critical sleight of hand.[20]

In Henry Jenkins's work on Star Trek fans, the trick of identification and
projection becomes obvious in his manner of translating the "empirical"
data of fan culture into his commentary on it. Jenkins is intent on proving
that Trekkies are not a collection of alienated and maladjusted cultural
dupes but a sort of peaceable kingdom functioning without the impositions of intellectuals. Surprisingly, however, as he describes the Trekkie
"community," it begins to resemble a sort of idealized research seminar
engaged in a fairly traditional form of literary study. "Organized fandom
is, perhaps first and foremost, an institution of theory and criticism, a
semistructured space where competing interpretations and evaluations of
common texts are proposed, debated, and negotiated and where readers
speculate about the nature of the mass media and their own relationship
to it."[21] Like traditional forms of literary study in the university, this one
is apparently well policed. Jenkins cites Kendra Hunter, a "long-time fan,"
who says that "Star Trek is a format for expressing rights, opinions and
ideals. Most every imaginable idea can be expressed through Trek. . . . But
there is a right way." As Jenkins puts it, "an individual's socialization into
fandom often requires learning 'the right way' to read as a fan, learning
how to employ and comprehend the community's particular interpretive
conventions" (89). This seems just as dictatorial and imposing as the policing of disciplinary boundaries or communal norms in the academy or the
social world usually is. In this light, it is not surprising that at least one fan
makes the equation between fandom and more traditional forms of social
and academic discipline explicit, saying that fandom made "TV viewing . . .
more like homework" (90). Yet Jenkins has nothing to say about the lines
of demarcation, discipline, and protocol—nor about the circuits of knowledge and power—employed to police and control these communities.

That is because he is intent on portraying fandom as a utopia for creative intellects. Thus, fan critics, not unlike critics of certain esoteric versions of Renaissance or modern literature (Shakespeare's and Joyce's exegetes come to mind), spend a good deal of time constructing time lines, plotting histories, expanding on the source materials, and attempting to influence producers and writers. Any academic literary intellectual would find much of this sort of work strangely familiar. Jenkins is quick to point out that such obsessive attention to detail in high-cultural artifacts is fairly common, but he has nothing to say about why this activity should be any more interesting when the question is the combination to Kirk's safe rather than, for example, the significance of Shakespeare's second-best bed or the accuracy of Joyce's map of Dublin.

For Jenkins there is nothing dreary about these fan enterprises. They become part of what he portrays as a productive and creative community, a nurturing and supportive collectivity. He makes fan writing, fan video production, and fan folk singing ("filking") the primary activities of the fan community. Here he describes two fans, Linda and Kate:

> For the "mundane" observer, what is perhaps most striking about this scene is the ease and fluidity with which these fans move from watching a television program to engaging in alternative forms of cultural production: the women are all writing their own stories; Kate edits and publishes her own zines she prints on a photocopy machine she keeps in a spare bedroom and the group helps to assemble them for distribution. Linda and Kate are also fan artists who exhibit and sell their work at conventions; Mary is venturing into fan video making and gives other fans tips on how to shoot better telepics. Almost as striking is how writing becomes a social activity for these fans, functioning simultaneously as a form of personal expression and as a source of collective identity (part of what it means to be a "fan"). Each of them has something potentially interesting to contribute; the group encourages them to develop their talents fully, taking pride in their accomplishments, be they long-time fan writers and editors . . . or relative novices. (154)

This is the intellectual's dream of a wholly organic community for whom the distinctions between analysis and creativity, reading and writing, consumption and production, blur into a utopian haze.

More astute at continuously interrogating her own active role as interpreter in the fan phenomena she describes, Constance Penley offers a similar account of Trekkies who produce "slash" stories and videos: "The group solidarity of these fans rests not only on the taboo nature of their work but also on their pride in having created a unique, hybridized genre that ingeniously blends romance, pornography, and utopian science fiction. They are also fiercely proud of having created a comfortable yet stimulating social space in which women can manipulate the products of mass-produced culture to stage a popular debate around issues of technology, fantasy, and everyday life. This, of course, is my version of it, based on a decade of familiarity with their work. The fans (who refer to me as 'one of the academic fans') would say they are just having fun."[22] The distance between Penley's account and the fans' account is intriguing, though not really surprising. Describing fan culture in the idealized terms of a perfected university seminar—a place in which cultural products and the issues they entail are subjected to widespread and lively debate and a multitude of decodings—is to pay fan culture a very high compliment. But we should never forget that this is a compliment within a value system that particularly or most reliably pertains to academic intellectuals who have internalized these ideals. Persuading popular audiences like Trekkies that their ideals include creative discursive decodings, unfettered debate on important and interesting issues, even democratic ideals and just social practices, that they are in fact like ours in the academy's left wing, would be an important task for intellectuals intent on coalition building to undertake.

In Jenkins, however, the construction of the fans' community takes a different turn, developing an uncanny resonance with the descriptions in evangelical discourse of the community of saints. A filk song by Julia Eclar that Jenkins cites captures something of this evangelical note:

> I was with the Midwest crowd
> Who stood in line for blocks.
> I cheered on the Reliant's end.
> I shed a tear for Spock's
> And we talked for three days running
> Of how Khan did push his luck.
> And I am saved!
> I am saved!
> I am saved! (Jenkins, 250)

Although he remarks elsewhere that filk "involves the skillful management of heteroglossia, the evocation and inflection of previously circulated materials" (253), Jenkins takes little note of this song's evangelical borrowings and seems uninterested in giving an account of what such borrowings in this context might mean, saying only that this "passionate song" "expresses sentiments shared by many within the fan community upon the release of Star Trek II: The Wrath of Khan" (250) and playfully evokes "religious imagery" (251).

In fact, Jenkins's persistent refusal to decode fan productions is the most frustrating aspect of his fascinating study. Rather than a refusal of interpretation or theorizing in the interests of empiricism, this is a refusal to occupy the place of the intellectual, who might be thought of as a fan with a secret decoder ring that projects meanings. That decoder ring gives the critic the power to interpret meanings that might not be apparent to everyone else.

With or without the secret ring, Jenkins does his share of projective decoding. He manages to shape his portrayal of fan culture into a mirror for, and a legitimation of, his own way of life. Structurally, this is similar to the claims Adorno and Horkheimer made for high art. Like Adorno, Jenkins decodes his object to suit his preconceptions of what its significance should be.

And in fact, the terms in which he decodes that culture would not be unfamiliar to the Frankfurt School. The strategy is not so much to contest the categories and criteria of evaluation but to demonstrate that fan culture fulfills their requirements. Thus fans are not passive media dupes; they are themselves artists, "engaged in alternative forms of cultural production" (Jenkins, 154). This is not so much, as in Baudrillard or de Certeau, an emphasis on consumption over production but an attempt to prove, in very traditional terms, that what looks like consumption actually is, for those who can see it, not only productive but production itself. If you want real intellectuals, Jenkins seems to claim, you will find them within the fan community and not among its critics. The fans, not the critics, possess the magic word of demystification and empowerment.

Yet at certain moments, Jenkins finds himself perilously close to uttering a critical statement himself, dangerously close to criticizing what he so wants us to admire. For example, after a long passage in which he explores the gendered differences in the way men and women tend to construct the meanings of texts, in which he celebrates the identification with characters and situations supposedly typical of women (most "fans" are female) over the analytical interrogation of authors supposedly practiced by most men, Jenkins finds himself forced momentarily to backtrack. Responding to David Bleich's claim, based on empirical research, that "women's reading practices insure a more comfortable, less alienated relationship to the narrative . . . than that required by masculine author-centered reading," Jenkins criticizes this finding as "deceptively utopian":

In practice, both the teller and the tale *are* often "radically other" for women within a world where publishing, broadcasting, and the film industry are all dominated by men; where most narratives center upon the actions of men and reflect their values; where most exist-

ing generic traditions are heavily encoded with misogynistic assumptions; and where educational institutions reward masculine interpretive strategies and devalue more feminine approaches. (Jenkins, 113)

Jenkins's own attempt to disown the intellectual's activity of critical decoding and to valorize, by way of contrast, a supposedly other gendered
reading practice of emotive identification leaves him in an uncomfortable
position. For if women readers take pleasure in identification and elabora-
tion, living inside the works they enjoy, that may be good. However, it may
also leave them open to the manipulations of a male-dominated culture
industry and its misogynistic traditions. At this point, identification must
break down, for if it did not, then Jenkins would be presenting us with a
subculture of cultural dupes rather than cultural masters.

I am not arguing that the female Trekkies Jenkins celebrates are actually dupes rather than successful manipulators of the media. I merely want
to point out that some intellectual function of critical distancing and analytical decoding is required to understand any aspect of culture, including
the culture of fans. This is true of the fans as well. Jenkins's attempt to
construct the fans he describes as the critical intellectuals he himself does
not want to be does not succeed in disguising his own shaping influence
everywhere in the descriptions of the phenomena he presents.

Even so inventive a decoder as Constance Penley sometimes wishes her
subjects into politically attractive progressive positions that there is no
reason to suppose they actually hold. In *Nasa/Trek* she writes: "A Trekker
can . . . , without apparent contradiction, adopt the precepts of IDIC, the
Prime Directive, and the peaceful use of technology while still exulting
in the American 'victory' in Grenada or enthusiastically supporting Star
Wars/SDI. But, in the main, most Trekkers use those precepts to create or
undergird a liberal humanistic or left libertarian ideology" (99). My point
is not that this is not the case but that there is nothing surprising about
the apparent inconsistency of embracing the peaceful use of technology
on the one hand and the Star Wars initiative on the other. This is precisely
what left liberalism and liberal humanism do all the time. This is, in fact,
mainstream American politics, the same politics that called a particularly
aggressive missile program "peacekeepers." The task for intellectuals, I
am arguing, is not simply to note these inconsistencies but to attempt to
make them tell by exploiting and expanding on these internal contractions
in order to persuade people, Trekkies or not, that abandoning aggressive
and wasteful programs like SDI is a good idea.

This question never emerges in Jenkins's argument. So intent is he on
constructing his object in terms of his own idealized self-image as a sort of
academic intellectual's utopia that he cannot pause to decode the messages

that might complicate his preconceived notions. This is particularly troubling in the passage on filk music. As an organic community, fan culture must of course have a folk tradition, "a spontaneous and on-going process of popular creation, one building upon community traditions but continually open to individual contribution and innovation" (Jenkins, 257). Thus, within the heart of electric media land, we reencounter premodern modes of folk production. Yet here in fandom's finest creations, one might decode the marks of pain and alienation that Jenkins labors so hard in his book to mask.

This is most evident in a single paragraph, crowded with references to songs whose lyrics he does not report and performances he does not describe. Some filk songs, Jenkins writes, "embrace . . . stereotypes only to push them to absurd extremes, relishing precisely the fan's self-proclaimed rejection of emotional restraint or social propriety."

> Fan songs speak with guiltless pleasure about the erotic fantasies ("Video Lust" [Davis and Garrett, 1989]) and loss of bodily and emotional control ("The Ultimate Avon Drool Song" [Lacy, 1989]), "Revenge of The Harrison Ford Slobber Song" [Trimble, 1985]); fans sing with ironic glee of lives ruined and pocketbooks emptied by obsessive collecting of media-related products, of houses overrun with fanzines. (Jenkins, 261)

In addition to guiltless pleasure over excess media indulgence and ironic glee about lives in disarray, would it be elitist to suspect that these songs encode internalized moments of self-resistance or mediated moments of self-loathing? Within the indulgences of fan culture there may be the marks of other cultures and of other pains that cannot be captured with a simple model of resistance or a utopian ideal of community structured as a sing-along. If these "sings" often "end with moments of communal laughter," then to describe that laughter as "born of warm recognition or playful transgression, of loving parody or biting satire, . . . a laughter whose primary function is creating fellowship," seems not to exhaust the possibilities (Jenkins, 260). One can only wonder at a model of interpretation that has no category for laughter expressive of rueful self-criticism, of anger misdirected or otherwise, of disappointment and despair. One can only wonder that a community devoid of these things can possibly offer any interest to anyone condemned to live in the late capitalist world most of us inhabit most of the time. In the intellectual's bag of tricks, community should not become the magic word that makes the world go away.

In fact, Jenkins cannot make the world go away. Near the end of his book, the world makes its presence felt. Indeed, at this moment, he sounds very much like Adorno:

Life, all too often, falls far short of those ideals. Fans, like all of us, inhabit a world where traditional forms of community life are disintegrating, the majority of marriages end in divorce, most social relations are temporary and superficial, and material values often dominate over emotional and social needs. Fans are often people who are over-educated for their jobs, whose intellectual skills are not challenged by their professional lives. Fans react against those unsatisfying situations, trying to establish a "weekend-only world" more open to creativity and accepting of differences, more concerned with human welfare than with economic advance. (Jenkins, 282)

Yet as he describes that weekend-only world, it sounds more and more like the mundane world to which he wants to contrast it, less and less like utopia and more and more like the space where we are:

Fandom, too, falls short of those ideals; the fan community is sometimes rife with feuds and personality conflicts. Here, too, one finds those who are self-interested and uncharitable, those who are greedy and rude, yet, unlike mundane reality, fandom remains a space where a commitment to more democratic values may be renewed and fostered. (Jenkins, 282)

Fandom, like the United States itself, is a sort of failed community. Its reported ideals—democracy, generosity, mutual respect, and group solidarity—these are the ideals of the dominant society as well, inculcated into every schoolchild in every civics class in the nation. The nation, like these fans, falls short. It is the falling short that usually attracts the critical intellectual's attention. Because Jenkins finally notes these things, one wonders why his model of fandom finds so little place for what could be a fascinating commentary on them. The pain here is barely discernible. Certainly its signs would be worth decoding.

Something like that project is what Constance Penley undertakes in her essay on Trekkie fan culture in the Grossberg, Nelson, and Treichler *Cultural Studies* collection and her book *Nasa/Trek*, which expands on the essay. She notes the questions that lead her, as an intellectual, to interrogate fandom, especially the production of slash fiction, and she also notes that the fans themselves ask similar questions:

Everything that was a question for me, from issues of genre—is K/S [Slash stories that retell *Star Trek* narratives by emphasizing a romantic relationship between Kirk and Spock] romance or pornography?—to the sexual orientation of the K/Sers, to the role of their fan activity in their daily lives, is in fact verbalized and contested by the fans themselves. It is a highly self-reflexive and self-critical fandom; their intellectual and political interests and anxieties are apparent in far more than merely symptomatic ways.[23]

So while Penley, like Jenkins—like any intellectual—projects herself onto her object of study, the model of intellectual work and intellectual respect she finds there is more complexly conflicted and politically ambivalent than those Jenkins purports to find. This, in turn, relieves Penley of what she experiences as a burden: "I do not feel so much as if I am *analyzing* the women in this fandom, as thinking along with them," she states, though she is quick to note that the ethics of writing about fan culture for a more general "mundane" world that is skeptical of fandom's protocols and hostile to homoeroticism remains an issue (Penley, "Feminism," 485).

This is not the place to offer an analysis or a critique of Penley's trenchant recomplication of the category of identification and the question of pleasure in studies of popular culture. But I do want to dwell, momentarily, on the anecdote and the question with which she ends her essay.

At a convention of slash writers, she attends a meeting devoted to dysfunctional families. This meeting is being held at the convention because the fans noticed that many of them came from dysfunctional families and seemed to be seeking within fandom the "unconditional acceptance one gets (supposedly) only from one's family." Reading a list of characteristics supposedly shared by children of alcoholic parents—isolation and fear, longing for approval, lack of self-consideration or a firm sense of identity—Penley, a visiting "academic fan," intervenes and does a bit of unsolicited decoding: "I finally spoke up to ask whether these descriptions weren't almost identical to those of the behavior of women in our culture because of their unequal treatment" ("Feminism," 492). One of the moderators agrees, but she immediately demurs, making it clear that she is not adopting a position that might be understood as feminist.

From this moment, Penley extracts some interesting and pressing questions about our place and status as intellectuals with reference to a popular audience that we both seek to construct and want to address:

We would indeed love to take this fandom as an exemplary case of female appropriation of, resistance to, and negotiation with massproduced culture. And we would also like to be able to use a discussion of K/S to help dislodge the still rigid positions in the feminist sexuality debates around fantasy, pornography, and S & M. But if we are to do so it must be within the recognition that the slashers do not feel they can express their desires for a better, sexually liberated, and more egalitarian world through feminism; they do not feel they can speak as feminists, they do not feel that feminism speaks for them. Fandom, the various popular ideologies of abuse and self-help, and

New Age philosophies are seen as far more relevant to their needs and desires than what they perceive as a middle-class feminism that disdains popular culture and believes that pornography degrades women. ("Feminism," 492)

Penley raises many important questions. Is feminism, identified as it often is with middle-class professional women, relevant to these underemployed fans? Is the work we do, as professional intellectuals, of interest to them? Penley suggests that it should be, because the questions that interest us also interest them. Why, then, aren't they interested? Why do they resist?

The answer Penley suggests is only partially satisfactory. Because we don't respect their culture, the fans can have no common ground on which to meet us. And yet there is a bind: if we are to proffer any version of the answers they claim to want, then our respect must also be tempered by critical distance. Penley suggests that these women find answers in pop cultural practices like New Age philosophies and ideologies of self-help. There is nothing, certainly, inherently wrong with that. If, however, we believe that we, as intellectuals, have better, more global, more empowering and productive answers to offer, then we need to engage with, and intervene in, the cultures we attempt to represent. This will require acts of decoding that can be presented as magic. Penley ends her essay with a question: "Are we ready, like the slash fans, 'to explore strange new worlds . . . to boldly go where no one has gone before?' " To which I would answer, yes, but bring your decoding rings and your magic projector. No appeal to empiricism or to populism can possibly replace them.

Dispelling Adorno's ghost

Today there cannot be a resurgence of the Frankfurt School. The theorist has no magic word to pronounce. Yet there can be no escape from the desire to pronounce it. Adorno may be exemplary, as Hohendahl has argued, not for the steadfast elitism or the despairing traditionalism of his position but for the inescapable and emblematic contradictions of his thinking: his tendency to rely on concepts—enlightenment, liberation, tradition—that his own analysis of violence, nonidentity, and manipulation had rendered suspect. These contradictions may begin to assume material form in recent debates about his legacy.

Hohendahl notes that Adorno's commitment to philosophical discourse is one aspect of his theorizing that makes him a doubtful candidate for relevance in the nineties. This is more than merely a matter of style, though the fact is that the convolutions and abstractions of German idealism and phenomenology seem considerably less sexy today than they once did. Indeed, the unfashionableness of philosophy today, the waning of high theory, has much to do with widespread, easily justifiable, and by now familiar suspicions of master discourses and the masters who claim the authority to pronounce them. This in turn, as David Harvey has suggested, may reflect alterations in the organization of production.

Especially significant here is the waning of industrial concentration and standardization that Harvey and others have called "post-Fordism." Fordism, with its totally administered, Taylorized, and rationalized approach to all aspects of production, left its stamp on Adorno's and Horkheimer's notorious denunciation of the culture industry at its Fordist apogee. Fordism also dialectically created the place from which its structures could be contested. A centralized and controlled mode of production offers an opportunity for autocratic and theoretical modes of demystification. Fragmentation of production, emphasis on the varieties of consumption, proliferation of economically viable subcultures rather than a mass-produced and unified mass culture—all these familiar aspects of the post-Fordist, postmodern moment leave no clearly demarcated position for totalization, in the Frankfurt School sense of total critique. Thus Jameson's urging of totality as the thought we must now think will probably not rally many.[24] Who are we—and where are we—to think this thought? Yet the irony of our situation may be that we cannot escape the rigors of totalization even when we believe we have most firmly renounced the desire for totality. Jameson makes a similar point when he says that "anti-systematic writing today is condemned to remain within the 'system' " (Late Marxism, 27).[25] Refusing to think the thought of totality may mean we are thought by it. Although thinking it may require, as Adorno and Jameson both suggest, a certain magic.

> Identity is, however, something like occluded system, totality forgotten or repressed, at the same time that it continues the more effectively to perform system's work. This is the sense in which the conscious reintroduction of system or totality comes as a solution to the closure of identity; it cannot free us from the latter's illusions and mirages, since no mere thinking can do that, but it suddenly makes these last visible and affords a glimpse of the great magic "spell" [der Bann] in which modern life is seized and immobilized. (Jameson, Late Marxism, 27–28)

Jameson's language suggests, though it is not what he wants to say, that the magic word of critical theory is itself a kind of mystification. What can break the spell that holds the world enthralled but a more powerful form of magic? The spell of critical theory, the magic of totalization, the power of projection, even if based on illusion, even if performed with the mirrors of the intellectual's own narcissism and the smoke of her confusion of herself with her objects, is a spell that critical intellectuals simply cannot break.

The Scientist: Disembodied Intellect and Popular Utopias

A whole category of philosophers spend their time predicting, i.e. awaiting, the last gasp of the sciences, in order to administer them the last rites of philosophy, *ad majorem gloriam Dei*. . . . But what is more curious is the fact that, at the same time, there will be *scientists* who talk of a crisis in the sciences, and suddenly discover a surprising philosophical vocation . . . in which they believe they are uttering revelations, although in fact they are merely repeating platitudes and anachronisms which come from what philosophy is obliged to regard as its history. — Louis Althusser, "Lenin and Philosophy"

Look who's talking

"Rocket scientists" may be the last intellectuals that the public takes seriously. Space, as Constance Penley tells us, is not only the final frontier; it may be the last utopia. This is one important reason that science, as she puts it, "is popular in America. An astonishing number of ordinary Americans take an extraordinary interest in exploring the human relation to science and technology." [1] Certainly no one in the last years of the millennium has done more to popularize space science than astrophysicist Stephen Hawking. Hawking's popularity rests on an ambivalent popular identification of science with utopian aspirations, of scientists as the last intellectuals who might manage to bespeak universal laws and therefore free us from contingency, from chance, from history, from politics. Hawking, whose intellectual prowess and physical debilities define his public image as pure mind, has been one figure in whom hopes about the human relation to science and to technology, hopes for a universal intellectual's realizing the structure of the universe, have been invested. He has become the figure of the scientist on which a vast popular audience has projected its utopian dreams. Nonetheless, a layperson's understanding of Hawking's theories and of the science he represents suggests that these popular investments are unlikely to yield profitable returns. Universal intellect, in the figure of Hawking and in his science, turns out to embody the full range of our usual contingent gendered and identity-bound problems. To consider how popular hopes get elicited, manipulated, and finally disappointed in the figure of the scientist as Stephen Hawking has come to represent it, I turn to Errol Morris's brilliant film on Hawking's life and work. The complex projections of Morris's film coincide remarkably with the complexities of popular identifications with the scientist's figure and with the utopian hopes his popularity represents.

The last words of Morris's film *A Brief History of Time* (1992) are emitted by the computer that Hawking, whose body is almost completely disabled by Lou Gehrig's disease, manipulates to simulate speech. These are also the final words of his best-selling popularization of contemporary cosmology, whose title Morris borrows. In the film, the words are voiced over a medium shot of Hawking propped in his wheelchair followed by close-ups of his hand on the computer control and of the chair's wheels and wires:

> If we do discover a complete theory, it should in time be understandable in broad principle by everyone, not just a few scientists. Then we shall all, philosophers, scientists, and just ordinary people, be able to take part in the discussion of . . . why it is that we and the universe exist. If we find the answer to that, it would be the ultimate triumph of human reason—for then we would know the mind of God.[2]

These shots, indeed Morris's entire film, capitalize on the peculiar place Hawking occupies in contemporary culture. Author of the best-selling popularization of theoretical physics in history, disabled figure of "a triumph of the human will that we can celebrate," Hawking, whose image hangs in London's National Portrait Gallery, is clearly "a curious kind of cultural icon."[3] Arthur Lubow has said, "The first glimpse of Stephen Hawking is always a shock. He's totally limp, a homunculus awaiting an animating spark." This homunculus, however, turns out to embody the animating spark of a fabled intellect (see Lubow, "Heart and Mind," 72). One might say that Hawking has come to represent science itself. That he speaks even in "real" life only in a sort of voice-over generated by his computer helps construct him as the contemporary icon of objective science. This portentous image nonetheless recalls a more comic version of the homunculus in recent cinema, the one for whom Bruce Willis spoke in *Look Who's Talking*. Could Hawking, like Bruce Willis, represent a particular masculine aggressiveness as well as the universalizing aspirations of the scientific intellect? What would that mean?

Errol Morris clearly banks on his subject's association with the universal. The final phrase of the movie accompanies an image that foregrounds Hawking's empty wheelchair (equipped with a bubble light from a police cruiser and a license plate that says "Stephen") against the starry firmament, against an image of the universe itself. Here too, however, something particular complicates the evocation of the universal. This composition evokes the recurring shot of a rotating bubble light in another of Morris's well-known films, The Thin Blue Line, which investigates the various and contradictory narrative reconstructions surrounding the murder of Dallas police officer Robert Wood. That film traces the pattern of coincidence and manipulation that lands an apparently innocent man, Randall Adams, in jail. The bubble light foregrounded in the final image of A Brief History of Time suggests a comparison of Hawking and his work with the thematics of the law, violence, and chance that organize the earlier film. Morris himself, in his promotional short The Making of "A Brief History of Time," has suggested that both films are ultimately about the same thing. But on which side of that "thin blue line" of the law, which in the words of the presiding judge at Adams's trial "separates the public from anarchy," does Hawking, as representative scientist, belong?

That judge misstated the case. The alternatives are not precisely anarchy and law but corporeal politics and abstract justice. The Thin Blue Line is about the manner in which the abstract universalism of the legal system continually yields to the pressures of sexual, economic, and racial prejudices. The politics of class, race, and perception in The Thin Blue Line juxtapose strangely with the mathematical constructs of theoretical cosmology in A Brief History of Time. Science, after all, is popularly assumed to be the antithesis of politics. If politics is a region of embodied conflict and determined subjectivity, science is supposed to be a realm of abstract law and universal order. Science, then, is perhaps the last location where a figure for the universal intellectual, the figure who, to paraphrase Foucault, "through his moral, theoretical and political choice . . . is . . . taken as the clear, individual figure of . . . universality," might be found.[4] Hawking, paradoxically aided by his physical disabilities, has become the contemporary representative of this universality, an icon for the universal intellectual in our time. As Errol Morris says, there is a millenarian aspect to Hawking's public image. "People want answers to cosmic questions, and Hawking isn't afraid to comply" (Lubow, 86). But why is Hawking's body, surrounded and foregrounded as it is by machinery and wires, the contemporary representation of the scientist around whom these dreams of a universal intellect take shape?

Both for those in the media (like Morris and Hawking himself) who have participated in producing the scientist as a universal intellectual and for those millions of middlebrow and middle-class readers who have enjoyed consuming this image, Stephen Hawking represents a dream of an intellectual capable of adjudicating the difference between the clarity of lawful order and the confusions of political life. Thus, the penultimate paragraph of *A Brief History of Time*:

> Up to now, most scientists have been too occupied with the development of new theories that describe *what* the universe is to ask the question *why*. On the other hand, the people whose business it is to ask *why*, the philosophers, have not been able to keep up with the advance of scientific theories. In the eighteenth century, philosophers considered the whole of human knowledge, including science, to be their field and discussed questions such as: Did the universe have a beginning? However, in the nineteenth and twentieth centuries, science became too technical and mathematical for the philosophers, or anyone else except a few specialists. Philosophers reduced the scope of their inquiries so much that Wittgenstein, the most famous philosopher of this century, said, "The sole remaining task for philosophy is the analysis of language." What a comedown from the great tradition of philosophy from Aristotle to Kant! (174)

Like Althusser, Hawking imagines a conversation between science and philosophy, though in his depiction of it, philosophy has failed to hold up its end. Science has the first and last word. This invocation of Kant's sublime—the starry sky above, the moral law within—situates Hawking and science at the center of a reconstituted public sphere. This would achieve the eighteenth century's dream of a rational debate conducted for or with the general public under the surveillance of a policing force of intellectuals whose special gifts and impersonal rationality fit them to be the guardians of universal truth and the interpreters of the Creator's mind. Hawking evokes a widespread desire to rediscover metaphysics within physics, a desire, as one commentator has said, that "goes hand in hand with rolling back the Copernican revolution and putting Man back at the centre of the universe, a reactionary project that makes the New Right look like tinkerers."[5] We have not seen exactly this configuration of intellectuals and imagined power since Pope wrote, "And God said let Newton be, and there was light."

Yet the sort of universal, rational, lawful, and nonviolent discursive space that the Newtonian universe seemed to promise is far different from the arena defined by relativity and quantum mechanics as Hawking explains them in his writings about physics. And as a popular icon of the intellectual poised against this universe, Hawking promises a very different sort of enlightenment: one that may, in the final analysis, involve the generation of more heat than light; one that is more closely related to the sort of language games Hawking seems to disparage in the passage quoted earlier than it is to either the putative rigor of complex mathematical equations or the reputed clarity and tranquillity of firm theological convictions. In those language games, the question of who is talking, the particularity of the speaker's identity and gender, is always important.

Popular science

Certain popular fantasies about scientists, certain utopian images of science, cluster around the figure of Stephen Hawking. As Lubow remarks, "Not since the public infatuation with Einstein's aureole of white hair has a scientist had such a popular following as Hawking" (86). He has, in fact, appeared with both Einstein and Newton in the 1993 season finale of *Star Trek: The Next Generation*. "Descent Part One" begins with the android Data playing poker on the holodeck with the three eminent scientists. The first two men are, of course, played by actors. Slouched in his wheelchair, manipulating his computer-driven voice synthesizer with the fingers of one crippled hand, Hawking plays himself. Why are they there? When a testy Newton, identifying himself as the founder of modern science, asks Data why he should be constrained to play a game of chance, Data responds as if he were a twentieth-century social scientist—the equivalent of what Newton's contemporaries would have called a moral philosopher.[6] Data says that he thought he could learn a lot about human nature by observing "three of history's greatest minds" playing poker. Thus, in a skewed way, the contest Althusser describes in which philosophy and natural science each struggle to pronounce the final word on the other's field is exemplified by Data's experiment, with its intricate weaving of scientific fact and narrative fiction. That poker involves elements of chance and the strategic construction of potentially persuasive narrative possibilities—that is, bluffing—seems wholly appropriate. Combinations of chance and of narrative construction are exactly what Hawking's science, like Morris's films, involves. Moreover, that the figure who takes the part of the humane philosopher investigating the intricacies of the scientific mind in this very human situation is, in fact, himself a machine is appropriate as well.

Each of these characters playing cards on the *Enterprise* has figured, for the popular mind, the image of a scientific intellect that may finally hold the answer to the related moral, theological, or metaphysical questions involving the relationship of the particular human imagination and situation to abstract universal principles. Each of the four great minds seated at the card table is embodied in a male form, and three represent intriguing combinations of masculine features and mechanical implementation.[7] Data, of course, is an android whose quest to become human figures in many

Star Trek: The Next Generation episodes. Hawking, as any visual image of him reveals, is sustained, cyborglike, by an array of prosthetic devices including his speech synthesizer. Less obvious but no less definite, Einstein, in keeping with popular fantasies concerning the brain lodged beneath that aureole of white hair, also represents a certain humanoid mechanization. As Roland Barthes described it: "Einstein's brain is a mythical object: paradoxically, the greatest intelligence of all provides an image of the most up-to-date machine, the man who is too powerful is removed from psychology, and introduced into the world of robots."[8] Einstein's intellect— which helped conceive both general relativity and quantum mechanics— resituates his organic being in the realm of the mechanical. Yet the force of his image as a powerful *man* may only be perfected by this remove.

Significantly, Morris's film about Hawking originated in his idea of making a film about the fate of Einstein's brain after the scientist's death.[9] Thus, the only purely "human" male playing cards is Newton himself. Once again, this seems appropriate. Since Newton's time—since, as the holodeck projection of Sir Isaac says, that apple hit him on the head (to which Hawking utters a synthetic groan, "Not the apple story again, Sir Isaac!") and suggested the possibility of reducing the multifarious phenomenal world to a single set of mechanical laws—the uncertainty of the interface between human being and mechanized function has been one of the primary sites for narrative, scientific, and philosophical speculation. In fact, Newton's name is most closely associated with two of the dominant myths of the industrializing West from the eighteenth century to the present day: the idea that the universe itself and human life within it are essentially mechanical, the recursive expression of a few underlying principles and reasonable laws; and the idea that the adventurous acquisitiveness of the individual mind might unlock the universe's secrets.[10] Behind these linked but antithetical images lurks a question: is human life the expression of abstract mechanical laws, or are those laws themselves the product or projection of an embodied human imagination? Moreover, as feminist critics of science have repeatedly demonstrated, the scientific imagination is not only embodied but gendered.[11] Around issues such as these, the dialogue Althusser describes between science and philosophy frequently takes place.

Even as Newton claims preeminence as the inventor of modern science, the science he invented has become strange to him. He does not recognize the twentieth-century physicists with whom he gambles as scientists at all. His aggravated question when Einstein miscalculates the bet he must make —"Can't you do simple math?"—indicates the distance between Newton's universal absolutes and the statistical and relativistic quantities his descendants manipulate. His first speech cuts short Data's attempt to explain a joke that Hawking tells, the punch line of which refers to one of general relativity's classical proofs: "Don't patronize me, Sir!"—as if Data had forgotten himself or his interlocutor. Seated at the table in his waistcoat and wig, Newton expresses an anger and contempt that stand in stark contrast to the affable techno-joshing of his twentieth-century counterparts.

Sir Isaac figures a moment in intellectual history and a moment in the history of intellectuals before the uncertainty principle in quantum mechanics and the disappointment of Enlightenment ambitions to rationalize human existence in the political and social realm suggested that chance and violence, not personal deity or eternal law, rule the universe. This was a time, unlike the present, when the laws of matter, motion, and society could be imagined as mechanically regular, ordinarily perceptible, and reasonably formalizable. The persistence of that ideal may well be what makes so attractive the affable meldings of masculine biology and mechanical engineering in the figures of Hawking, Einstein, and Data—figures who contrast sharply with the cantankerously human and oddly impotent "father" of Western science. Although advances in theoretical physics are unlikely to shed any unambiguous light on the mechanisms and dysfunctions of common life, the popular wish persists that the man of science, because of the abstract precision of his brain, might shed light on the dark confusions of embodied existence and might, like an idealized and universalized patriarch, bring order to the everyday chaos of existence.[12] It is this hope that Hawking manipulates when he agrees to take up the theological riddles that contribute significantly to his commercial successes. In doing so, however, it is distinctly possible that he is only bluffing.

Certainly Hawking is aware of the fantasies surrounding him and is intent on manipulating them. Of Hawking's appearance on Star Trek: The Next Generation, The Star Trek Encyclopedia tells the following story:

Professor Hawking's appearance on Star Trek was the result of a visit he made to Paramount Pictures to promote his motion-picture version of A Brief History of Time. At Paramount, he made known his dream of visiting the Enterprise. Hawking not only got to visit the sets, but he persuaded Star Trek's producers to let him make an appearance on the screen. While passing through the Main Engineering set, Hawking paused near the warp engine, smiled, and said, "I'm working on that."[13]

Hawking was promoting Morris's film during that visit to Paramount Pictures. He gives ample evidence of knowledge about his public image and masterfully manipulates his own publicity. In Black Holes and Baby Universes, he gives the following precise and perceptive account of his career based on his reading of the reviews of his worldwide best-selling book:

I found most of the reviews, although favorable, rather unilluminating. They tended to follow the formula: Stephen Hawking has Lou Gehrig's disease (in American reviews), or motor neurone disease (in British reviews). He is confined to a wheelchair, cannot speak, and can only move x number of fingers (where x seems to vary from one to three, according to which inaccurate article the reviewer read about me). Yet he has written this book about the biggest question of all: Where did we come from and where are we going? The answer that Hawking proposes is that the universe is neither created nor destroyed: It just is. In order to formulate this idea, Hawking introduces the concept of imaginary time, which I (the reviewer) find a little hard to follow. Still, if Hawking is right and we do find a complete unified theory, we shall really know the mind of God. (In the proof stage I nearly cut the last sentence in the book, which was that we would know the mind of God. Had I done so, the sales might have been halved.)[14]

Hawking is no doubt right that the theological twist he added to the book's conclusion, the same phrase with which Morris ends his film, contributed substantially to his popularity.[15] Hawking also notes that the implications of his own cosmology leave no place in the universe for any such transcendental entity as God's mind.

This raises an obvious question: why does the public's interest in Hawking so far exceed the limits of what his science purports to do? This misdirected interest or misplaced hope is what he manipulates. Although a few theologians have bothered to take issue with his theories, his ex-wife Jane correctly asserts that "he is delving into realms that really do matter to thinking people and in a way that can have a very disturbing effect on people . . . and he's not competent" (Lubow, 86). She, of course, considers herself an expert on his incompetence. In 1988 she told a reporter that after nursing him for a quarter of a century, her role now was "simply to tell him that he was not God." Apparently no one told the *Newsweek* reporters who ended their piece on Hawking with the following: "But if Hawking finds the parallel universe on the other side of a black hole, no one will begrudge him deification there."[16] That deification is what the final image of Morris's film—the empty wheelchair with its bubble light and license plate, an odd chariot for a strange god, superimposed on the starry firmament—attempts to construct.

Documenting science

Morris's film, constructed around images of a debilitated man in a wheelchair, furnishes a compelling contemporary representation of the universal intellectual. Because of his disability, all Hawking's lines in the film are edited in as voice-over. Morris has referred to Hawking as a nontalking talking head. In the late twentieth century, an era of explicit and seemingly relentless articulations between the corporeal and the political, the fantasy of the universal intellectual involves the fantasy of a disembodied voice. That such a voice should require the interposition of a certain prosthetic technology is not surprising.

Western science has often attempted to engineer the abstraction of thought through the interposition of technology, the use of certain observational instruments such as the camera. The intercession of apparatus between concept and articulation, identity and expression, finds a familiar analogue in the apparatus of the cinema analyzed in a classic essay by Jean-Louis Baudry. Near the beginning of "Ideological Effects of the Basic Cinematographic Apparatus," Baudry remarks on the coincidence of the invention of optical machinery and the origins of Western science, "whose birth coincides exactly with the development of the optical apparatus which will have as a consequence the decentering of the human universe, the end of geocentrism (Galileo)." But lest this too well known story of the decentering of the human universe by the end of geocentrism remain deceptively simple (since there is nothing simple about it), Baudry goes on to suggest a paradox that actually makes the problem of this shift apparent. "The optical apparatus camera obscura," he writes, "will serve in the same period to elaborate in pictorial work a new mode of representation, *perspectiva artificialis*. This system, recentering or at least displacing the center (which settles itself in the eye), will ensure the setting up of the 'subject' as the active center and origin of meaning." [17]

In this paradox—that in the decentering of the universe (the removal of the human world from the eye of God) emerges a recentering of the human subject and its active eye—resides the problem and the fear that motivates the line of philosophers, especially Kant, to whom Hawking refers and among whom he and physics aspire to a place. For despite the attempts of the New Right to undo the Copernican revolution by putting God back at the center of the universe, the tendency of Copernicus's insight has always been to locate humanity there, a tendency that poses more problems than it solves. To what sort of place in contemporary space-time might a universal intellectual such as Hawking represents aspire, if the meaning and character of the Newtonian void has also shifted and become somewhat too full of human significance to afford any comfort to the legislative mind in its search for the eternal, objective principles of law and order?

The comfort of objectivity has often been the explicit desire of cinema. As Brian Winston notes, "There is a powerful argument, grounded in centuries of modern scientific inquiry, for seeing the camera as no more and no less than a device for representing the world of natural phenomena, a device like any other." [18] Winston also remarks that the aim of Direct Cinema, for example, was, like the avowed aim of science, to remove the problem of the observer as much as possible from the circuit of observation. He cites Leacock, who in 1964 wrote:

> When you make an electrical measurement of a circuit, you do it with a volt-meter. Now the moment you do that, you change the circuit. Every physicist—and I used to be one—knows this. So you design your volt-meter so that very little goes through it. And in a very sensitive situation you need very much less going through it.[19]

The objectivity of the observation is predicated by the reduction of subjectivity's embodiment. Yet as Heisenberg's uncertainty principle indicates, such effects, the effects of the subjective viewer's inevitable embodiment in and through the situation observed, are ineluctably part of the situation of observation. As we have long known, we usually imagine the camera as an invisible instrument of masculine desire. Yet the game in cinema, as in science (at least up through the moment of classical physics), has been to imagine the origin of the gaze, technological or otherwise, as disembodied—and hence universalized—reason: reason unlimited by the embodied subject, the corporeal, the corporate, the political. This is why the figure of the scientist in Western popular culture has long been the figure of a disembodied man, or the figure of a man whose attention to the material and social world, to his own body and to others, is defined by his distracted attention to the problems of an immaterial or purely intellectual realm. This is the significance of Einstein's well-known forgetfulness about wearing socks and of his unkempt hair. In the contemporary world, no figure has more compellingly captured this oddly gendered disembodiment than the figure of Stephen Hawking, a fact that is evident in Morris's film.

Morris assumes the epistemological riddle, the ideological recognition of scientific apparatuses, already inscribed in the history of documentary film's theory and desire and makes it, in both The Thin Blue Line and A Brief History of Time, part of the subject he records.[20] The question of documentary—its relation to the real, to representation, to the body, and to politics—is the question Morris's film articulates with reference to Hawking's figure and his science. As Michael Renov puts it, documentary, with its recontextualization of elements plucked from the lived world, raises "the question of the adequacy of a representational system as a stand in for lived experience," a question that only becomes more complex if, as Morris's films remind us, lived experience itself is a representational system.[21] This applies to the microunits of an individual life as much as to the macrounits of history itself. Thus Morris cuts from images of the firebombing of London around the time of Hawking's birth to pictures of the infant scientist in his parents' arms. The voice-over of his mother's recollections concerning the German attacks and her son's birth is followed by the physicist's synthesized voice asking, "How real is time?" Both the film and its subject suggest that time is ultimately as real as the representations of it that we construct. One can see this in the film's first images.

After the credits and over music by Philip Glass, the screen goes momentarily blank. One hears the clicking of what will turn out to be the computer that Hawking uses to drive his voice synthesizer. Then the screen is filled by the same image of a starry firmament that will end the film. A new strain of music sounds before the synthesizer asks, "Which came first, the chicken or the egg?" Suddenly a large, startled-looking hen's head pops into the bottom center of the frame. The disembodied voice continues: "Did the universe have a beginning, and if so, what happened before then? Where did the universe come from, and where is it going?"

Morris structures this shot around the ineluctable gap structured into representation itself: the absurdity of the chicken's staring eyes, the sublimity of the cosmic void, the clicking of Hawking's prosthetic apparatus, the first synthesized words, "Which came first, the chicken or the egg?" We sense here, as Trinh T. Minh-ha puts it, that "what is put forth as truth is often nothing more than a meaning. And what persists between the meaning of something and its truth is the interval, a break without which meaning would be fixed and truth congealed." [22] That interval in which meaning is unfixed and the truth becomes fluid is the space of politics and of the body. It is in the body, as Donna Haraway explains, that the objective meets its limitations, and those limitations are political. Given the embodied nature of all vision, the gaze of objectivity in science and documentary, the "gaze from nowhere," is "the gaze that mythically inscribes all the marked bodies, that makes the unmarked category claim the power to see and not be seen, to represent while escaping representation. This gaze signifies the unmarked position of Man and White." [23] The attempt to fix meaning requires an attempt to universalize mind by removing it from the particularities of the body. This, however, always entails the surreptitious reinscription of the corporeal specificities of Man (and White) as universals.

Prosthetic gender

As Morris's film traces Hawking's progressive debilitation, the scientist becomes increasingly available to the imagination as a more and more perfect instrument of observation, a more and more perfect embodiment of pure mind. He also becomes an increasingly evident index of a paradox.

The ability to represent—and therefore to make real—the observations he makes becomes, in the attenuation of his physical apparatus, more and more problematic. His physical body yields, therefore, not to the transcendent negativity of no body but to the increasingly elaborate prostheses that constitute his presence in the world. These remind us on the one hand of the singularity of his predicament and on the other of the prosthetic nature of all corporeality in its relationship to consciousness.

As Arthur Lubow observes, Hawking's popular image "is the model of pure mind unleashed from body." This is an image those close to him resist; "He's not a machine," as one friend remarked (Lubow, 74). Being a machine here means being free from the limitations and vicissitudes of the body, as if prosthetic devices simply made the body and its gender disappear. Thus, in the melding of mind and machine, Hawking, like Einstein and Data, appears to be the perfect image of mental prowess. And yet momentary consideration reveals that the intellectual as Hawking represents him is not disembodied at all. Hawking's physical apparatus is essential to his public image, and not only because "No one can resist the idea of a crippled genius," as Hawking himself has remarked.[24] The articulation of his mental processes with the prosthetic is what makes them sexy. If he is, as Errol Morris's wife suggests, "the Mick Jagger of theoretical physics" (Lubow, 74), the sexiness of Hawking's presence may be a function of its dispersal in time and space.

His project is most often described in the popular press in explicitly masculine terms. On the back of my copy of A Brief History of Time, for example, the following sentences appear: "Professor Hawking leads us on an exhilarating journey to distant galaxies, black holes, alternate dimensions—as close as man has ever ventured to the mind of God. From the vantage point of the wheelchair in which he has spent more than twenty years trapped by Lou Gehrig's disease, Stephen Hawking has transformed our view of the universe. . . . A Brief History of Time is the story of the ultimate quest for knowledge: the ongoing search for the tantalizing secrets at the heart of time and space." Even despite the use of "man," which makes the gendered address of these sentences explicit, the description identifies the book as an adventure-quest fantasy, a popular "boy's" genre. In that genre, however, the hero moves the muscular concentration of his body across vast reaches of space and time. This is precisely what Hawking, of course, cannot do. His mind may roam the reaches of the universe, but his body remains "here," though here its presence is dispersed among the various prosthetic components that enable him to live and to speak. The voice synthesizer through which he must articulate his thoughts, for example, dislocates the origin of his utterances in temporal, spatial, and societal matrices, entailing not only a gap between conception and communication but a dislocation of his English accent—the mark of his national character, education, and class origins—by what Hawking himself describes as an American twang that originates in California, where the speech unit is made.

As Lubow remarks: "The voice does sound vaguely American, but mainly synthetic—somewhat reminiscent of Arnold Schwarzenegger's Terminator" (72). Is it simply fortuitous that the apparent model of pure mind unleashed from body should recall the contemporary icon of overbearing masculinity, a masculinity realized in its articulation with machinery? Here, at the intersection of body and prosthesis, one reencounters the problematics of gender, of corporeal politics, and of violence that the dream of the universal intellectual promised to transcend. If Hawking recalls Schwarzenegger's machine-tooled physique and flattened diction, it is because the very strangeness of Hawking's figure—the blurring of the boundaries between his body and the technology that both compensates for and expresses its disabilities—paradoxically but inevitably recalls more familiar images of masculine power.

I am inclined to take Hawking not as the exceptional case, as he is always presented, but as the typical and emblematic instance of the position and nature, the displacement and denaturing, of the universal intellectual at this time.[25] Since the eighteenth century, the modern intellectual, the figure of universalized specificity, has always occupied the site of an intersection and dispersal between organic processes and mechanical devices. The modern intellectual depends on and, in fact, is constructed by the availability of cheap and widely disseminable media such as print. This, as Habermas notes, is the "decisive mark" of the bourgeois public sphere, the "published word."[26] Print is not only a technology enabling the more efficient pursuit of an ongoing project (the dissemination of information, for example) but also—as Michael Warner has noted—the constitutive mechanism of that project. For the intellectual in the bourgeois public sphere, that project entails a certain disembodiment or decorporealization of thought.

As Warner puts it, "the validity of what you say in public bears a negative relation to your person. What you say will carry force not because of who you are but despite who you are." Science, with its attempt to disembody its subjects through instrumentation, is only the most marked development of this tendency. Yet as Warner also notes, abstraction through technologies of representation does not construct so much a decorporealized presence as a public prosthetic body, and one that is gendered. "For the ability to abstract oneself in public discussion has always been an unequally available resource. . . . Self-abstraction from male bodies confirms masculinity. Self-abstraction from female bodies denies femininity."[27] When Hawking's daughter Lucy remarks, as reported in Lubow's review, that "I don't think I've got quite his strength of mind . . . which means he will do what he wants to do at any cost to anybody else," she indicates more a specifically gendered politics of aggressive (rather than abstract) masculinity than the understanding of the scientist as "the model of pure mind unleashed from body" that commentators love to celebrate. More to the point, as one of Hawking's associates remarks, the expression of that will is definitely embodied in the form of Hawking's prostheses. "His wheelchair is not just an aid, but a weapon." "Almost everyone's first contact with him is metal" (Lubow, 76). Here a certain ambivalence typical in representations of Western scientists becomes evident in the representations of Hawking: on the one hand, a disembodied and desexualized mind; on the other, the hero of a specifically macho sort of adventure in which, despite his debility, Hawking manages to play a commanding and physically demanding part.

In the decorporealization of Hawking's mind, we reencounter the corporeal politics of his situation, both domestic and professional. In Morris's film, this emerges visually in the remarkable division of labor evident in the gender specificity of topics as they are divided among the talking heads. The phantasmatic decorporealization of the mind's body is realized as a series of demands for physical caretaking met, most often, by the women who surround Hawking (see "Why Past Is Past," 53). As Hawking puts it in the autobiographical essay "My Experience with ALS," "Jane managed to help me and bring up two children without outside help." Meanwhile, all the physicists are men. The cosmos, as a site for the adventure of the mind, seems to be an exclusively masculine realm.

In an interview that appears near the end of Morris's film, John Wheeler, the American physicist who first renamed "gravitationally completely collapsed objects" "black holes," describes one phenomenon by which the force of a black hole becomes evident by comparing it to men in dark evening clothes waltzing with women in white ball gowns in a darkened hall. The men would be invisible, but their presence could be detected by the movements of the women as they spin around the floor. This describes the presence and force of masculinity itself, which hides behind a rhetoric of universality that renders it invisible, manifesting itself most clearly in its powerful deformation of the feminine. The thematics of Wheeler's example for the observational verification of the existence of black holes— the invisible men in the darkened waltz and the orbiting women dressed in white—develops the thematics of masculinity and its tendency to exert itself most powerfully at the point where it approaches total invisibility. Thus, one might argue—somewhat poetically—that the black hole is masculinity itself, and that Stephen Hawking is the ultimate embodiment of this metaphor. This does not mean that masculinity is not subject to observation, as Hawking's work on the radiation of energy and information from black holes (which are not quite black) indicates. It does mean that masculinity may best be studied indirectly, in the manner in which its workings distort the field of inquiry or construct the objects to be investigated. It is fitting that in Hawking's office hangs a portrait of Marilyn Monroe, an actress whose work and appearance he has long admired: "I suppose you could say she was a model of the universe," Hawking has "joked" (White and Gribbin, 282). In this joke, the model of the universe and the model of the universal get figured as the object of masculine desire and the masculine desiring subject respectively. But, of course, this is not necessarily a joke at all.

Deformed singularity as universal intellect,
or just another guy

Hawking's joke suggests that the physicist is finally just another guy. But what does that suggest about the hopes popularly associated with the figure of the universal intellectual that Hawking's own singularity is taken to represent? As Hawking has more recently argued, "Black Holes Ain't So Black," and singularities are neither completely singular nor entirely entombed in the inert masses of their own bodies. Black holes emit radiation. They therefore broadcast energy and information, participate in or possess entropy; yet they do all this with a difference. For they still represent, according to Hawking, not a continuity in but a rupture of the space-time of the universe in that the information or energy emerging from the quantum phenomena on the horizon of the black hole is in no necessary way linked or traceable to the information or energy going into the black hole. From what comes out of a black hole, there is no certain way to tell what went in. A black hole is therefore a rift in the history of time. The principle of emission from the singular point of the black hole, then, is one that involves both displacement and the quantum smear of indeterminacy. Physicists must forgive a lay reader who finds in this image of the phenomenon an image of the universal intellectual himself, who, far from being the locus of a singular law that discovers the link between the present and the past, is rather the shifter for an indeterminate number of conflicts and projections, not the legislator of politics but one important site where politics occurs.

While this may seem to open onto a familiar postmodern dilemma about the death of the intellectual and the end of politics, I want to qualify these assertions. They are founded on a distorted notion of what the relation of the intellectual to politics has been and will no doubt continue to be. Pace Baudrillard and the apocalypticists of postmodernity: the configuration of the intellectual as outside the limits of the phenomena observed and represented—as imagined in the model of objectivity common to science and philosophy—is not for the West simply the configuration that makes possible the social and the political. This configuration is more profoundly a dream of escaping from society and politics. This has been true since Plato invented metaphysics and dialectics as an alternative to democracy and rhetoric. The discovery of Truth—in metaphysics as in physics—was to end the otherwise endless constructions and contestations of polemic, opinion formation, and action that are the political itself. Postmodernity's condition, skepticism about the adequacy of intellectuals' representations of the material, the social, the masses, history, et cetera, to some incontrovertible, absolute, and hence non- or apolitical preexistent truth or reality, does not foreclose the political or the social, as Baudrillard claims.[28] Postmodernity opens the entire field of intellectual endeavor to social and political vicissitudes.

The revision of the theory of the black hole seems to me analogous to an equally suggestive revision concerning the origin and end of the universe itself, a revision that involves the concept of what physicists call "imaginary time." I approximate this idea most closely to the Garden of the Forking Paths designed by Borges, in which different and myriad interconnecting and divergent networks of unfolding time express all narrative possibilities and probabilities in the universe. This involves the concept of "sum over" histories. As Hawking describes this idea, it figures a universe in which narratives remain linear but proliferate with quantum irregularity. "This gives a whole family of possible histories for the universe. There would be a history in which the Nazis won the Second World War, though the probability is low. But we just happen to live in a history in which the Allies won the war" (Black Holes, 130). In imaginary time, the real singularity posited at the universe's beginning disappears into the virtuality of a quantum smear of possibilities, so that as Morris's film indicates, the sharply pointed cone of space-time in an expanding universe must be redrawn so that the end becomes what one physicist calls "a beautiful bowl." But what does this beautiful bowl contain? On the one hand, the problem of the breakdown of natural law at the point of the singularity that made the origin unavailable to science is resolved by the smearing away of the singularity itself. On the other hand, the very concept of law and legislation—the dream of a lawful creator that has occupied the West since the Enlightenment—gets smeared as well. For if the universe has no singular origin, it also has no determinate end and no place for a creator, a law, or an intelligence not susceptible to the vagaries of quantum mechanics, uncertainty, virtual bodies, and corporeal politics. As Hawking puts it, "So long as the universe had a beginning, we could suppose it had a creator.

But if the universe is really completely self-contained, having no boundary or edge, it would have neither beginning nor end: it would simply be. What place, then, for a creator?" (*A Brief History of Time*, 141). In that beautiful bowl at the origin and end of space-time, physics rediscovers the image of a world it projects rather than uncovers.

As Hawking says, the nearest approach science can make to a fundamental principle, the anthropic principle, suggests that the universe exists as it does because only within these parameters could it make us possible. "According to this theory," he explains,

> there are either many different universes or many different regions of a single universe, each with its own initial configuration and, perhaps, with its own set of laws of science. In most of these universes the conditions would not be right for the development of complicated organisms; only in the few universes that are like ours would intelligent beings develop and ask the question: "Why is the universe the way we see it?" The answer is then simple: If it had been different, we would not be here! (*A Brief History of Time*, 124–25)

This also suggests that in a modification of Kant's Copernican revolution, we understand the universe as we do because the apparatuses of our perception and cognition, the projections of our thinking and positioning, construct it so around us. Or as Hawking asks: "How can we know what is real, independent of a theory or model with which to interpret it?" (*Black Holes*, 46). In this view of the universe, human significance is not removed from the cosmos; it is placed at its center in a particularly terrifying—because ultimately ungrounded—form. The intersection of coincidence and law, gender and intellect, is revealed to be the place where thought occurs, the locus of the intellectual's activities. But that activity must also be understood to be an aspect and a continuance of the phenomena it was supposed to arrest.

All this, again, is suggested in the final image of Morris's film, the wheelchair with the police bubble in the foreground, poised before a starry sky. What came first, the chicken or the egg? The wheelchair or the cosmos? The apparatus of cognition or cognition's object? Does the last word belong to science or philosophy? "Man" or machine? In the quantum smear of origins and ends and the uncertainties of a law that cannot finally be disembodied or clearly distinguished from occurrences of chance and violence, these riddles mark a space that is never voided of the material of politics.

7

The Professional: Science Wars and Interdisciplinary Studies

Albert Einstein meets the nutty professor

The recent "science wars" between scientists and humanists over science studies tell us little about science and even less about science studies. They reveal a lot, however, about the conflicts and crises within academic professions and among academic intellectuals about the status and prerogatives of expertise. In the public perception, the contestants have never been equals. On the one hand, people sometimes still look to scientists engaged in arcane research for political wisdom or cosmic insight, areas where humanists and philosophers might traditionally claim expertise. On the other hand, audiences often seem to enjoy representations of literature professors as fools to be mocked and pilloried for their naive political commitments and wacky theories. Thus Albert Einstein once offered his ruminations on peace and war to an attentive world, and Stephen Hawking, more recently, retails his speculations on the relation between theoretical physics and "the mind of God"; but who wants to hear what literary theorists and cultural studies types have to say, not only on issues of general interest but most particularly on the topic of science? Many humanists still tend to define themselves by their ignorance of, and antipathy toward, science. And yet the work of humanists, especially those few who study science, may be more important for the ethical and democratic culture of contemporary society than popular attitudes and current publicity seem to warrant.

The popular urge to humanize scientists may well reflect a desire to domesticate the terrors often associated with their work. For example, the film *IQ* (1995) asks us to imagine Einstein and other émigré physicists at the Princeton Institute for Advanced Studies in the Cold War fifties as lovably eccentric, elderly gentlemen with broad, comic accents who are so sentimentally wise and humane that they are willing to suspend their research to make a match between Tim Robbins's car mechanic and Meg

Ryan's graduate candidate in theoretical mathematics. Despite her pro forma identification with science, the primary business of Ryan's character is the feminine task of finding the proper mate. The schmaltzy antics of the distinguished scientists as they become manipulative yentas wise in the ways of the human heart do not negate or subvert the imposing masculinity of their brain power evident in their mastery of abstruse specialties so closely related to the sublime terrors of the atomic bomb: they draw attention to it. The film underlines this gender dynamic by ridiculing the feminized prissiness of Ryan's unsuitable fiancé, a psychologist whom she will learn to despise, whose soft-science discipline the physicists mock by calling him "the lesser professor." The car mechanic she learns to prefer may be uneducated, but he is very manly. This is an attribute the film asks us to join the physicists in admiring. What stake does the public have in imagining these men, whose expertise lies in the cold mathematical abstractions of theoretical physics and cosmic apocalypse, as possessing beyond the boundaries of their discipline a generalized life wisdom that would legitimate their interference and meddling?

When humanists consider the work that scientists do, scientists on the defensive have little trouble characterizing humanists as nutty professors — hopelessly out of their dim-witted depths, comical in their pathetic pretensions, devoid of common sense, prissy and feminized in their hysterical insistence on political correctness. This is the burden of Paul Gross and Norman Levitt's *Higher Superstition: The Academic Left and Its Quarrel with Science*.[1] Like other conservative cultural critics, they accuse literature professors of not understanding their own disciplines, much less the extraordinary rigors of scientific inquiry or the common tribulations of everyday life and practical politics. From their vantage point in the "hard" sciences, these authors ridicule the "lesser professors" in the humanities and social sciences who, like wayward women or undisciplined children, presume to intrude their frivolous opinions on serious matters that they are ill-equipped to understand.

Recent events have brought this asymmetry between science and science studies into sharp focus. In the spring of 1996, *Lingua Franca*, a journal primarily addressed to academic professionals, printed an article by New York University physicist Alan Sokal in which he reported the results of an "experiment" he had conducted in the field of cultural studies.[2] Sokal had successfully induced the editors of *Social Text*, a well-known quarterly in cultural studies, to publish an article purporting to describe the hermeneutics of quantum gravity. The author now gleefully revealed that the essay had been a hoax, filled with pseudoscientific gibberish that any scientifically literate reader should immediately have detected. According to Sokal, the experiment proved not only a "decline in the standards of rigor in certain precincts of the academic humanities" but a fundamental zaniness in the epistemological underpinnings of cultural studies in general and science studies in particular. That the editors had placed the ersatz piece in a special issue of the journal devoted to work in science studies and the generally hostile reaction to the field by science professionals such as Gross and Levitt made Sokal's point even sharper. The essay could not have been better placed. No saboteur's monkey wrench could more effectively have stuck in the works.

As *Lingua Franca*'s editors put it in their introduction to Sokal's exposé, "the interdisciplinary university is not always a peaceful place" (Sokal, 63). Interdisciplinary studies in general and science studies in particular are likely to be battlefields where the heat of conflict generates most of the light. The reasons for this involve the participation of scientists in the public sphere, the limits of specialization in the U.S. academy, and the relationship of intellectuals to political and social tensions in contemporary U.S. culture.

Concerns about the relationship of intellectuals to politics, according to Sokal, motivated his hoax. Its success, he claims, demonstrates the unacceptably low standards of argument and evidence that are characteristic of a certain segment of the academic Left. This lack of rigor especially characterizes those nonscientists engaged in the cultural study of science. It is not only a problem in itself, Sokal contends, but a symptom of more fundamental debilities. As Sokal explains, he is concerned especially with a "particular kind of nonsense and sloppy thinking: one that denies the existence of objective realities." His concerns with such thinking are "both intellectual and political." As he explains, "Intellectually, the problem with such doctrines is that they are false (when not simply meaningless). There *is* a real world; its properties are *not* merely social constructions; facts and evidence *do* matter. What sane person would contend otherwise?" And he attempts to illustrate how his experiment proves the rightness of his critique of idealist epistemology on the Left. Because the *Social Text* editors liked his ersatz conclusion about "postmodern science" and progressive politics, they "apparently felt no need to analyze the quality of the evidence, the cogency of the arguments, or even the relevance of the arguments to the purported conclusion" (63–64). That may be true, but in Sokal's *Lingua Franca* exposé, both the cogency of his arguments and the relevancy of those arguments to his conclusions are also flawed.

I don't want to dwell on Sokal's own lack of rigor except insofar as it is symptomatic of more general problems of greater interest, so I will summarize. First, he offers no sign that he is familiar with, or can position his argument among, the various philosophical opinions, epistemological problems, and ontological issues informing what he calls "social constructivist" or "subjectivist" thinking. For Sokal, for instance, in a way that would have surprised Bishop Berkeley or Hegel, idealism and social constructivism are simply identical. Second, Sokal offers no argument why these positions must be considered simply wrong, except for the unsupported, question-begging statement that they are all wrong and no sane person could possibly disagree. (One imagines that similar arguments were offered by religious dogmatists against Copernican cosmologies: "The sun moves around the earth! What sane person could contend otherwise?") Third, he offers no explanation of how admitted lapses by the editors of *Social Text* come to possess any general epistemological or ontological significance at all. Is he claiming that social constructionists (to coin a nearly meaningless collective noun) are incapable of editing a learned journal, following professional paradigms, thinking logically, or being empiricists? The history of Western thought—indeed, the history of empiricism since, at least, Montaigne and Hume—suggests otherwise. I do not mean to suggest that skepticism in general, or Montaigne and Hume in particular, are simply right, only that there is a long history of argumentation on these issues that Sokal fails to engage either as history or as argument in his polemic. Moreover, his two claims about the carelessness of his editors and the errors of their allegedly fundamental assumptions do not form an argument because they have, strictly speaking, nothing to do with each other. To claim that particular views of "reality" and evaluations of "truth" are social constructs does not make those views or evaluations any less concrete or real in the contexts they structure.[3] Assumptions about epistemology do not in this case, or in any other, determine editorial practice. Nor do social constructionist beliefs or relativism disable leftist critiques of mystifications promoted by the powerful in the realms of history, sociology, economics, politics, or science. As we shall see, one of those mystifications may well be the false idea that any one discipline or profession possesses the key to an objective reality that entitles its experts to legislate policy for their less gifted or credentialed fellow citizens.[4]

Why then is the slap at social constructionism in cultural studies added to the purported findings of Sokal's experiment? The answer, I believe, has to do with the material conditions of academic professions, the questions of interdisciplinarity, and the nature of intellectual work at this time. It has less to do with fundamental questions of science, epistemology, and ontology than Sokal and other scientists want us to think.

That their better-paid and more institutionally powerful colleagues in the hard sciences currently face hard times still surprises many academic humanists who have themselves gotten used to being the academic departments that are internally in crisis and institutionally besieged. Whether crises in the sciences herald science's end, as some have claimed, they certainly mark a shift in public perceptions of science; and the material expressions of this shift are quite real.[5] Research money and jobs, like all such resources within the university, by all accounts have become more scarce. The Cold War's end has eased some of the national security state's urgent need to compete on all fronts in a bipolar world, removing some of the apparent legitimacy of large-scale commitments to "pure" research. Increasing pressure on universities to credential students for competitive life in the capitalist economy similarly devalues disciplines without direct applications to business or technology. The so-called hard sciences, for the first time in fifty years, find themselves lumped with the humanities as less important and less well funded departments in universities increasingly devoted, even at the undergraduate level, to programs in engineering and management.

For those of us in the humanities, this is not so much a reason to gloat as it is a cause for concern. Dorothy Nelkin understates the case when she says that "when academic institutions are generally under siege, dividing the academy into warring factions in this way is extraordinarily counterproductive."[6] And yet the so-called science wars continue and seem to escalate. She attributes the heated rhetoric typical of those like Alan Sokal who seek to defend science from perceived threats from science studies to "the typically defensive response of endangered institutions that seek to seal their doors in an effort to preserve their purity and security in the face of external intrusion" (Nelkin, 94).[7] Such defensiveness does not, however, characterize only scientists. Given current conditions within the U.S. academy, no one should be surprised that a degree of defensive panic characterizes those who speak for science studies as well. Such defensiveness and panic may be the irreducible condition of these debates.

The real world

Despite continued popular fascination with science, the prestige that it long enjoyed as the perceived vanguard of perpetual progress is waning.[8] The "endless frontier of science," opened by the 1945 Vannevar Bush report that recommended large-scale government investment in research, is closing.[9] The state's resources for science, the material bases of the postwar "social contract" between science and the government, are drying up. As belief in the endless promise of scientific "advances" becomes more difficult to maintain, the willingness to commit money from reduced budgets to fund scientific research weakens as well. As Nelkin notes, this is no doubt a contributing factor in the somewhat overheated and largely misdirected strife of the so-called "science wars," because " 'outsiders' who study science are convenient scapegoats, and waging war is an easy way for scientists to avoid critical self-inquiry, to deflect responsibility and blame."[10] Scientists, like humanists, increasingly feel themselves besieged.

Increasingly scientists feel they receive insufficient respect from the public at large. Perhaps there is, as Gerald Holton has claimed, a "rebellion against science at the end of the twentieth century" (3). Perhaps, as Holton also claims, this rebellion is recognizably romantic, even Blakean, a dangerous antirationalism dressed up as postmodern skepticism or New Age piety. Yet as Holton admits, in recent decades, images of science in the public sphere have not always been edifying. Popular books like *Betrayers of the Truth: Fraud and Deceit in the Halls of Science* as well as congressional and government agency reports have publicized various incidents of scientific misconduct and fraud.[11] Whether such reports exaggerate corruption and malfeasance among scientists, the willingness, even eagerness, of the public to believe that they do not requires consideration. Such a belief seems to indicate an erosion of popular faith in scientists and in science. That scientists often appear in public as "experts" offering scientific evidence supporting contending sides in emotional public debates — for and against the safety of nuclear power, the carcinogenic and addictive properties of cigarettes, the wholesomeness of food additives, the reliability of DNA testing — has no doubt contributed to widespread perceptions that they, like most other members of a frankly capitalist society, have their price and can produce findings that suit their employers. Scientists in these cases do not seem like the disinterested servants of truth and apolitical acolytes of method they often claim to be. The truths they produce seem either too complex or too easily twisted to be of much use to a public that needs unambiguous answers and effective solutions.

Public distrust of science and of scientists does not necessarily amount to an urge to abandon the projects of rationalism and research central to science's and the West's most flattering self-representations in favor of New Age mysticisms or ancient folk beliefs. As Sandra Harding, whose feminist studies of science have drawn more than their share of fire from panicky scientists, puts it:

Feminist and antiracist science studies have called for more objective natural and social sciences, not less objective ones! They want sciences that are competent at detecting the culture-wide presuppositions that shape the dominant conceptual frameworks of disciplines and public discourse. Such presuppositions, if unexamined, function as evidence, "laundering" sexism or racism or class interests by transporting them from the social order into the "natural order."[12]

Harding's comments are characteristic of the current critique of science as well as of the popular uneasiness about science. She has often been presented as the representative of science study's worst excesses by the project's attackers. Yet there is nothing either antiscientific or, in the most conventional construction of the term, anti-Western in her work. Science-inspired hopes as much as science-inspired fears motivate her and many other popular and academic critics of science. Their criticisms are often a demand that science deliver on its promises rather than an attack on its founding assumptions.

Nonetheless, Harding comes in for an especially vituperative attack in Gross and Levitt's *Higher Superstition*, where they attempt to defend physics from Harding's claim that aspects of its practice may, like the society as a whole, be inflected by gender (Gross and Levitt, 126–32). The energy of this attack is symptomatic. This reading of Harding has more to do with the authors' ideological and political positions than with the actual content of her argument. On affirmative action, for instance, Gross and Levitt offer the following: "The only widespread, *obvious* discrimination today is against white males" (110). Their representation of beleaguered "white males," a group whose earning power and control of positions of authority in the university and in society at large is affirmed by every set of "scientific" statistics published, depends wholly on metaphors and images. Ironically, this is precisely the sort of evidence that, when feminist analyses of science are the issue, the authors derogate as trivial. This is especially evident when Gross and Levitt cross disciplinary boundaries to become TV critics:

> Who has not looked sidewise at the screen and seen a beautiful young woman (political correctness in the media does not yet frown upon "lookism"), high heels, lipstick and all, leaping about with her 9-mm. Beretta held, two handed, in the approved barrel-up manner, dodging around corners, stalking a murderous criminal? Who has not seen her straddle and handcuff the oaf, toward the end of the show? Who has not seen the impenetrably tough, young woman lawyer face down a crooked male judge in court, and then, as a sop to story line and the *connectedness* of women, make a lonely phone call to her mother, or her sister, late that night? (Gross and Levitt, 123–24)

As the absence of specific examples or the rudiments of argument (not to mention the utter disregard of the varied work by professional critics in the academic field of television studies that might support, contradict, or complicate their position) makes clear, this is not argument but diatribe. That more than a note of hysteria creeps into Gross and Levitt's display of explicitly manly disdain when the topic is feminism specifically or women more generally seems especially strange when they are claiming to defend reasoned argument and dispassionate inquiry as ungendered categories. Although they claim that science is gender free, they use representations of women (and of a distinctly feminized—in their estimation—popular culture) to reassert the gendered identity of hard science as a masculine enterprise.

Gender issues aside, however, there is one specific aspect of the contemporary critique of science that scientists frequently find particularly troublesome. While defenders of science frequently bemoan science studies for its purported relativism and its tendency to raise political questions involving gender, they often seem most troubled by a certain populist strain notable in the work of several writers.

The idea that science, in a variety of external and internal ways, is socially conditioned (an idea that even Gross and Levitt cannot actually deny) becomes most aggravating when coupled with demands that science be made more "democratic," more responsive and serviceable to the communities around it, less the exclusive property of money and power elites. Andrew Ross, for example, speaking as a "sober relativist," can claim that "we all operate within the framework of our own patched-together rationality," specific to our local "cultural environment," whether "we" are a "Western laboratory scientist" or a "rainforest shaman." From the perspective of scientists or of shamans, this claim is fairly banal. It becomes more threatening, though, when Ross brings his argument to a point and attempts to stick the experts with it:

> The unjustified conferral of expertise on the scientist's knowledge of, say, chemical materials, and not on the worker's or the farmer's experience with such materials, is an abuse of power that will not be opposed or altered simply by demonstrating the socially constructed nature of the scientist's knowledge. That may help to demystify, but it must be joined by insistence on methodological reform—to involve the local experience of users in the research process from the outset and to ensure that the process is shaped less by a manufacturer's interests than by the needs of communities affected by the product. This is the way that leads from cultural relativism to social rationality.[13]

Ross makes sensible recommendations: what sane person could think otherwise? But before anyone points out that he has here made explicit the link between cultural relativism and the critique of scientific rationality that Sokal found so problematic (and the existence of which I earlier denied), I want to point out that Ross's actual recommendations and his purported relativism are, in this instance, unrelated.

There is nothing relativistic or contrary to the paradigms of experimental science about the recommendation that methodologies for field testing various agents require improvement and that those who work in the actual fields being tested may, although they are neither research scientists nor credentialed experts, have valuable knowledge worth incorporating into these studies to better serve a wider community's interest in a safer environment.[14] The claim to cultural relativism here and the appeal to the socially constructed nature of science does no real work in this part of the argument. The problem, from the point of view of credentialed experts being asked to listen more attentively to, and perhaps to share power with, the noncredentialed, is precisely the apparent erosion of the authority that the certificates, institutions, and procedures of the expert confer. These recommendations threaten the prerogatives of the professional scientist, not the metaphysics of his or her research.

A social constructionist view has, strictly speaking, no implications for the legitimacy or validity of science, though Sokal believes that such a view does.[15] Attempting to illustrate his claim that physical reality, unlike "theories" of physical reality, is not at bottom "a social or linguistic construct," Sokal writes that "anyone who believes that the laws of physics are social conventions is invited to try transgressing those conventions from the windows of my apartment" (Sokal, 62). This is a very old argument, and it invites several responses. The first, and least relevant to the question of legitimacy and validity, is the reminder that the "law of gravity" is itself a descriptive construct, an artifact of human intelligence, and a cultural expression of a historical moment. It is not "reality itself" and in itself does not cause a body to fall from a twenty-first-story window, though it does, in certain contexts, provide an interesting and useful explanation of how—if not necessarily why—this happens. The second and more pertinent point is that whatever the ultimate epistemological validity or ontological grounding of the law of gravity may be, usefulness, not metaphysics, determines its scientific validity.

In fact, science, insofar as it believes itself to be a pragmatic, empirical enterprise, need take no interest in metaphysics at all because metaphysics, by definition, cannot be empirical. How the world appears to us and why the world appears to us as it does are two different orders of speculation. The phenomena of the world and the meaning of those phenomena are only contingently related. Meanings can be constructed and can construct the world in a variety of ways.

There is, however, a practical implication of the scientific critique of metaphysics. If the value of science must be measured by pragmatic arguments rather than by pious appeals to an undemonstrable and unscientific metaphysics of truth, then scientists have—and have had for some time—a real, as opposed to a philosophical, problem. For society at large, the blessings of science are widely perceived to have been mixed. Stanley Aronowitz summarizes the implications of the long tradition of criticism and analysis in the history and philosophy of science as follows:

The sum of these investigations is to bring science and scientificity down to earth, to show that it is no more, but certainly no less, than any other discourse. It is one story among many stories that has given the world considerable benefits including pleasure, but also considerable pain. Science and its methods underlie medical knowledge, which, true to its analytic procedures, has wreaked as much havoc as health on the human body; and it is also the knowledge base of the war machine.[16]

What this means, pragmatically, is that scientists should now expect to defend the worthiness of their work in public rather than retreating behind irrelevant claims about science's universality as the sole path to true enlightenment and prudent policy.[17]

What one hears in the science wars—and one hears it from the defenders of science and of science studies as well—is the instinctive defensiveness of experts who fear that their claims to special authority in the domain of their credentialed expertise are being questioned.

The question of expertise also figures prominently in the response to Sokal that Andrew Ross and Bruce Robbins framed on behalf of *Social Text*. Ross and Robbins are careful to note that at least one member of the editorial board "was unconvinced that Sokal knew very much about what he was attempting to expose," and to explain that whereas his essay "would have been regarded as somewhat outdated" if it had been the work of a humanist or social scientist, as "the work of a natural scientist it was unusual, and, we thought, plausibly symptomatic of how someone like Sokal might approach the field of postmodern epistemology."[18] Ross and Robbins are understandably more concerned that a nonspecialist could have gotten the best of them on their own turf—producing a hoax that mimicked their own professional languages and procedures well enough to fool them—than they are about the scientific illiteracy with which Sokal charges them. They are specialists in science studies, not in science.

What one hears on both sides of the science wars is the lament of an intellectual priesthood faced with a blaspheming laity. Despite protests by scientists, this, and not relativism, is the problem. As Feyerabend puts it, "Relativism is often attacked not because one has found a fault, but because one is afraid of it. Intellectuals are afraid of it because relativism threatens their role in society just as the Enlightenment once threatened the existence of priests and theologians."[19] Defensiveness is what both sides in the so-called science wars share, even though science studies people sometimes claim to defend relativism and their critics purport to attack it.

It just might be that science studies may be something scientists really should fear, but not because of any relativist, constructivist, or perspectivist epistemology underpinning it. Rather, as another issue of *Lingua Franca* suggests, it may just be that science studies is gaining prestige and even a measure of power in the United States. In an article on Bruno Latour, David Berreby documents the spread of science studies programs, sometimes supported by grants from the National Science Foundation, at prestigious U.S. universities such as UC San Diego, MIT, and Cornell.[20] Berreby also notes that in 1994 the NSF awarded a National Medal of Science to sociology of science pioneer Robert Merton, the first time the foundation has awarded its prestigious medal to a sociologist (Berreby, 26–27). Concerning claims by those like Gross, Levitt, and Lewis Wolpert that only specialists in a given field can judge the wider effects or ecological implications of research in the field, a British science studies scholar reports that "ideologues such as Wolpert [and by implication Gross and Levitt as well] remain marginal to policy making, while regulatory experts have been in dialogue with science studies—as represented by me, for example."[21] Scientists in the United States must find this prospect especially alarming. If science studies, to borrow a term from Latour, opens the black box of scientific truth and makes visible the untidy pragmatics of scientific production, then scientists no longer find themselves the sole group empowered or entitled to determine what counts as valid and worthy in their discipline and what does not.

Any professional would find such a prospect alarming, literary professionals not excepted: witness the strong reactions to the culture wars attacking curricular revision, multiculturalism, feminism, identity politics, and "theory." Each of these is currently a professional issue of considerable interest to practitioners in the humanities and social sciences. The "culture wars" saw laypeople in the form of right-wing public intellectuals and politicians such as Dinesh D'Souza, Roger Kimball, William Bennett, and Lynne Cheney suggest from outside the profession that such enterprises were neither valid nor worthy. Arguments justifying these activities beyond simple evocations of expert knowledge and professional privilege need to be, and are being, made.[22] But professionals will always feel that being required to make such arguments threatens their authority and prestige.

In the current battle, science studies partisans have not sufficiently noted a peculiar reversal of roles that appears when one considers the conflict in this light. If the science wars continue the cultural wars, they also shift the places of the players with regard to questions of specialized expertise and professional power. In the struggles over culture, nonspecialists such

as D'Souza, Kimball, and others attacked—sometimes in explicitly populist or faux populist terms—what professional academic literary specialists were doing in their research and teaching. They demanded, in effect,
more influence in determining how these scholars were allowed to com-
port themselves. In the science wars, critics of science, even when they are
academic professionals from other disciplines, find themselves characterized and positioned as ignorant outsiders carping about the privileges and
protections empowering those they criticize. In both cases, those whose
professional prerogatives are being questioned respond sharply. In both
cases, evocations of professionalism emerge as crucial elements in the
argument, as crucial as the apparent content of the disputes.

Philosopher kings and other professionals

A professional humanist might have made the following reply to Alan
Sokal's attack: That you could perpetrate such a hoax, that you could utter
phrases ironically that your audience took seriously, is an expression not
so much of your own cleverness or of the debility of your readers but of
the nature of language. Perhaps your intended hoax was not a hoax in fact.
Your intention to write a hoax does not control the meaning of what you
have written any more than your desire for a simply available reality outside
human ways of constructing or knowing reality can master the uncertainties expressed by quantum theory. God plays dice with language as well
as with the world, and we, who are not God, frequently cannot even distinguish clearly between the two. We have a problem, that is, distinguishing between the world and the representational apparatuses that make it
available to us. This problem is at least as old as philosophy itself. Such a
response would have been possible, but it would have been largely beside
the point as well.

Two hundred years ago, Dr. Johnson attempted to refute Berkeley's skeptical idealism, which held that the world has no existence apart from our
perceptions of it, by giving a rock in his path a hard kick and declaiming, "I
refute it thus." In the same manner, Alan Sokal invites any who would deny
the independent existence of the law of gravity to jump from his apartment
window on the twenty-first floor. The fact is, such simple demonstrations
never persuade people not already convinced that skepticism need never
trouble the philosophical or moral certainties with which they dwell.

Our professional humanist, and Sokal and Johnson as well, have confused levels of analysis. No one has ever seriously doubted (I almost wrote
that no sane person could ever doubt) that actions in the world, a kick at a
stone or a leap from the twenty-first floor, yield certain predictable consequences—for example, a violent impact. Trouble occurs when one pauses

to ask why this seems to be so. I say "seems to be so" because to insist, simply, that "it is so" would be to beg the question, to assume as already solved the problem whose solution one pretends to seek. Such question begging forecloses the sorts of inquiries that many philosophers and some scientists find interesting: Is it so? Is it necessary that it is so? What does it mean that it should be so?

Where do these questions come from? Why do we ask and argue about things that seem so certain? If I can be certain (and I don't doubt that I can be, but what does *that* mean?) that if I kick a stone or jump out of a high window I will stub my toe or splatter on the sidewalk, what more do I (or anyone else) need to know? Where does the intellectual work called "science" or "philosophy" come from? How do we know when to take certain interrogative utterances "seriously" and when someone is using them to pull our leg?

Humanists tend to respond with generalities about the restlessness of the human spirit and the ceaseless questing of the human mind. They also respond with moral platitudes about professional ethics and trust within the academic community. These sentiments, uttered by intellectuals, are self-serving and unconvincing, the equivalent of kicking a stone or jumping from a window, a question-begging attempt to end rather than further an argument. Wonderment and curiosity are fine things, but they are too whimsical to sustain prolonged and painful interrogations of phenomena that might, if unquestioned, appear so simple and reassuring. Similarly, when professionals evoke the ethics of their own disciplines in response to critics, it is usually to say, "Go away and leave us alone."

C. S. Peirce, an American philosopher, one of the founders of pragmatism and no wild-eyed skeptic, once speculated that all thought begins with the discomfort of doubt. That alone doesn't tell us much more than any other bromide. Where does doubt come from? Here Peirce is interesting. He suggests that doubt, the discomfort at the origin of thought, comes from other people. Questioning, after all, is a social phenomenon.[23] The agony that is thinking is, as Socrates and Heidegger knew, an agon, a struggle with—though not always against—an opponent. Thinking is at its base both social and political. What does this imply about the distinction between politics and science to which so many subscribe?

In the humanist's conventional gesture, let us indulge in a philological excursus, since philology might be considered the first and most fundamental of the human sciences. Let us consult the dictionary to focus better the meaning of the word "science," around which the positions in the science wars revolve. The OED yields an embarrassment of riches. In fact, one finds there the grounds on which the war between science and philosophy is now being fought. "Science" is *Philos*, knowledge as opposed to belief or opinion, knowing, simply and self-evidently, what is what. It is by definition "theoretical" knowledge, absolute and universal "truth," and is contradistinct from "art" (as in contemporary divisions of arts and science in U.S. universities), "opinion," and "belief," for these are matters of historically specific dogmas, habitual skills, and traditional metaphysics that are the result of ungrounded speculation. Science, therefore, is or should be a theoretical, abstract discipline based on, and taking as its object, general laws or abstract forms. It is distinct from history, from tradition, from habit, from metaphysics. It is distinct, in short, from the political realm of opinion and from the arts appropriate to opinion, most notably, the arts of rhetoric, of argumentation, of persuasion. Science, unlike these other arts, depends not on argument but on demonstration, not on persuasion but on self-evidence. It is not a realm for debate. It is not democratic.

Those with a taste for philosophy will recognize in this dictionary entry yet one more footnote to Plato. He wrestled with the problem of knowledge and opinion in *The Republic*. For philosophers to be legitimate kings, knowledge (science), and not opinion (rhetoric), must rule the day. However, one should add, the state in which the philosopher king would legislate is an antidemocratic, even totalitarian, utopia for experts. Plato's *Republic* may be thought of as the first treatise on modern state organization, the first project for intellectuals, the first program for specialization. Lenin may have been reading Plato as much as Marx.

In Plato's scheme, talent, training, and specialization produce the ideal social order. Individuals are selected by objective criteria to occupy a place among the moneymaking, military, or ruling classes and then trained assiduously to perform the unique and specialized functions of the order to which they belong. "Justice," the well-ordered functioning of the state, depends on each practitioner performing the tasks (and no others) for which he or she has been trained. The ruin of the city—the confusion of wisdom and the loss of truth—results from the chaotic state in which no one knows one's place or the limits of one's competence: "This meddling brings the city to ruin. . . . That then is injustice. And let us repeat that the doing of one's own job by the moneymaking, auxiliary, and guardian groups, when each group is performing its own task in the city, is the opposite, it is justice and makes the city just." [24] Thus in Plato we also find the first critique of disciplinary boundary crossing. Philosophy, science itself, may be thought of as the ultimate specialization, and any incursions into the field by those who by training and inclination belong to other professions are not only unwise but also unjust. Uncontrolled interdisciplinarity brings the republic to ruin.

Certainly the moralized tone and globalized claims of Plato's critique of boundary crossing or hubris are echoed in the science wars. However, before one rushes to embrace Plato's position and rule not only poetry but interdisciplinarity out of the public sphere, one should consider the rigidity and mendacity of the institutions Plato imagines would be necessary to protect the boundaries of specialization and power in his ideal city. Certainly the republic would not be the city of democratic deliberation and of free exchanges of ideas that contemporary scientific academic communities claim to be; nor would it be a community in which—I would claim—thinking itself would be possible.

If Plato's version of an ideal social and political order based on professional specialization seems sensible to twentieth-century Americans, it is no doubt because life in the United States, as Burton Bledstein notes, has since the middle of the nineteenth century undergone a pervasive professionalization often undertaken according to "scientific" principles that taught laypeople "the hygienic way to bathe, eat, work, relax, and even have sexual intercourse."[25] What Max Weber believed was "The Uniqueness of Western Civilization"—the rationalization of society in a capitalist economy combining instrumentalized reason and bureaucratic structures dividing and compartmentalizing labor on the basis of operationally defined expertise—Bledstein analyzes as a characteristically middle-class and quintessentially American mode of life.[26]

It is, however, a mode of life whose political valences are ambiguous. On the one hand, professionalism democratizes power by legitimating its exercise not through birth or position but by the universally (in theory at least) acquirable attributes of skill, knowledge, and credentials. As Bledstein points out, professionalism provides "an orderly explanation of basic natural processes that democratic societies, with their historical need to reject traditional authority," require (Bledstein, 90). Central to Bledstein's thesis, then, is the "active relationship between higher education and the legitimacy of social power in America" (129). On the other hand, professionalization creates enormous opportunities for abuses and corruption, for antidemocratic concentrations of power in the hands of self-defined elites who hold themselves to be unaccountable to the general public.[27]

The tendency of professions to become self-defined, vertically organized enclaves separate from the rest of society is, according to Bledstein, the essence of their authority. That authority, "derived from a special power over worldly experience, a command over the profundities of a discipline," laypeople were incapable of comprehending: "Professionals controlled the magic circle of scientific knowledge which only the few, specialized by training and indoctrination, were privileged to enter, but which all in the name of nature's universality were obligated to appreciate" (Bledstein, 90). Thus, if as Bledstein argues, "science as a source for professional authority transcended the favoritism of politics, the corruption of personality, and the exclusiveness of partisanship" (which is precisely what Plato hoped it would do), it brings with it problems of power, exclusivity, and corruption of its own (90). The tension between the democratic and authoritarian tendencies of professional culture is one source of friction between science and its critics today.

The ambivalence of professional culture with respect to democracy is not all that makes it dangerous. The history of the twentieth century suggests that it is the separation of moral, ethical, or political reflection from the specified tasks of the specialist that causes problems. Those who have criticized cultural relativism often make a rhetorical gesture toward the horrors of National Socialism, claiming that the relativist can find no response adequate to Hitler's fanaticism. This gesture is usually meant to end discussion and to terrorize the opposition. And yet, considered dispassionately, relativism is a precisely appropriate caution against totalitarian absolutism, just as multiculturalism furnishes a reasonable critique of desires for racial, ethnic, or cultural purity. Any reasonable discussion of these crucial issues should take into consideration the fact that the horrors Germany perpetrated are attributable, as sociologists and historians have noted, only in part to the racist ideologies of National Socialism. The grim operational efficiency of the Final Solution was produced by a thoroughly modern culture organized around professional specialization and bureaucratic compartmentalization. Thus, as Hannah Arendt pointed out, Eichmann found a place in the Nazi hierarchy not because he was a particularly committed ideologue or an especially heartless killer but because he made himself into an "expert on the Jewish Question," an individual possessed of specialized knowledge and experience that allowed him efficiently to organize and carry out the tasks assigned to him in a thoroughly professional manner. For Eichmann, the fact that the task assigned involved the concentration, transportation, and extermination of human beings was unfortunate but inessential. He was, after all, an expert on logistics. He was not responsible for the plans he so effectively executed.[28] Science, knowledge of precise and definable sorts as opposed to opinion, the possession of specialists and professionals as opposed to the laity, does not guarantee and in fact cannot prevent horrendous injustices. National Socialism was a modern version of Plato's republic gone mad.

In our world, unlike Plato's, few sane people any longer believe that virtue, morality, and justice can be objects of knowledge rather than topics of opinion. In this world, with its manifold competing claims and increasingly abusive differentials of power, more and more people withhold unquestioning approbation from the scientists of all disciplines and resist the charismatic allures of the specialists.[29] Yet as the culture and science wars indicate, such resistance can itself be both morally and politically ambiguous. Democratization itself does not guarantee any particular politics at all. Although National Socialism concentrated power in the hands of specialists, it was also legitimated by wide populist appeals.[30] It may furnish one troubling example where the elite specialist and the majority found themselves in accord. Popular democracy does not in itself make fascism unthinkable. Where, between the field of the specialist and the general will, is the space for critical intervention; and is that intervention the work of specialists, academic or otherwise, and is it itself always simply democratic?

Interdisciplinarity as threat

One hears a lot about interdisciplinary studies, but I don't think we know what they are. Terri Reynolds, then a graduate student in comparative literature at Columbia University, joined the fray following Sokal's disclosure by participating in a forum on the topic in *Lingua Franca*. She pointed out that Sokal's article did not masquerade as "straight cultural criticism," "sociology of science," or "science" but as "interdisciplinary work." As such, she claimed, she could not recognize it. She then attempted to describe what interdisciplinary work should be: "The point of interdisciplinary endeavor is that work done in one field may be used to elucidate material in another. . . . They function as *cognitive* metaphors: unexpected associations that reorganize a familiar conceptual field and allow us to behave differently within it." She concluded, "Interdisciplinary work, then, is always translation—from one specialized discourse into another.[31] Reynolds's work, on relativity, quantum mechanics, and literary culture, sounds fascinating, but as she describes it, it is not interdisciplinary. She follows the most traditional practices of the academic literary scholar, the borrowing of "cognitive metaphors" from other disciplines—the thematization of other areas of knowledge such as history, psychoanalysis, philosophy, anthropology, or "science"—to shed a different light on the literary field. These metaphors may appear in the contents of works of fiction or in the rhetoric and textuality of a variety of discourses. The work in all these cases remains—even at its most revolutionary or unsettling—solidly within the discipline to which it is addressed, the discipline whose professional members are empowered to sanction or sanctify the work and its author, the discipline whose paradigms and discursive conventions the individual practitioner can challenge or transform but never simply ignore, the discipline (in this case) of literary studies, with its specialized objects and characteristic gestures.

There is, however, an actual interdisciplinarity at work in the current science wars, one that tends to provoke accusations of violent expropriation and professional transgression. The metaphorics of translation and elucidation across disciplinary boundaries seem inappropriate here, for these excursions are likely to generate more heat than light. This is not to say that they may not, finally, elucidate much about our contemporary intellectual and institutional scene. Sokal's original essay, with its mingling of metaphysics, physics, and politics, is as Reynolds suggests a parody of interdisciplinarity. As such, it succeeds in raising certain questions. For example, is interdisciplinarity always, to an important extent, parodic? And, if so, is the parody of or about professionalism?

Stanley Fish, who took a prominent position in the Sokal affair with an Op-Ed piece in the *New York Times*, has very definite ideas about interdisciplinarity and its relation to professionalism.[32] According to Fish, not only is a strong sense of interdisciplinarity difficult, even impossible, to maintain, but were it possible it might be professionally suicidal. He takes his own profession as a literary scholar as an example. "Literary work," he argues in *Professional Correctness*, "like any other, can always surrender its distinctiveness to a political agenda, but when it does, it has not found its true form; it has lost the form that gave it distinctive life" (82). This is because, as Fish goes on to explain, any profession in current institutional contexts (the U.S. university, for example), "unless the enterprise is bent on suicide . . . will still present itself, both to the outside world and to its members, as uniquely qualified to perform a specific task" (19). The rewards for successfully making that claim are considerable, even fundamental, for on that claim rests the claim to "a space at the table of enterprises," the very existence of the discipline or profession itself: "An enterprise that can make good on that claim will in an important way be autonomous, not autonomous in the sense of having no affiliations with or debts to other enterprises . . . but autonomous in the sense of having primary responsibility for doing a job society wants done" (19–20). This task-specific expertise is what disciplines and the professionals who work within them depend on. This is because, in Fish's antiessentialist and socially constructivist view, there is nothing natural about disciplines or their objects: "The vocabularies of disciplines are not external to their objects, but constitutive of them. Discard them in favor of the vocabulary of another discipline, and you will lose the object that only they call into being" (85). Construed in the vocabulary of discourse analysis, the real-world objects about which scientists claim to discover truths seem to disappear. This seems clear, but in the light of this clarity, another question becomes visible. If language and disciplinarity are powerfully linked, if so much depends on disciplinary boundaries, why do academic intellectuals, both literary and scientific, so often seek to escape the limits that simultaneously circumscribe and enable their differing expertise? Why do more general political questions so often intrude on the local politics and prerogatives of academic specialists?

One might, as Fish does, attribute the desire of academic intellectuals to be effective in the wider world to what he calls megalomania. Academic intellectuals believe first that they are smarter and better informed than other people and second that their disciplinary skills and practices are central or should be central to what goes on in other academic and nonacademic fields. Against the megalomania of this belief, Fish offers a defense of specialized knowledge in all areas.[33] Like Andrew Ross and other critics of scientific knowledge and the pretensions it often exhibits to being the repository of absolute truth, Fish emphasizes "local experience" and the expertise inherent in specific and various practices against any one claim to universality, truth, or efficacy. But in Fish's polemic, the point is not to undermine the power of professions (scientific and technological professions certainly included) but to reaffirm their exclusivity and power within their specific domains. In Fish's view, all professions remain and must remain what Bruno Latour calls black boxes, machines that produce "truth" whose inner workings stay invisible to outsiders.[34] Are, therefore, the incursions of science studies scholars into science and scientists into cultural studies simply illegitimate? Is all this fear and loathing on both sides of the disciplinary divide simply mistaken?

I want, at the risk of a little megalomania of my own, to advance the claims of literary intellectuals. Those involved in the hermeneutic trades, where, as Fish declares, the crucial disciplinary question is "What does it mean?" and the "what"—the object of study—can remain largely unspecified, are not so easily circumscribed. Their specific disciplinary orientation involves the prying open of the black boxes where meaning is made. This is not to say all such efforts are necessarily legitimate, only that they can provoke anxiety when their practitioners make claims on other fields, like science. Skilled methods of construal often have considerable resonance in other areas. Questions of meaning tend to occur at all levels of personal, social, and political life. If that is the case, then (especially in societies and in a global environment where different ways of construing meaning, different cultural and professional ways of constructing and engaging the world, are increasingly in contact and in conflict) in such contexts, skill at construing and persuasively constructing meanings is crucial. As Zygmunt Bauman has suggested, in the postmodern public sphere, as intellectuals renounce the traditional roles as legislative authorities that they can no longer credibly play, they may become interpreters within and between ever more diverse and fractious communities.[35]

Yet like some versions of interdisciplinarity, this view of the intellectual's function in contemporary society too easily masks a certain violence and resistance characteristic of acts of construal. As the culture and science wars suggest, contact between various disciplines and segments of professional and public life is likely not to be marked by harmonious understandings based on faithful or disinterested acts of translation. Acts of translation, like other forms of interpretation, tend to be interesting in direct portion to the degree that they are interested. And because interests often clash, they also tend to be contestatory and even violent.

In this light, the science wars may be understood as a clash between disciplinary predispositions, each claiming to be central, each apparently mutually exclusive. For if the professional routines of disciplines not only act on but actually produce the objects of disciplinary study—be they literary "texts" or experimental "findings"—then when the issue is the relationship between disciplines, the objects of each can easily seem to disappear when viewed from the "angle" of the other. This is one reason why, as Liz McMillen notes in her report on the science wars in the *Chronicle of Higher Education*, "Much of what many scholars in the humanities take for granted, such as the analysis of discourse, causes alarm among scientists."[36] One might add that the opposite is also true.

Here the hysteria these disciplinary crossings sometimes provoke among scientists begins to be legible. In the terms of literary criticism, my profession, its meaning becomes construable. Of all professions on the contemporary scene, science has long made the strongest claims to be the legislative arbiter of the world. The scientists' claim to be philosopher kings, in the minds of some like Sokal or Gross and Levitt, depends on the concrete and neutral existence of a natural world and the natural adequation of their work as scientists to that world. If science is to rule the public sphere and enjoy the perquisites of money, privilege, and power that attend that ruling, then science must present itself not as a discipline—in Feyerabend's terms, one way of humanly invented and culturally dependent knowing among others—but as a natural kind. Science must claim to be the universal protector and sole purveyor of the un(re)constructed truth about the world. However, if there is no un(re)constructed truth (which is not to say that there are no useful constructed truths), then the discipline that takes ways of construing as its object and its method may make claims that from within the discipline of science seem especially frightening. One such claim would be that there are no unreconstructed truths. Scientists seem to feel that this claim makes the work they do and the truths they produce impossible. Instead, I would say, that if these claims can be made persuasively about science, then they alter nothing about science's most inner working. Experimental methods, mathematical abstraction, and rigorous review by peers remain powerful and in place. These claims would, however, make univocal appeals to science's unique prestige and power in the wider public sphere questionable, open, that is, to public interrogation and demands for justification.

Certainly science does not find itself in the tight place it currently occupies because of science studies. As we have seen, most writers in the field claim, quite rightly, that the current panic about science studies is a symptom of quite other maladies: the internal and external crises in research protocols, government funding, and academic retrenchment we began by noting. As Nelkin puts it: "One is hard put to find any correlation between historical or sociological analysis of science and changes in science policy" (94–95). But science studies seems to have made some contribution to, or at least made a systematic reflection of, a more general, altered understanding of science's place and status; and that, for scientists at least, is troubling.

Those like Stanley Fish who emphasize the self-contained unity and limited translatability of disciplinary skills have difficulty explaining these anxieties. If, as Fish argues, "in relation to a strongly enforced territoriality, the language of literary theory is not subversive, but irrelevant: it *cannot be heard* except as the alien murmurings of a galaxy far away" (*Professional Correctness*, 91), then what is all the worry about? Such a view of professionalism and its relationship to specialized fields seems neither accurate nor adequate to describe what goes on in the science wars particularly and cultural studies generally. Here, negotiations of power and squabbles over influence between professionals and laypeople, or between professionals from different fields who are then laypeople in each other's respective domains, are the central issue. Arguments about what counts as evidence and as argument, disagreements about what specialists know and don't know, and contestations about what knowledge in specific contexts means are themselves evidence that the murmurings from alien galaxies have become both more proximate and more threatening. Despite the protests and pranks of Sokal and others, in a democratic rather than a Platonic republic, that is the way things ought to be.

CONCLUSION

Tattered Maps

Unpopular intellectuals

In his remarkably evenhanded description of the present state of American universities and their unpopularity, Donald Kennedy uses the film *Quiz Show* (Redford, 1994) to make a point about the degree to which popular perceptions about academic professionals have changed in the last decades. Today, he notes with dismay, few would be shocked by the sort of scandal that beset Charles Van Doren after he was caught cheating on the TV game show 21 because few today believe in the honesty or integrity of academics. "The relationship between universities and their public is more dependent on trust than on anything else. For this reason, perhaps, mendacity is viewed as the least forgivable blot on academic duty." According to Kennedy, this is why the exposure of Van Doren's cheating led to "a national scandal of extraordinary proportions." Kennedy ends the anecdote by noting that "today, alas, the public would react to such a revelation both more calmly and more cynically."[1] While Kennedy may be right that this change reminds us "of the degree to which truth-telling is the linchpin of academic trust" and "how serious a threat to the public's confidence in the value of scholarship is the belief that its pursuit is marred by personal interest, greed, or dishonesty" (210), I do not find this account of "higher education's fall from grace" to be completely persuasive.

First, since it is unlikely that universities will ever be or have ever been populated by secular saints, academic careers will continue to be—as they have always been—touched by personal interest and the desire for personal gain. Why shouldn't they be? Dishonesty is another matter. However, although research misconduct in the sciences may be a problem that, as Kennedy puts it, some "popular books decrying contemporary universities have given . . . loving attention" (210), research misconduct is not what has altered public perceptions of professors in the humanities. Certainly, right-wing critics from D'Souza to Bennet to Cheney have decried an assault on

Western values and canonical authors and the prevalence of a paralyzing skepticism and relativism in college English departments. But these accounts, as we have seen, are factually ill founded and logically inconsistent. More important, they are also beside the point. If public appreciation of work in the humanities has waned, it is probably because the cultural capital that the humanities have traditionally purveyed no longer exchanges for convertible currency at very high rates. Thus, the corporate executive who serves as regent for the Massachusetts State University system can say in public that 90 percent of the research not in the hard sciences conducted in the university he heads is "nonsense"—by which he means unlikely to be of use in increasing the efficiency of industry or the personal earning power of graduates—and the reaction of the public is neither bewilderment nor outrage but general approbation. Everyone can multiply his or her own examples of such institutional and popular disrespect.

That the cultural capital of the humanities has declined in value is the point that John Guillory makes, and I find his observation painfully persuasive, though I cannot honestly say that I think it is altogether a bad thing. The snob value of class accreditation has never been the most attractive aspect of what an education in the humanities can provide, nor is the society that would honor such credentials a particularly enlightened place. In a more democratic society, literary and cultural studies have other things to offer. In a democratic society, they should be valued parts of—indeed, central to—the education of each citizen. As Kennedy suggests, academic, like civic, duty has something to do with truth telling, even if the truth told is the difficult truth that there may be no easily definable single or universal truth to which all parties in an argument or a community can refer. This truth is not, as conservative critics would charge, the end of values or of the West or of community itself; it is, as I have already suggested, a continuation of the West's best traditions and the point from which any ethically serious consideration of values or judgment or community must take its departure.

This is where intellectuals in the university find themselves during the culture wars that continue to simmer in the public sphere. The valuable lesson that one might draw from the culture wars is that when intellectuals seek to speak the truth to power, especially when that truth involves their own position and task, they must do so in a field that has frequently been defined by the falsehoods and distortions of those they must oppose. Intellectuals must choose the truth. For this reason, and in this special sense, I would argue that Dinesh D'Souza, William Bennet, Lynne Cheney, and others who have sensationalized and distorted the situation of cultural intellectuals in the academy today may not accurately be described as intellectuals at all. They seek not to speak the truth to power but rather to promulgate falsehoods on power's behalf. To be an intellectual means to assume a certain tradition and certain traditional values that are frequently associated with, but not uniquely available through, the Enlightenment. It means attempting to promulgate those values, projecting them (and ourselves) into the world and onto our objects, hoping to make them and us and those we hope to serve prevail. To attempt to work without or in opposition to those values, to seek to avoid or obscure the problems and paradoxes involved in intellectual work, is to cease to be an intellectual at all. And without intellectuals there can be no politics, progressive or otherwise.

Teaching and intellectual work generally cannot always be popular. Good teachers and responsible intellectuals do not necessarily make their constituents comfortable or happy, especially if one of their important functions is to engage students and the public in the painful practice of interrogating their own prejudices and assumptions. As Henry Louis Gates Jr. and Cornel West put it, being an intellectual "does not necessarily mean being loved; loving one's community means daring to risk estrangement and alienation from that very community, in the short run, in order to break the cycle of poverty, despair, and hopelessness that we are in, in the long run." [2] Professors, unlike other purveyors of services, cannot always be judged on the basis of customer satisfaction. Their relation to the popular is and must remain vexed. The paradoxes of the intellectual's position cannot be wished away by romanticized populisms of the Left or of the Right. Intellectuals frequently antagonize the very people for whom they purport to speak in the name of "common" values and "shared" commitments, like justice and freedom, that are themselves the points of contention.

Rigor among the ruins

The real problem in recent polemics about the academy is the problem of intellectuals. What roles do they feel themselves capable of playing in contemporary society, what roles do they actually play, and how are those roles articulated within the institutional context of the American university? For better or worse, the university has become the base of operations for most cultural and scientific, critical and traditional intellectuals today.

The putative passing of critical intellectuals in particular from positions of prominence in the political and cultural lives of the general community to more marginalized places in universities has occasioned much notice, anxiety, mourning, and celebration. One should remember that reactions to this passing have been most evident among intellectuals themselves, who may perhaps be forgiven for finding their own status in the world of such absorbing and momentous significance. There has been, however, widespread confusion about what that significance might be.

Not surprisingly, I find an appropriate figure for the legacy of the Enlightenment and the place of intellectuals in contemporary societies within my own special sphere of intellectual expertise—literature. A short story by Jorge Louis Borges, I think, says it all—or will say it all once, drawing on my institutional authority as a professional interpreter, I have explained the story for my readers.

"Del Rigor en la Ciencia" is so short that I will quote it whole, for in fact it is little more than a fragment. It begins with three dots, the typography of the fragment, referring to and marking the absence of a larger totality:

Del Rigor en la Ciencia

. . . En aquel Imperio, el Arte de la Cartografía logró tal Perfección que el mapa de una sola Provincia ocupaba toda una Ciudad, y el mapa del Imperio, toda una Provincia. Con el tiempo, esos Mapas Desmesurados no satisfacieron y los Colegios de Cartógrafos levantaron un Mapa del Imperio, que tenía el tamaño del Imperio y coincidía puntualmente con él. Menos Adictas al Estudio de la Cartografía, las Generaciones Siguientes entendieron que ese dilatado Mapa era Inútil y no sin Impiedad lo entregaron a las Inclemencias del Sol y de los Inviernos. En los desiertos del Oeste perduran despedazadas Ruinas del Mapa, habitadas por Animales y por Mendigos; en todo el País no hay otra reliquia de las Disciplinas Geográficas.—Suárez Miranda: Viajes de Varones Prudentes, Libro Cuarto. Cap. XLV, Lérida, 1658.[3]

Of Rigor in Knowledge

. . . In that Empire, the Art of Cartography reached such Perfection that the map of a single Province filled a whole City, and the map of the Empire, a whole Province. With time, these Extravagant Maps no longer sufficed, and the College of Cartographers created a Map of the Empire, which filled just as much space as the Empire itself and coincided precisely with it. Less addicted to the Study of Cartography, later Generations understood that such an extended Map was Useless, and not without Impiety they abandoned it to the Inclemency of the Sun and the Rains. In the wilderness of the West the tattered Ruins of the Map remain, inhabited by Animals and by Beggars; in the entire Country there is no other relic of the Geographical Disciplines.

This is the story of the Enlightenment's special topography, its historical and geographic ambitions, its protracted crisis and decline, its ubiquitous persistence. If enlightenment, as Plato, Kant, Marx, Horkheimer, Adorno, and many others have claimed, signifies the universalizing ambitions and ameliorating hopes that give the West its particular shape, and if—as Borges's legend suggests—the West is now a wilderness in which only the tattered ruins of the universalizing map remain, then we can see why the universal seems so difficult to locate today. Its ruins are where we live, like the beggars and the beasts who inhabit Borges's fragment. He does not fail to suggest the links between intellectual pretensions and imperial ambitions—the desire to map the world originates in and eventually dominátes and subverts a political state he calls an empire. In this empire, the cartographers of knowledge seek to rule the map, seek to reduce the world to their universal mapping of it. Ironically, they succeed. Yet their attempt to impose a universal Enlightenment also fails and inevitably falls to tatters. What remains?

Borges's parable twists ever so slightly the familiar plot that entwines the intellectual's ambitions to subjugate reality to a universalized mapping of knowledge and the failure of that desire to subjugate local traditions and particular modes of knowing. If this is a story about the ultimate failure of reason to impose a universal rule on the world, it is also a story about the persistence of community not only in opposition to but also engaged with the map of the universal that attempts to dominate it. If the map of Enlightenment presents the world as a totalizing spatialization, the map of mapping presents us with various histories, diachronic unfoldings, narrative constructions. These define communities. Frequently community has been the touchstone by which contemporary thinking seeks to orient itself. If specific communities have replaced the universal as the grounds of intellectual work, it is not surprising that community has assumed some of the imperative values and universalizing ambitions that intellectuals still seek to represent.

Borges reminds us that thought is not a disembodied, immaterial essence. Thinking is a socially mediated and historically embedded function that involves specific groups or classes—the displaced, priestly cartographers of Borges's fragment or the professional intellectuals in our world whose orientation and position now seem unclear. But to approach this fable and these matters in this fashion is to do so in too general and universalizing a fashion. It is to forget the intellectual's special locale among the parti-color fragments of Enlightenment, that place whose name itself is one of those persistent fragments of universalizing ambition: the university.

In fact, Borges's story represents an almost perfect figure for the modern American university, the institution that Bill Readings describes as a "university in ruins."[4] Here the different disciplines of a projected universal map of science as intellectuals dreamed it a hundred years ago are charted onto the quadrangles and departments of the campus. These days most of those departments—in the humanities and in the sciences—have lost any sense of obvious or natural correspondence with the titles under which they continue to live. Many who inhabit these departments feel themselves, whether they will admit it or not, to be dwelling in a ruined edifice—metaphoric or real—and most peer out of their particular gap in the fabric of knowledge's map with a certain fear and mistrust of the other beggars across the quad. This sort of bunker mentality does no one much good.

It may seem strange to speak of the West, its ideas, and institutions as a tattered ruin at this moment of their apparent triumph. The Cold War's end promised the progress of a new world order establishing the eternal reign of liberal values. Yet the apparent demise of Marxism's world-historical pretensions in the failures of Eastern Europe should give everyone pause. Right-wing critics and left-wing apologists who have imagined that Marxism, one of the greatest attempts at a universal map of knowledge, was simply liberalism's opposite—an aberrant other that threatened to impose its brutal grip on the West—forget that Marxism emerged from deep within the hopes and aspirations of the West's Enlightenment. Marxism's failure, if that is what we have witnessed, is a failure of Enlightenment hopes and aspirations. When defenders of the West call on us to celebrate this, what are we supposed to celebrate?

Insofar as this failure indicates the failure of enlightened attempts to comprehend and explain the world, to map knowledge in a comprehensive and useful manner, to project the world as a function of an intellectual's understanding of it, the fall of Marxism and the reality of the injustices, lies, and brutal stupidities perpetrated in its name remain problems for progressive intellectuals everywhere. They call, or seem to call, the possibility of being a progressive intellectual into question. Conservative critics often remark with some derision that Marxism survives only in the humanities departments of Western universities. That is largely true and perhaps right. Marxism finds itself there among other remains of the Enlightenment—along with liberalism and imperialism, which are in little better shape with regard to the figure they have made and continue to make in the world. Our task is to salvage and shore up what is best among these.

The irreducible heterogeneities of the world, the multiplicities of contending cultures and viewpoints, have torn the map of Enlightenment universals. Yet the fragments of the Enlightenment persist, and they remain indispensable. They help us, in our specific communities either in the academy or beyond its walls, locate ourselves and orient our projects. There is no need to mourn. Without pretensions to universality, Enlightenment ideals of justice, equality, and compassion are more useful to progressives than they have ever been. For intellectuals, there is certainly no need to despair. The life that goes on in the university, the pedagogy we conduct amid the ruins, is different from, livelier and more rigorous than, what the various legends of the truth's decline and the intellectual's demise have led us to believe. On the Right and on the Left, critics afflicted by or affecting a melancholy disposition occasioned by a failed modernity tend, in their confusion, to miss this point. For those who get it, the values of the Enlightenment still furnish the patches of brightness by which we choose our way.

NOTES

Introduction: fundamental confusion

1 Some representative works on each of these topics are Jean-François Lyotard, *The Post-modern Condition* (Minneapolis: University of Minnesota Press, 1984), and *Tombeau de l'intellectuel et autres papiers* (Paris: Gallimard, 1984); Russell Jacoby, *The Last Intellectuals* (New York: Basic Books, 1987); Todd Gitlin, *The Twilight of Common Dreams* (New York: Henry Holt, 1995); Arthur Schlesinger, *The Disuniting of America* (New York: Norton, 1992); Andrew Ross, *No Respect: Intellectuals and Popular Culture* (New York: Routledge, 1989); Alvin Gouldner, *The Future of Intellectuals and the Rise of the New Class* (New York: Seabury Press, 1979); Bruce Robbins, *Secular Vocations: Intellectuals, Professionalism, Culture* (London: Verso, 1993); and Michael Bérubé, *Public Access: Literary Theory and American Cultural Politics* (London: Verso, 1994), and *The Employment of English: Theory, Jobs, and the Future of Literary Studies* (New York: New York University Press, 1998).

 Two attitudes toward intellectuals shape most recent commentary. The first celebrates or mourns or attempts to analyze—depending on the critic—the death of the intellectual and the advent of postmodernity frequently defined as a "postintellectual culture." (The phrase is Donald N. Wood's. His title, *Post-intellectualism and the Decline of Democracy: The Failure of Reason and Responsibility in the Twentieth Century* [London: Praeger, 1996], captures the tone of his polemic.) The work of Jean-François Lyotard, Michel Foucault, Zygmunt Bauman and a certain characteristically populist strain in contemporary cultural studies evident in the work of Andrew Ross, Janice Radway, Constance Penley, Paul Bové, and others offer a few familiar examples of this tendency. The second attitude holds to a more triumphalist view of intellectuals and sees in them the hopes for progress in the perfection of modernity and social justice. Jürgen Habermas, Henri-Bernard Levy, Todd Gitlin, and cultural critics such as Bruce Robbins, Cary Nelson, and Michael Bérubé reflect, though sometimes only implicitly, this latter view. I find myself drawn toward each of these positions and sometimes have difficulty telling them apart. If my position in this book stands as a middle ground, it is shaped by compromise formation rather than compromise. This is to say that my position is shaped by, and symptomatic of, irreducible conflicts within and between discourses about intellectuals rather than by a harmonious synthesis of them.

2 Carl Boggs, *Intellectuals and the Crisis of Modernity* (Albany: State University of New York Press, 1993), 3; hereafter cited in text.

3 See Antonio Gramsci, "The Formation of Intellectuals," in *The Modern Prince and Other Writings* (New York: International Publishers, 1957), 118; hereafter cited in text.

4 Bruce Robbins, "Introduction: The Grounding of Intellectuals," in *Intellectuals: Aesthetics, Politics, Academics*, ed. Bruce Robbins (Minneapolis: University of Minnesota Press, 1990), ix–xxvii. He elaborates this argument further in *Secular Vocations: Intellectuals, Professionalism, Culture*.

5 George Konrad and Ivan Szelenyi, *The Intellectuals on the Road to Class Power*, trans. Andrew Arato and Richard E. Allen (New York: Harcourt Brace Jovanovich, 1979). The widespread influence of Konrad and Szelenyi's work reminds us that those who celebrate the intellectual's death have reason and to some extent history on their side. The collapse of the Leninist party states in Eastern Europe is a complex and overdetermined phenomenon, but the lesson most frequently read in the rubble is the failure of both intellectuals and specialists to effectively plan or pragmatically administer the progressive society they sought to create. Because the failures that lead to the collapse were long evident, critical intellectuals who opposed the state—dissident Eastern European intellectuals— have long played a crucial and somewhat complicated part in the self-imaginings of their counterparts in the West. See, for example, my "The Intellectual in Uncivil Society: Michnik, Poland, and Community," *Telos* 88 (summer 1991): 141–54.

6 Konrad and Szelenyi, *The Intellectuals on the Road to Class Power*, 14; hereafter cited in text.

7 Zygmunt Bauman, "Legislators and Interpreters: Culture as the Ideology of Intellectuals," in *Intimations of Postmodernity* (London: Routledge, 1992), 1.

8 Alvin Gouldner, *The Future of Intellectuals and the Rise of the New Class* (New York: Seabury Press, 1979), 83; hereafter cited in text.

9 Lawrence Goodwyn, to take one example, has offered intriguing rehabilitations of populism in a series of historical analyses. See *Democratic Province: The Populist Movement in America* (New York: Oxford University Press, 1976), *The Populist Movement: A Short History of the Agrarian Revolt* (New York: Oxford University Press, 1978), and *Breaking the Barrier: The Rise of Solidarity in Poland* (New York: Oxford University Press, 1991).

10 Stuart Hall, for example, has said of the Birmingham Centre and of British cultural studies generally: "I tried on many occasions, and other people in British Cultural Studies and at the Centre especially have tried, to describe what it is we thought we were doing with the kind of intellectual work we set in place in the Centre. I have to confess that, though I've read many, more elaborated and sophisticated, accounts, Gramsci's account still seems to me to come closest to expressing, what it is I think we were trying to do. Admittedly, there's a problem about his phrase 'the production of organic intellectuals.' But there is no doubt in my mind that we were trying to find an institutional practice in cultural studies that might produce an organic intellectual" ("Cultural Studies and Its Theoretical Legacies," in *Cultural Studies*, ed. Lawrence Grossberg, Cary Nelson, and Paula Treichler [New York: Routledge, 1992], 281; hereafter cited in text). The problem with the concept of organic intellectuals in which I am particularly interested here has more to do with populist interpretations of the concept than with Gramsci's complex ruminations on the topic. For a full account of cultural studies as an articulation of Gramscianism, see David Harris, *From Class Struggle to the Politics of Pleasure: The Effects of Gramscianism on Cultural Studies* (New York: Routledge, 1992).

11 Adolph L. Reed Jr., *W. E. B. Du Bois and American Political Thought: Fabianism and the Color Line* (New York: Oxford, 1997), 17–18; hereafter cited in text.

12 See James Gilbert, *Designing the Industrial State: The Intellectual Pursuit of Collectivism in America, 1880–1940* (Chicago: University of Chicago Press, 1972). Christopher Lasch offers a similar account of the transformation of American reform movements and their antidemocratic tendencies around the turn of the century. Along with a willingness to use government to control the populace, Lasch identifies "a tendency to see cultural issues as

inseparable from political ones; so that 'education,' conceived very broadly, came to be seen not merely as a means of raising up an enlightened electorate but as an instrument of social change in its own right. Conversely, the new radicals understood the end of social and political reform to be the improvement of the quality of American culture as a whole, rather than simply a way of equalizing the opportunities for economic self-advancement. It is precisely this confusion of politics and culture, so essential to the new radicalism, that seems to me to betray its origins in the rise of the intellectual class; for such a program, with its suggestion that men of learning occupy or ought to occupy the strategic loci of social control, has an obvious appeal to intellectuals" (The New Radicalism in America, 1889–1963 [New York: Norton, 1965], xiv).

13 Lyotard notes this absence of a historical agent or critical subject to be one distinguishing mark of the postmodern condition (The Post-modern Condition, 13).

14 Antonio Gramsci, "Two Editorials from Ordine Nuovo," in The Modern Prince and Other Writings, 21.

15 Similarly, in "The Southern Question" Gramsci imagines the forging of links between the disparate and conflicted regions of the north and south to require the intervention, of a sort only problematically organic, of intellectuals who rise above the regional identities of either grouping. See The Modern Prince, esp. 50–51.

16 On the history of Jacobinism and its complex centrality to conceptions of intellectual work, especially on the Left, see Boggs, Intellectuals and the Crisis of Modernity, esp. 1–96.

17 Edward Said, Representations of the Intellectual (New York: Pantheon Books, 1994), 13; hereafter cited in text.

18 Allan Bloom, The Closing of the American Mind: How Higher Education Has Failed Democracy and Impoverished the Souls of Today's Students (New York: Simon and Schuster, 1987); Dinesh D'Souza, Illiberal Education: The Politics of Race and Sex on Campus (New York: Free Press, 1991); Samuel P. Huntington, The Clash of Civilizations and the Remaking of World Order (New York: Simon and Schuster, 1996); Todd Gitlin, The Twilight of Common Dreams; Christopher Norris, Uncritical Theory: Postmodernism, Intellectuals, and the Gulf War (Amherst: University of Massachusetts Press, 1992); Terry Eagleton, Ideology: an Introduction (New York: Verso, 1991). See also Jürgen Habermas, The Philosophical Discourse of Modernity: Twelve Lectures (Cambridge, Mass.: Polity Press, 1987).

19 I would add that this is especially true when intellectuals most explicitly attempt to deny it, as we shall see in our consideration of populism and fandom in cultural studies in chapter 5.

20 Robbins, Secular Vocations, 23.

21 As Robbins puts it, "If there is not ultimate foundation or grounding, the activity of seeking after and contending over groundings and foundations does not therefore ground to a halt" (25). In fact, it remains the central turning point of many of the conflicts we join.

22 Max Horkheimer and Theodore Adorno, Dialectic of Enlightenment, trans. John Cumming (New York: Continuum, 1989).

23 This is because the historical and cultural conditions that enabled the formation of such vanguards have changed. See Boggs, Intellectuals and the Crisis of Modernity; Zygmunt Bauman, Legislators and Interpreters: On Modernity, Post-modernity, and the Intellectuals (Oxford: Basil Blackwood, 1987); and Lyotard, The Post-modern Condition and Le Tombeau de l'intellectual.

24 Although Boggs and Gouldner deny the Jacobinism of scientists and engineers, a notable Jacobin tendency has lately appeared among the technocrats, one based on a claim to unimpeded access to universal truth of interest to all peoples, a truth that should furnish the basis for all politics. See, for example, Paul R. Gross and Norman Levitt, The Higher

Superstition: The Academic Left and Its Quarrel with Science (Baltimore, Md.: Johns Hopkins University Press, 1994); and Alan Sokal, "A Physicist Experiments with Cultural Studies," *Lingua Franca* (May–June 1996): 62–64. I will consider this phenomenon more closely the final two chapters.

25 See, for example, Lyotard, *The Post-modern Condition* and *Le Tombeau de l'intellectual*. See also Bauman, *Legislators and Interpreters*.

26 Bernard Yack, *The Fetishism of Modernities* (Notre Dame, Ind.: University of Notre Dame Press, 1997), 5; hereafter cited in text. Yack quotes Lyotard, *The Post-modern Condition* (82), and Gianni Vattimo, *The Transparent Society* (Baltimore, Md.: Johns Hopkins University Press, 1992), 8.

27 A claim he distinguishes carefully from Habermas's less persuasive claim that modernity is an unfinished project we should seek to complete, since for Yack modernity is not a project.

28 Ross, *No Respect: Intellectuals and Popular Culture*, 211.

29 Bill Readings, *The University in Ruins* (Cambridge: Harvard University Press, 1996), 102. Fredric Jameson, of course, expresses a similar sense of cultural studies in "On 'Cultural Studies,'" *Social Text* 11, no. 1 (spring 1993): 17–52, and *Postmodernism, or The Cultural Logic of Late Capitalism* (Durham, N.C.: Duke University Press, 1991).

30 Cary Nelson, *Manifesto of a Tenured Radical* (New York: New York University Press, 1997), 65–66; hereafter cited in text.

1 Publicity: black intellectuals as inorganic representatives

1 Stuart Hall, "Cultural Studies and Its Theoretical Legacies," in *Cultural Studies*, ed. Lawrence Grossberg, Cary Nelson, and Paula Treichler (New York: Routledge, 1992), 281; Fredric Jameson, "On 'Cultural Studies,'" *Social Text* 11, no. 1 (spring 1993): 17–52. See also Cary Nelson, who offers a critique of cultural studies' identification with populism in "Always Already Cultural Studies," in *Manifesto of a Tenured Radical* (New York: New York University Press, 1997), 52–74. See also David Harris, *From Class Struggle to the Politics of Pleasure: The Effects of Gramscianism on Cultural Studies* (New York: Routledge, 1992).

2 Robert S. Boynton, "The New Intellectuals: African American Intellectuals," *Atlantic Monthly*, March 1995, 60.

3 Michael Hanchard, "Intellectual Pursuit: By Ignoring Our Social and Political History, We Have Impoverished Debate about 'Black Public Intellectuals,'" *Nation*, 19 February 1996, 2.

4 Russell Jacoby, *The Last Intellectuals: American Culture in the Age of Academe* (New York: Basic Books, 1987).

5 Adolph L. Reed Jr., "What Are the Drums Saying, Booker? The Current Crisis of the Black Intellectual," *Village Voice*, 11 April 1995, 31; hereafter cited in text as Reed, "Drums."

6 Adolph L. Reed Jr., *W. E. B. Du Bois and American Political Thought: Fabianism and the Color Line* (New York: Oxford, 1997), 4–5; hereafter cited in text as Reed, *Du Bois*.

7 Gerald Early, "Black like Them," *New York Times Book Review*, 21 April 1996, 7; hereafter cited in text.

8 Arthur M. Schlesinger, *The Disuniting of America: Reflections on a Multicultural Society* (New York: Norton, 1992), 118; hereafter cited in text. For a critique of Schlesinger's position that associates it with the nativist logic of American racists, see Stanley Fish, "Bad Company," in *There's No Such Thing as Free Speech, and It's a Good Thing Too* (New York: Oxford University Press, 1994), 80–88. Schlesinger, according to Fish, has forgotten his own immigrant and Jewish origins. Patricia Williams notes that such forgetting seems typical

of "the amalgamated 'white' middle class of today [which seems to have] . . . lost its sense of derivation from the poor, the tired, the hungry, huddled masses who so threatened the ruling classes of a century ago" (*The Rooster's Egg: On the Persistence of Prejudice* [Cambridge: Harvard University Press, 1995], 67–68; hereafter cited in text).

9   Ernest Renan, "What Is a Nation?" in *Nation and Narration*, ed. Homi K. Bhabha (New York: Routledge, 1990), 11; hereafter cited in text.

10 Frank Shuffelton, introduction to *A Mixed Race: Ethnicity in Early America* (New York: Oxford University Press, 1993), 5. See also *Diversity and Unity in Early North America*, ed. Philip D. Morgan (New York: Routledge, 1993).

11 *The Frederick Douglass Papers: Series One*, vol. 4, ed. John W. Blassingame and John R. McKivigan (New Haven, Conn.: Yale University Press, 1991), 256.

12 For Douglass's designation as "representative colored man" in the United States see Peter F. Walker, *Moral Choices: Memory, Desire, and Imagination in Nineteenth-Century American Abolition* (Baton Rouge: Louisiana State University Press, 1978), 210. Douglass's views and experience of Egyptians and of Africans as well as African Americans were decidedly shaped by the dominant Eurocentric prejudices of his time. See Waldo F. Martin, *The Mind of Frederick Douglass* (Chapel Hill: University of North Carolina Press, 1984), esp. 207–13. As Martin puts it, in a chapter entitled "A Composite National Identity," "Douglass's assimilationism embodied this pivotal conflict" between "Afro-American race pride" and "an Anglo-American vision" (213). Bell hooks has written that "Douglass and other black male activists allied themselves with white male patriarchs on the basis of shared sexism" (*Ain't I a Woman: Black Women and Feminism* [Boston: South End Press, 1981], 90).

13 Henry Louis Gates Jr., *Thirteen Ways of Looking at a Black Man* (New York: Random House, 1997), 201; hereafter cited in text as Gates, *Thirteen Ways*.

14 *Narrative of the Life of Frederick Douglass, an American Slave* (New York: Signet, 1968), xv.

15 Toni Morrison, *Playing in the Dark: Whiteness and the Literary Imagination* (Cambridge: Harvard University Press, 1992), 45; hereafter cited in text.

16 Patricia Williams, *The Alchemy of Race and Rights: Diary of a Law Professor* (Cambridge: Harvard University Press, 1991), 3; hereafter cited in text as Williams, *Alchemy*.

17 This may be most evident in the work of bell hooks, who has most persistently insisted that she speaks for—even as she wants to create—a revitalized African American community that will in turn revitalize American community as a whole. *Killing Rage: Ending Racism* (New York: Henry Holt, 1995), for example, begins with an account of hooks's fury at a racist and sexist incident suffered on a plane flight and ends with a utopian vision of a "beloved community": "In a *beloved community* solidarity and trust are grounded in profound commitment to a shared vision. Those of us who are always anti-racist long for a world in which everyone can form a *beloved community* where borders can be crossed and cultural hybridity celebrated. Anyone can begin to make such a community by truly seeking to live in an anti-racist world. If that longing guides our vision and our actions, the new culture will be born and anti-racist communities of resistance will emerge everywhere. That is where we must go from here" (272). Ironically, and significantly, hooks has been noted and taken to task for her polemics against other intellectuals and her tendency to ignore the contributions of other black feminists. See, for example, Michele Wallace's review of *Killing Rage*, "Bell Hooks, Line, and Sinker: Black Feminist or Poststructuralist Oprah?" in *The Voice Literary Supplement*, November 1995, where she remarks, "What hooks is doing here is what I call eating the other. Yes people of color can eat the other too" (21). I mention this because the utopian vision of community too often obscures the fact that communities are places where crucial conflicts happen. Attempts to

represent community, while they often seem to offer the hope of ending conflict, usually become the focus of it.

18　Cornel West, "Black Strivings in a Twilight Civilization," in *The Future of the Race*, by Henry Louis Gates Jr. and Cornel West (New York: Knopf, 1996), 71. References to *The Future of the Race* hereafter cited in text.

19　W. E. B. DuBois, "The Talented Tenth," in Gates and West, *The Future of the Race*, 133.

20　Michele Wallace offers a similar critique of bell hooks in "Bell Hooks, Line, and Sinker," 19–24.

21　Nell Irvin Painter, "*The Future of the Race*," *Nation*, 6 May 1996, 38.

22　See bell hooks, *Ain't I a Woman: Black Women and Feminism*; see also Michele Wallace, *Black Macho and the Myth of the Super Woman* (New York: Dial Press, 1978).

23　bell hooks and Cornel West, *Breaking Bread: Insurgent Black Intellectual Life* (Boston: South End Press, 1991), 21; hereafter cited in text.

24　Robin D. G. Kelley, *Yo' Mama's DisFUNKtional! Fighting the Cultural Wars in Urban America* (Boston: Beacon Press, 1997), 2; hereafter cited in text. Kelley is quoting here from Dinesh D'Souza, *The End of Racism: Principles for a Multiracial Society* (New York: Free Press, 1995), 24.

25　Andrew Ross, *No Respect: Intellectuals and Popular Culture* (New York: Routledge, 1989), 226.

Chapter 2　Pedagogy: enlightened instruction as oppressive discipline

1　See, for example, Roger Kimball, *Tenured Radicals: How Politics Has Corrupted Our Higher Education* (New York: Harper, 1990); Dinesh D'Souza, *Illiberal Education: The Politics of Race and Sex on Campus* (New York: Free Press, 1991); Lynne V. Cheney, *Telling the Truth: A Report of the State of the Humanities in Higher Education* (Washington, D.C.: National Endowment for the Humanities, 1992); Richard Bernstein, *Dictatorship of Virtue: Multiculturalism and the Battle for America's Future* (New York: Knopf, 1994).

2　The inaccuracies, omissions, and bias that structure D'Souza's and Kimball's accounts have by now been widely documented. See, for example, John K. Wilson, *The Myth of Political Correctness: The Conservative Attack on Higher Education* (Durham, N.C.: Duke University Press, 1995). See also the collection *Beyond PC: Toward a Politics of Understanding*, ed. Patricia Aufderheide (St. Paul, Minn.: Graywolf Press, 1992). Todd Gitlin, himself a critic of the contemporary academy, exposes many of the exaggerations and distortions in right-wing polemics; see *The Twilight of Common Dreams: Why America Is Wracked by Culture Wars* (New York: Henry Holt, 1995), 166–99; hereafter cited in text. See also Michael Bérubé, *Public Access: Literary Theory and American Cultural Politics* (London: Verso, 1994), esp. 13–27. More theoretical responses are collected in *The Politics of Liberal Education*, ed. Darryl J. Glen and Barbara Herrnstein Smith (Durham, N.C.: Duke University Press, 1992). See also Stanley Fish, *There's No Such Thing as Free Speech, and It's a Good Thing Too* (New York: Oxford University Press, 1994); hereafter cited in text as Fish, *Free Speech*. An attempt to stage exchanges between Left academics and their conservative critics is recorded in *Higher Education under Fire: Politics, Economics, and the Crisis of the Humanities*, ed. Michael Bérubé and Cary Nelson (New York: Routledge, 1995).

3　Andrew Ross, *No Respect: Intellectuals and Popular Culture* (New York: Routledge, 1989), 210–11.

4　Statistics indicate that whatever capital a four-year degree once had on the labor market is, like the value of most labor capital in our economy, steadily declining. In 1970 the median annual income for all male workers aged twenty-five to thirty-four with a bachelor's degree was $41,045 in 1995 constant dollars. In 1994 it was $32,116. Women lost slightly less ground over this time period but still lagged far behind their male counterparts in earning power. In 1970 the median income for all women with bachelor's degrees was 27,608; in 1994 it was 25,655. Black and Hispanic college graduates of both sexes did even worse. Only white women did slightly better. For all categories including white women, the erosion in earning power has been especially rapid since 1989. Meanwhile, the cost of getting this education keeps rising at a pace that outstrips inflation year after year; and year after year the rising cost of education gets more and more attention from the press. In this environment, students more often seek those departments and degrees that seem to promise more readily convertible forms of capital. From 1971 to 1993, the number of bachelor's degrees granted decreased in the humanities and social sciences by 15 percent and in the natural sciences by 30 percent. What, after all, do you do with a physics major? Meanwhile the number of degrees awarded in business management increased by more than half (U.S. Department of Education, National Center for Education Statistics, *The Condition of Education, 1996*, NCES 96-304, ed. Thomas M. Smith [Washington, D.C.: U.S. Government Printing Office, 1996], 260, 266–67). There is an increased disparity between those who earn a bachelor's degree and those who don't. In most categories, those with bachelor's degrees earn around 50 percent more, and females with bachelor's degrees earn close to twice what their less credentialed counterparts make. These trends, which reflect the declining living standards and increasingly stressed and anxious position of the American middle classes, are the material dimension of the crisis in the humanities. The humanities in particular and the liberal arts in general don't pay, or don't pay enough, or so most Americans believe. For most people, the sizable investment represented by an undergraduate degree is too important to risk on culture.

In fact, as John Guillory has argued, the important cultural capital the humanities once purveyed—a certain proficiency in the use of standard English, a certain polish of style and taste—is one that the modern technological managers no longer believe they need. John Guillory, *Cultural Capital: The Problem of Literary Canon Formation* (Chicago: University of Chicago Press, 1993), 45–46, see also 79–82. Guillory thus argues against Bourdieu's influential analysis of taste as a means of maintaining distinction and structuring social hierarchies (Guillory, 332–40).

5 The phrase, of course, is Arthur Schlesinger's. See *The Disuniting of America: Reflections on a Multicultural Society* (New York: Norton, 1992).

6 Paradoxically these local loyalties reemerge at a moment when capital is becoming more and more globalized, more and more unified, and more and more beyond effective local or even national control. See, for example, Robert Reich, *The Work of Nations: Preparing Ourselves for 21st-Century Capitalism* (New York: Random House, 1992), and Paul Smith, *Millennial Dreams: Contemporary Culture and Capital in the North* (London: Verso, 1997).

7 Patricia Williams, *The Rooster's Egg: On the Persistence of Prejudice* (Cambridge: Harvard University Press, 1995), 112. For a reading of the complex relations one might posit between talk shows and public opinion, see Paolo Carpignano, Robin Anderson, Stanley Aronowitz, and William Frazier, "Chatter in the Age of Electronic Reproduction: Talk Television and the 'Public Mind,'" in *The Phantom Public Sphere*, ed. Bruce Robbins (Minneapolis: University of Minnesota Press, 1993), 93–120.

8 See Zygmunt Bauman, *Legislators and Interpreters: On Modernity, Postmodernity, and the Intellectuals* (Oxford: Basil Blackwood, 1987), and Jean-François Lyotard, *Le tombeau des intellectuals et autres papiers* (Paris: Gallimard, 1984).

9 Rey Chow, *Writing Diaspora: Tactics of Intervention in Contemporary Cultural Studies* (Bloomington: Indiana University Press, 1993), 101.

10 Paul Lauter, " 'Political Correctness' and the Attack on American Colleges," in Bérubé and Nelson, *Higher Education under Fire*, 84–85.

11 Jeffrey Herf, transcribed interview in "Money, Merit, and Democracy at the University: An Exchange," in Bérubé and Nelson, *Higher Education under Fire*, 171.

12 Bérubé, *Public Access*, 21; hereafter cited in text.

13 Bérubé is, I believe, completely right to argue that "what truly endangers the future of higher education, then, are the PC wars in tandem with the growing mad-as-hell taxpayer outrage at the professional autonomy of faculty, an outrage most effectively expressed as the demand that universities curtail professorial research and require more undergraduate instruction from their employees," and to point out that this critique "vastly overestimates the size of its target" (*Public Access*, 21).

14 Rey Chow, *Writing Diaspora*, 14. Gayatri Spivak makes a similar point in her controversial article "Can the Subaltern Speak?" when she writes, "The banality of leftist intellectuals' lists of self-knowing, politically canny subalterns stands revealed; representing them, the intellectuals represent themselves as transparent," in *Marxism and the Interpretation of Culture*, ed. Cary Nelson and Lawrence Grossberg (Houndmills: Macmillan, 1988), 275. As Bruce Robbins comments, intellectuals pretending to refuse the institutional privileges of power are also attempting to evade their institutional and societal responsibilities. They primarily avoid "self-knowledge." See *Secular Vocations: Intellectuals, Professionalism, Culture* (London: Verso, 1993), 205. Similarly and with greater philosophical density, Wendy Brown has explored and criticized the centrality of concepts of injury to contemporary identity politics. See *States of Injury: Power and Freedom in Late Modernity* (Princeton, N.J.: Princeton University Press, 1995).

15 Paulo Freire, *Pedagogy of Hope: Reliving Pedagogy of the Oppressed*, with notes by Ana Maria Araiyo Freire, trans. Robert R. Barr (New York: Continuum, 1994), 80; hereafter cited in text.

16 Paul V. Taylor, *The Texts of Paulo Freire* (Bristol, Pa.: Open University Press, 1993), 53–54; hereafter cited in text.

17 John L. Elias, *Paulo Freire: Pedagogue of Liberalism* (Malabar, Fla.: Krieger Publishing, 1994), 104; hereafter cited in text.

18 Henry Giroux and Paulo Freire, introduction to *Critical Pedagogy and Cultural Power*, by David Livingston et al. (New York: Bergin and Garvey, 1987), xi.

19 Henry Giroux, *Theory and Resistance in Education* (South Hadley, Mass.: Bergin and Garvey, 1983), 155; hereafter cited in text.

20 Gerald Graff and Gregory Jay, "A Critique of Critical Pedagogy," in Bérubé and Nelson, *Higher Education under Fire*, 206–7; hereafter cited in text.

21 Michael Warner, "No Special Rights," in Bérubé and Nelson, *Higher Education under Fire*, 285; hereafter cited in text.

22 Andrew Ross, *No Respect*, 229; hereafter cited in text. Bruce Robbins has offered a thorough and persuasive critique of these romantic narratives in *Secular Vocations*.

23 Allan Bloom, *The Closing of the American Mind: How Higher Education Has Failed Democracy and Impoverished the Souls of Today's Students* (New York: Simon and Schuster, 1987), 62; hereafter cited in text.

24 Bérubé continues to remember and to forget the troublesome absence of necessary links between culture and politics in his later book *The Employment of English: Theory, Jobs, and the Future of Literary Studies* (New York: New York University Press, 1998), where on the one hand he offers such admissions as "And when critics on the cultural Left point out that none of this [training in theory] is necessarily inconsistent with the project of giving students mere ideological obfuscation or training them in quietism, my impulse is to

agree—and then to suggest in return that if one desires guarantees that one's teaching and writing can never be put in the service of ideological obfuscation or quietism,
one would be better off not wasting time with the humanities in the first place" (108);
and even more pointedly, "The simple ugly fact is that if 'the aesthetic' is truly (relatively) autonomous from instrumental uses of language, and if the university is truly
(relatively) autonomous from state power, then we cannot predict whether the knowledges produced in these precincts will be put to laudatory or regrettable ends" (162).
Yet he can go on to call for "a practice of cultural studies that articulates the theoretical
and critical work of the so-called public intellectual to the movements of public policy"
(224). His early admissions make such an articulation seem highly unlikely to have much
persuasive force if they are to be grounded only in the professional work of cultural
critics.

25   Frank Lentricchia, *Criticism and Social Change* (Chicago: University of Chicago Press, 1983),
     5. Lentricchia, whom Bérubé frequently seems to echo, also looks for the links between
     culture and the work of cultural intellectuals and politics: "My presiding contention is
     that our potentially most powerful political work as university humanists must be carried
     out in what we do, what we are trained for. We might do it very well because we have the
     technical knowledge of the insider. We have at our disposal an intimate understanding of
     the expressive mechanisms of culture. We know how culture works; we know, or should
     know, that culture does *do* work. I would go so far as to say that those of us in the univer-
     sity who conceive of our political work mainly in those other ways I have listed, and not
     as activity intrinsic, specific to our intellectuality (our work as medieval historians, for
     example) are being crushed by feelings of guilt and occupational alienation" (7). While
     this is a useful corrective to the current romanticization of the "public intellectual," it
     begs the difficult and problematic question of what the work culture does actually is, and
     also how culture does it.

Chapter 3   Community: pragmatism as a profession of anxiety

1   Dinesh D'Souza, *Illiberal Education: The Politics of Race and Sex on Campus* (New York: Free
     Press, 1991); Todd Gitlin, *The Twilight of Common Dreams: Why America Is Wracked by Culture
     Wars* (New York: Henry Holt, 1995). A simple solution to the problem of contested values
     is just what D'Souza and Gitlin want. Each manifests a persistent longing for transcen-
     dent truths that would constitute a position above the fray from which these conflicts
     might be adjudicated. Each blames the academy for having abandoned the search for,
     and the belief in, these truths. D'Souza, for example, offers the following: "This new
     breed of scholars in the humanities tends to denigrate the idea that a text has any inher-
     ent meaning; on the contrary, it asserts that all interpretations are valid. Anything goes.
     'There is no knowledge, no standard, no choice that is objective,' says Barbara Herrn-
     stein Smith, a former president of the Modern Language Association who now teaches
     English at Duke. 'Even Homer is a product of a specific culture, and it is possible to
     imagine cultures in which Homer would not be very interesting' " (157). For his part,
     Gitlin cites a "very intelligent young woman," a Berkeley graduate student circulating a
     protest leaflet, who tells him that "there is no 'truth,' . . . there are only truth effects."
     He explains what she meant: "She meant that propositions are no more than rhetori-
     cal, 'discourse all the way down,' judged 'true' only arbitrarily. But why should there
     be universities, other than to convey status and take unemployed youth off the streets,
     if all they do is hurl around transient and arbitrary statements?" (157). For my part, I
     would describe what D'Souza, Gitlin, and the graduate student all are doing as hurling

around transient and arbitrary statements intended to gain a rhetorical advantage. I am not particularly shocked, nor am I dismayed, that such activities go on within American universities or in the community at large. They are part of our intellectual and deliberative processes. But some statements are altogether too arbitrary. Logic, after all, has always been a part of rhetoric.

2 Gerald Graff sketches the history of canon and curricular revision in literary studies in *Professing Literature: An Institutional History* (Chicago: University of Chicago Press, 1987); see also Robert Scholes, *The Rise and Fall of English: Reconstructing English as a Discipline* (New Haven, Conn.: Yale University Press, 1998).

3 Bill Readings, *The University in Ruins* (Cambridge: Harvard University Press, 1996), 117–18; see also 44–53 and 63–118. Hereafter cited in text.

4 Zygmunt Bauman, *Legislators and Interpreters: On Modernity, Post-modernity, and Intellectuals* (Oxford: Basil Blackwood, 1987), 146; hereafter cited in text as Bauman, *Legislators*.

5 Samuel Weber, for example, notes that "whenever the codes and conditions that have assured the consensus necessary for communication begin to change radically or to break down, attention is inevitably drawn to the question of institutions." As he goes on to specify, the issue of communities in much contemporary critical discourse is an aspect of the question of institutions. See *Institution and Interpretation* (Minneapolis: University of Minnesota Press, 1987), 33.

6 D'Souza quotes Gates as follows: "Ours was the generation that took over buildings in the late sixties and demanded the creation of black- and women's studies programs, and now, like the return of the repressed, we have come back to challenge the traditional curriculum" (*Illiberal Education*, 56).

7 See Stanley Fish, *Surprised by Sin: The Reader in "Paradise Lost"* (New York: St. Martin's Press, 1967), and *Self-Consuming Artifacts* (Berkeley: University of California Press, 1972).

8 Stanley Fish, "Commentary: The Young and the Restless," in *The New Historicism*, ed. H. Aram Veeser (New York: Routledge, 1989), 315. This essay has been reprinted in *There's No Such Thing as Free Speech* (New York: Oxford University Press, 1994), 256; hereafter cited in the text as *Free Speech*. The title of Fish's essay, "The Young and the Restless," indicates that he finds these anxieties to be overly self-dramatizing. I find that Fish's resistance to overdramatization exists uncomfortably with his characterization of persuasion, his master term, as a dramatic act.

9 Stanley Fish, *Doing What Comes Naturally* (Durham, N.C.: Duke University Press, 1989); hereafter cited in text.

10 See, for example, the collection *Disciplinarity and Dissent in Cultural Studies*, ed. Cary Nelson and Dilip Parameshwar Gaonkar (New York: Routledge, 1996).

11 Habermas, operating at a high level of abstraction flavored by his own turn to linguistics and communicative action, criticizes poststructuralism generally and Jacques Derrida in particular in terms that remind us of Stanley Fish's pragmatic defense of disciplinary boundaries. "If, following Derrida's recommendation, philosophical thinking were to be relieved of the duty of solving problems and shifted over to the function of literary criticism, it would be robbed not merely of its seriousness, but of its productivity. Conversely, the literary-critical power of judgment loses its potency when, as is happening among Derrida's disciples in literature departments, it gets displaced from appropriating aesthetic experiential contents into the critique of metaphysics. The false assimilation of one enterprise to the other robs both of their substance. . . . Whoever transposes the radical critique of reason into the domain of rhetoric in order to blunt the paradox of self-referentiality, also dulls the sword of the critique of reason itself. The false pretense of eliminating the genre distinction between philosophy and literature cannot

lead us out of this aporia." Jürgen Habermas, *The Philosophical Discourse of Modernity: Twelve Lectures*, trans. Frederick G. Lawrence (Cambridge: MIT Press, 1990), 210. Philosophy is the realm of problem solving, literature is the realm of aesthetic experience; rhetoric and self-referential critical reason must not be confused; the genre distinction between literature and philosophy must be maintained: Fish would agree with many of these formulations except, notably, Habermas's crucial attempt to isolate reason from rhetoric and to render its transcendence the critical lever of a still working modernity.

12 Fish retraces and discusses his development of this stabilizing notion of interpretive communities in *Is There a Text in This Class?* (Cambridge: Harvard University Press, 1980), where he writes, "meanings are the property neither of fixed and stable texts nor of free and independent readers but of interpretive communities that are responsible both for the shape of a reader's activities and for the texts those activities produce" (322). This ability of communities to recuperate propriety and to regulate meaning, if only momentarily, begins to alter in *Doing What Comes Naturally.*

13 At other times, as in his essay "Rhetoric," Fish presents the debate between Plato and the Sophists as the endless battle between philosophy and rhetoric that Western thought repeatedly wages (471–502). I am not interested in explicating the theory of pragmatism as a metaphysics. A. O. Lovejoy did that quite brilliantly in his essay "The Thirteen Pragmatisms," which deals with the incoherences of pragmatism, especially as espoused by William James. See *The Thirteen Pragmatisms and Other Essays* (Baltimore: Johns Hopkins University Press, 1963); hereafter cited in text. I have no intention of writing an essay that might be called thirteen ways of looking at a Fish. Fish himself does too good a job at pointing out the necessary and temporary assumptions underlying any beliefs to be himself an interesting subject for such an analysis. See, for example, *Doing What Comes Naturally*, 29–30.

14 Fish will not take "at face value the boundaries that separate disciplines and render their respective activities discrete from one another." "In fact," he writes, "neither disciplines nor the activities they enable are discrete; they exist in networks of affiliation and reciprocity that can sometimes be glimpsed (as they are here) in footnotes that reveal how a position taken in one corner of the institutional world is authorized by and authorizes in its turn positions of a similar kind taken elsewhere. Given the structural interdependence between disciplines, the effects of a piece of writing will always extend to contexts apparently far removed from the ones explicitly addressed" (*Doing What Comes Naturally*, 310–11). Yet if this is true—and it seems to be empirically so—then how can one erect the carefully exclusionary lines between literary criticism and philosophy, interpretations and accounts of interpretation, intended contexts and their extensions, that Fish argues for so energetically while performing other sections of *Doing What Comes Naturally?*

15 Quoted in Fish, *There's No Such Thing as Free Speech*, 194.

16 Samuel Weber notes that in *Is There a Text in This Class?* Fish's argument is more a symptom of, than a cure for, anxiety (*Institution and Interpretation*, 35).

17 C. S. Peirce, *The Philosophical Writings of Peirce*, ed. Justus Buchler (New York: Dover, 1955), 247–48. Frank Lentricchia sees a similar contentiousness at the heart of William James's pragmatism: "James' vision of pragmatism is irreducibly a vision of heterogeneity and contentiousness—a vision strong for criticism, self-scrutiny, and self-revision that never claims knowledge of a single human narrative because it refuses belief in a single human narrative and refuses the often repressive conduct resulting from such belief." See Lentricchia, "The Return of William James," in *Ariel and the Police: Michel Foucault, William James, Wallace Stevens* (Madison: University of Wisconsin Press, 1988), 109.

18 Lentricchia's point that the drive to theory is inescapably a part of thought—a point he

ventures on the authority of William James—is a nice one (see "The Return of William James," esp. 123–33).

19 Bruce Robbins has argued that the relation of any profession to the world around it is always incorporated into the structure of the profession itself and that Fish tends to slide into a spatialized formalization of the literary profession he discusses. *Secular Vocations: Intellectuals, Professionalism, Culture* (London: Verso, 1993), 103–5.

20 On this aspect of the profession and Fish's reflections on it see Samuel Weber, "The Debt of Criticism: Notes on Stanley Fish's *Is There a Text in This Class?*" and on institutions of interpretation in the humanities, see "Ambivalence: The Humanities and the Study of Literature," both in *Institution and Interpretation*.

21 On the redefinition of the nation-state in the global economy, see Robert Reich, *The Work of Nations: Preparing Ourselves for 21st Century Capitalism* (New York: Vintage, 1991); for an interpretation of shifts in nationalist sentiments due to changes in postcolonial demographics, see Tom Nairn, *The Breakup of Britain and New Nationalism* (New York: New Left Books, 1977). On the relationship between the growth of nationalism and the development of capitalism, see Fernand Braudel, *Civilization and Capitalism, 15th–18th Centuries* (New York: Harper and Row, 1984); Eric Hobsbawm, *The Age of Empire, 1875–1914* (New York: Pantheon, 1987); J. H. Hayes, *The Historical Evolution of Modern Nationalism* (New York: Macmillan, 1948); Boyd C. Shafer, *Nationalism: Myth and Reality* (New York: Harcourt, Brace and World, 1955). Whether the era of nationalism as an effective means of economic organization has come to an end is, of course, intensely debated. See Paul Smith, *Millennial Dreams: Contemporary Culture and Capital in the North* (London: Verso, 1997); James Fallows, *More like Us: Putting America's Native Strengths and Traditional Values to Work to Overcome the Asian Challenge* (Boston: Houghton Mifflin, 1989); Michael L. Dertouzos, Richard K. Lester, and Robert M. Solow, *Made in America: Regaining the Productive Edge*, the report of the MIT Commission on Industrial Productivity (Cambridge: MIT Press, 1989); and Paul Krugman, *The Age of Diminished Expectations: U.S. Economic Policy in the 1990's* (Cambridge: MIT Press, 1990). Popular consciousness and anxieties concerning these issues registered in the popularity of Michael Crichton's best-selling *Rising Sun* (New York: Knopf, 1992), a novel that adapted the mechanics of the Cold War thriller—with all of its anxious speculation on identity and identification—to tell the story of market competition between the United States and its new/old archrival, Japan.

22 Richard Rorty, *Contingency, Irony, Solidarity* (Cambridge: Cambridge University Press, 1989), xv; hereafter cited in text as Rorty, *Contingency*.

23 Richard Rorty, *Achieving Our Country: Leftist Thought in Twentieth-Century America* (Cambridge: Harvard University Press, 1998), 148 n. 8.

24 On a similar topic, see my "Making a Stand: Standpoint Epistemologies, Political Positions, Proposition 187," *Telos* 108 (summer 1996): 93–104.

25 This, of course, has been one of the central thematics of speculation on the postmodern. On the relationship of commodity circulation to social reproduction, see, for example, Michel Foucault, "Truth and Power," in *Power/Knowledge: Selected Interviews and Other Writings, 1972–77* (New York: Pantheon, 1980), 126–33; see also Zygmunt Bauman, *Legislators and Interpreters*.

Chapter 4 Culture: western traditions and intellectual treason

1 Fredric Jameson, "On 'Cultural Studies,'" *Social Text* 11, no. 1 (spring 1993): 17–52; hereafter cited in text. The book reviewed was *Cultural Studies*, ed. Lawrence Grossberg, Cary Nelson, and Paula Treichler (New York: Routledge, 1992).

2 Ironically, Fredric Jameson's "On 'Cultural Studies' " and Samuel P. Huntington's "The Coming Clash of Civilizations, or The West against the Rest" both appeared during the summer of 1993. This is one index of how widespread the current academic and political focus on culture is. Samuel P. Huntington, "The Coming Clash of Civilizations, or The West against the Rest," *New York Times*, 6 June 1993; hereafter cited in text as "Coming Clash." Huntington's essay then became the basis for a lead article, "The Clash of Civilizations?" in *Foreign Affairs* 72, no. 3 (summer 1993): 22–49, hereafter cited in text as "Clash of Civilizations"; and of his book, *The Clash of Civilizations and the Remaking of World Order* (New York: Simon and Schuster, 1996), hereafter cited in text as *Clash of Civilizations*. I will refer to all three versions of Huntington's argument in this chapter.

3 In one reviewer's words, this article provoked "the most intense response to anything [in *Foreign Affairs*] . . . since George Kenan wrote on Soviet containment in the 1940s." Amyn B. Sajoo, "Latent Contests of Culture Are Surfacing," *Bangkok Post*, 30 March 1997, 2. The book in which Huntington later elaborated this thesis has been a notable commercial success for a major commercial press, selling more than fifty thousand copies in the first months of its publication. Hardy Green noted that the book was an example of how commercial presses could still make money in an increasingly competitive environment ("Superstores, Megabooks—and Humongous Headaches," *Business Week*, 14 April 1997, 92).

4 Andrew Ross, *Real Love: In Pursuit of Cultural Justice* (New York: New York University Press, 1998), 213.

5 For an especially trenchant critique of the purportedly baleful political tendencies of contemporary critical skepticism and an attempt to defend poststructuralism from becoming a "thoroughgoing relativist creed," see Christopher Norris, *Uncritical Theory: Postmodernism, Intellectuals, and the Gulf War* (Amherst: University of Massachusetts Press, 1992), and *What's Wrong with Postmodernism: Critical Theory and the Ends of Philosophy* (Baltimore: Johns Hopkins University Press, 1990); as well as Terry Eagleton, *Ideology: an Introduction* (London: Verso, 1991). See also Todd Gitlin, *The Twilight of Common Dreams: Why America Is Wracked by Culture Wars* (New York: Henry Holt, 1995).

6 Richard Rorty, "On Ethnocentrism: A Reply to Clifford Geertz," in *Objectivity, Relativism, and Truth: Philosophical Papers*, vol. 1 (New York: Cambridge University Press, 1991), 204.

7 Richard E. Rubenstein and Jarle Croker coined the phrase "warmed over Cold War pie" in a review of *The Clash of Civilizations* in *Foreign Affairs* 96 (September 1996): 113.

8 In his book, Huntington uses world maps to illustrate his point. See *The Clash of Civilizations*, 22–27. His frankly simplified modeling of the world and of civilization has drawn a good deal of fire. Rubenstein and Croker, for example, describe Huntington as deeply confused and contradictory about the monolithic character of global civilizations. Versions of this criticism of Huntington's thesis are fairly common. For instance, the editors of *Defense and Foreign Affairs: Strategic Policy* (31 January 1997) said that "Huntington and the 'mainstream' academics who follow him have finally understood the importance of culture as part of the strategic mix, only to have reduced the complexity of its role to absurd simplicity. . . . neither the West nor any other block of cultures is unified, and nor are they axiomatically confrontational" (22). William Pfaff, in his syndicated column, slammed the book as "curiously ignorant in its treatment of history and politics, and a disastrous guide to thinking about international affairs and national policy." Nonetheless, other commentators commend Huntington for putting culture on the map, so to speak, and for focusing Western attention on the real enemies, Islam and China abroad, multiculturalism and secularism at home. See, for example, Daniel Ben Yaakov, "Conflictual Relations," *Jerusalem Post*, 6 March 1997, 3; and Richard Piper, "The Clash of Civili-

zations?" *Commentary* 103, no. 3 (March 1997): 62. In one bizarre moment, Yaakov also commends Huntington for attempting to shore up the weakness of the "WASP elites" in the United States. Nonetheless, as Michael J. Mazarr points out, "Culture is the newest fad sweeping the literature on international relations, security studies, and international economics" ("Culture in International Relations," *Washington Quarterly* 19, no. 2 [spring 1996]: 177). See also Fouad Ajami, "The Clash of Civilizations," *Foreign Affairs* 72, no. 3 (fall 1993): 2. However controversial, Huntington is an eminent figure, and his position has provoked a huge volume of debate worldwide.

9 Jameson notes such triumphalism in Cary Nelson, "Always Already Cultural Studies," *Journal of the Midwest Modern Language Association* 24, no. 1 (1991): 24–38; See also Michael Bérubé, *Public Access: Literary Theory and American Cultural Politics* (London: Verso, 1994), 137–60.

10 See Fredric Jameson, *Postmodernism, or The Cultural Logic of Late Capitalism* (Durham, N.C.: Duke University Press, 1991), x; hereafter cited in text as Jameson, *Postmodernism*. Cultural studies, Jameson notes, has particularly vexed relations with history. See "On 'Cultural Studies,'" 18–19.

11 Like Huntington, Jameson takes an ambivalent view of the importance of nationalist ideology in mapping the globe and notes the end of bipolarity in world affairs: " 'Nation' today ought to be used as the word for a term within a system, a term which ought now always to imply relationality (of a more than binary type)" ("On 'Cultural Studies,'" 48). He continues, "It being understood that 'national' is now merely a relational term for the component parts of the world system, which might also be seen as the superposition of various kinds of space (local and regional as well as national, the geographical bloc as well as the world system itself)" (49–50).

12 Bruce Robbins, *Secular Vocations: Intellectuals, Professionalism, Culture* (London: Verso, 1993), 206.

13 Fredric Jameson, "The Antinomies of Postmodernism," in *The Seeds of Time* (New York: Columbia University Press, 1994), 43–44.

14 Huntington seems to forget what the ontological status of his model is. He quickly confuses it with reality, and his model becomes not heuristic but prescriptive. At the beginning of his second chapter, he abandons the language of pragmatics and paradigms to assert a bald-truth claim for the unique adequacy of his global map and strategy. Echoing Marx's dictum about class struggle, and enjoying the irony, Huntington writes that "human history is the history of civilizations. It is impossible to think of the development of humanity in any other terms." At the same time, Huntington offers the contradictory information that "civilization" itself has not always existed as a concept but was invented by French theorists in the eighteenth century and is genetically and inextricably intertwined with the history and legitimation of European colonialism (*Clash of Civilizations*, 40–41). Clearly it is not impossible to think of the development of humanity in any other terms, since throughout most of human history and even today we have done just that.

15 Zygmunt Bauman, *Intimations of Postmodernity* (London: Routledge, 1992), 39.

16 Weber, writing in the first decade of the twentieth century, surveyed a world dominated by the imperial powers of Western Europe, especially the Protestant cultures of England and Prussia. He developed a thesis linking culture and power and grounding that understanding in religion. "For Weber, the world-view of a religion is the single most important factor by means of which culture shapes social life." Ralph Schroeder, *Max Weber and the Sociology of Culture* (London: Sage Publications, 1992), 43.

17 Max Weber, *The Protestant Ethic and the Spirit of Capitalism: The Relationship between Religion*

and the Economic and Social Life in Modern Culture (New York: Charles Scribner's Sons, 1958), 26–27. Which is not to say that the connections between the various social spheres and phenomena in Weber is ever given with the sort of aspiration toward totalizing method evident in Marx, for instance. The links between social forces remain, for Weber, somewhat contingent and always related to the intellectual labor of forging them. Huntington is not so careful. See Schroeder, Max Weber and the Sociology of Culture, 6–11. Richard Rorty has claimed to find a basis for compassionate politics in the Judeo-Christian foundations of the West: "For it is part of the tradition of our community that the human stranger from whom all dignity has been stripped is to be taken in, to be reclothed with dignity. This Jewish and Christian element in our tradition is gratefully invoked by freeloading atheists like myself" ("Postmodernist Bourgeois Liberalism," in Objectivity, Relativism, and Truth, 202). Interestingly, Jameson has paid considerable attention to the value of Weber's vocation as an intellectual and has generated a rather different and more politically complex reading of Weber than the one that subtends Huntington's worldview. See Fredric Jameson, "The Vanishing Mediator, or Max Weber as Storyteller," in The Ideologies of Theory: Essays, 1971–1986, vol. 2 (Minneapolis: University of Minnesota Press, 1988); see also Bruce Robbins, Secular Vocations, 118–27.

18   Ajami, "The Clash of Civilizations," 2; hereafter cited in text.

19   Huntington's view of Islam, in particular, as a monolith seems more indebted to the work of cultural intellectuals such as V. S. Naipaul than it does to social science research. See V. S. Naipaul, Among the Believers: An Islamic Journey (New York: Knopf, 1981). One fascinating countering example among many possible may be found in the work of anthropologist Akbar S. Ahmed. See, for example, his Postmodernism and Islam: Predicament and Promise (New York: Routledge, 1992), and the essays collected in Islam, Globalization, and Postmodernity, ed. Akbar S. Ahmed and Hastings Donovan (New York: Routledge, 1994). See also Mohammed Bamyeh, The Ends of Globalization (Minneapolis: University of Minnesota Press, forthcoming).

20   Richard Rorty, "Cosmopolitanism without Emancipation: A Response to Jean-François Lyotard," in Objectivity, Relativism, and Truth, 215.

21   Michael Ignatieff, Blood and Belonging: Journeys into the New Nationalisms (New York: Farrar, Straus, and Giroux, 1994), 23; hereafter cited in text.

22   Ignatieff, "Fault Lines," New York Times Book Review, 1 December 1996, 13.

23   Attempts to retool Cold War anxieties for a world dominated by multinational capital have occurred in popular culture as well as in the rarefied environment of political science. For example, Michael Crichton's Rising Sun (New York: Knopf, 1992), both the book and the movie, attempted to adapt the paranoia of the Cold War thriller to the realities of capitalist competition between the United States and Japan. It provides a ready index of how difficult the translation of Cold War paranoia to the new world order can be. The Cold War thriller, perhaps best exemplified by the film The Manchurian Candidate (1959), was replete with anxieties concerning American identity, personal agency, traditional values, and Anglo-Saxon masculinity—the sense that all cherished Western institutions and icons from the American flag to Abraham Lincoln could be co-opted and contaminated by racially and ideologically foreign agents. Rising Sun attempts to evoke some of the same fears. But it finally collapses because the Japanese, while they are racially and culturally different from European and African Americans, turn out to be guilty of nothing more nefarious than greater skill and discipline in the ruthless struggle of globalized capital deployment and accumulation in which "we" are engaged. Their only characteristic "evil" turns out to be their business acumen. If this provokes anxiety, it is of a different order than the lush paranoia that flourished during the Cold War.

24 James Shapiro, "From Achebe to Zydeco: Two African-American Scholars Have Produced a 'Dictionary of Cultural Literacy' for the 1990s," *New York Times Book Review*, 2 February 1997, 7.

25 It is significant that the studies of U.S. civilization he cites—Charles A. Beard and Mary R. Beard's *The Rise of American Civilization* and Max Lerner's *America as a Civilization*—date from 1927 and 1957 respectively. His views seem out-of-date, and more recent considerations of non-Western influences on Western culture find no place in Huntington's argument. See, for example, Ronald Takaki, *A Different Mirror: A History of Multicultural America* (Boston: Little Brown, 1993), and Michael Kamen, *People of Paradox: an Inquiry Concerning the Origins of American Civilization* (New York: Knopf, 1972). More recently, Kamen has focused on the problem of tradition in a heterogeneous democracy; see *Mystic Chords of Memory: The Transformation of Tradition in American Culture* (New York: Knopf, 1991); hereafter cited in text as Kamen, *Mystic Chords*.

26 U.S. culture has never identified itself apart from the dynamics of cross-cultural conflict. As Frank Shuffelton puts it: "America was ethnic from the beginning, and to fail to understand this is to risk always the misconception that later immigration is a dilution or contamination of some supposed founding ethnic purity" (introduction to *A Mixed Race: Ethnicity in Early America*, ed. Frank Shuffelton [New York: Oxford, 1993], 6–7).

27 If Huntington imagines the West to be such a club, Richard Rorty also thinks that each of us should have a club where "you will be comforted by the companionship of your moral equals" at the end of the day spent in the conflictual negotiations of civil society. I don't think that such clubs can actually exist in any meaningful way without participating in the violence of intolerance and exclusion that Rorty deplores. Uncritical acceptance is not an option, but neither is it possible to avoid conflict. See Richard Rorty, "On Ethnocentrism: A Reply to Clifford Geertz," in *Objectivity, Relativism, and Truth*, 209.

Chapter 5   The critic: cultural studies and Adorno's ghost

1 Peter Uwe Hohendahl, *Prismatic Thought: Theodor W. Adorno* (Lincoln: University of Nebraska Press, 1995), 243.

2 Fredric Jameson, *Late Marxism: Adorno, or The Persistence of the Dialectic* (London: Verso, 1990); hereafter cited in text. Peter Uwe Hohendahl comments that the reception of Jameson's polemic was mixed and conflicted. See Hohendahl, *Prismatic Thought*, 13–16.

3 Hohendahl makes the case for this rapprochement quite persuasively in *Prismatic Thought*. Jameson seems more intent on maintaining distinctions (see *Late Marxism*). Michel Foucault, of course, said before he died, "If I had known about the Frankfurt School in time, I would have been saved a great deal of work. I would not have said a certain amount of nonsense and would not have taken so many false trails trying not to get lost, when the Frankfurt School had already cleared the way." See Michel Foucault, "Um welchen Preis sagt die Vernunft die Warheit? Ein Gespräch," *Spuren* 1 (1983): 24, cited in Rolf Wiggershaus, *The Frankfurt School: Its History, Theories, and Political Significance*, trans. Michael Roberston (Cambridge: MIT Press, 1995), 4; hereafter cited in text. Jameson, noting a similar remark in another interview, dismisses it as "a moment of abandon" (*Late Marxism*, 9). See also Michel Foucault with Gerard Ravlet, "Structuralism and Poststructuralism," *Telos* 55 (spring 1983): 195–211. Others who have been concerned to conflate or distinguish critical theory with postmodernist modes of thought include Russell A. Berman, *Modern Culture and Critical Theory: Art, Politics, and the Legacy of the Frankfurt School* (Madison: University of Wisconsin Press, 1989), 220. Two other very different books published the same year deal with similar topics. Mark Poster's *Critical Theory and Poststruc-*

turalism: *In Search of a Context* (Ithaca, N.Y.: Cornell University Press, 1989) "attempts," as its author announces, "a rapprochement between the tradition of critical social theory as developed by the Frankfurt School and other continental theorists, including Jean-Paul Sartre, and French poststructuralism, especially as practiced by Michel Foucault" (1). Douglas Kellner's *Critical Theory, Marxism, and Modernity* (Baltimore: Johns Hopkins University Press, 1989) makes a historical survey of critical theory's development since the 1930s because he believes that "a reconstructed Critical Theory can continue to be significant in the future" (vii). Each of these writers feels with some urgency that relations between critical theory and Marxism, Marxism and emancipation, emancipation and enlightenment, need to be reconsidered. See also, for example, Martin Jay, *Marxism and Totality: The Adventures of a Concept from Lukacs to Habermas* (Berkeley: University of California Press, 1984), esp. 510–37; Seyla Benhabib, *Critique, Norm, and Utopia* (New York: Columbia University Press, 1986); Peter Dews, *Logics of Disintegration: Post-structuralist Thought and the Claims of Critical Theory* (London: Verso, 1987).

4 As Hohendahl has noted, these oppositions are frequently remarkably less stark in Adorno's work than in the work of those who charged him with adherence to elitist, traditional, or high-cultural positions. See Hohendahl, *Prismatic Thought*, 119–48.

5 As Hohendahl says, "Here Adorno and Horkheimer play the role of heavies who have, without much respect for details, developed a totalizing theory of mass culture, based on questionable notions of the development of twentieth-century capitalism. Exclusively preoccupied with an outdated and outlandish conception of high culture, they fail to address the interaction between social groups and their (popular) cultures" (*Prismatic Thought*, 9).

6 Umberto Eco, *Travels in Hyperreality* (New York: Harcourt, Brace, Jovanovich, 1986), 150.

7 Jim Collins, *Uncommon Cultures: Popular Culture and Post-Modernism* (New York: Routledge, 1989), 1–42, hereafter cited in text; John Storey, *Cultural Studies and the Study of Popular Culture* (Athens: University of Georgia Press, 1996).

8 Andrew Ross, *No Respect: Intellectuals and Popular Culture* (New York: Routledge, 1989), 227.

9 *The Cultural Studies Reader*, ed. Simon During (London: Routledge, 1993), 29, 20.

10 Simon Frith, "The Cultural Study of Popular Music," in *Cultural Studies*, ed. Lawrence Grossberg, Cary Nelson, and Paula Treichler (New York: Routledge, 1992), 179.

11 Dick Hebdige, *Subculture: The Meaning of Style* (London: Methuen, 1979), 1–19.

12 Judith Williamson, "The Problems of Being Popular," *New Socialist*, September 1986, 14–15; cited in Meaghan Morris, "Banality in Cultural Studies," in *Logics of Television: Essays in Cultural Criticism* (Bloomington and Indianapolis: Indiana University Press, 1990), 14.

13 Ien Ang, "Wanted: Audiences: On the Politics of Empirical Audience Studies," in *Remote Control: Television, Audiences, and Cultural Power*, ed. Ellen Seiter, Hans Borchers, Gabriele Kreutzner, and Eva-Maria Warth (New York: Routledge, 1989), 105; hereafter cited in text. See also David Morley, *The "Nationwide" Audience: Structure and Decoding* (London: British Film Institute, 1980); and Lawrence Grossberg, "Critical Theory and the Politics of Empirical Research," in *Mass Communication Review Yearbook*, vol. 6, ed. Michael Gurevitch and Mark R. Levy (Newbury Park, Calif.: Sage, 1986), 86–106.

14 Janice Radway, *Reading the Romance: Women, Patriarchy, and Popular Literature* (Chapel Hill: University of North Carolina Press, 1984); hereafter cited in text.

15 Tania Modleski, *Feminism without Women: Culture and Criticism in a "Postfeminist" Age* (New York: Routledge, 1991), 45. Ien Ang, *Watching "Dallas": Soap Opera and the Melodramatic Imagination*, trans. Della Cooling (London: Methuen, 1985). Meaghan Morris points out that cultural studies often legitimates itself by constructing popular subjects as critical intellectuals who themselves possess the insights and resistance that theorists once

claimed. "Cultural studies," she writes, "posits a 'popular' subject 'supposed to know' in a certain manner, which the subject of populist theory then claims to understand . . . or mimic" (25). For those burdened with the intellectual's task of representation, it is a relief to find that each audience subculture is a form of resistance and a reconstitution of community. (As Eco might say, "Ah, what luck!") This relieves the critic of the necessity of criticizing (unless it is to criticize other critics who just don't get it) and redefines the intellectual's task as empirical description and occasional celebration. It requires little argument or evidence to condemn those who would criticize these pleasures. Morris has found such a predisposition to be common in cultural studies. As she puts it, "There is a process going on . . . of discrediting. . . . the voices of grumpy feminists and cranky leftists ('Frankfurt School' can do duty for both)" (25).

16 John Fiske, *Reading the Popular* (New York: Routledge, 1991), 2; hereafter cited in text.

17 John Fiske, *Power Plays, Power Works* (London: Verso, 1993), 5.

18 Wendy Brown, *States of Injury: Power and Freedom in Late Modernity* (Princeton, N.J.: Princeton University Press, 1995), 21–22.

19 Zygmunt Bauman makes this point in *Intimations of Postmodernity* (New York: Routledge, 1992), 2.

20 In her critique of the populist strain in cultural studies, Morris describes how this trick works: "What takes place is first, a citing of popular voices (the informants), an act of translation and commentary, and then a play of *identification* between the knowing subject of cultural studies and a collective subject, 'the people' " (22–23). Identification here is also projection. Criticism is reserved for those who refuse to enter into this circuit: "The argumentative rhetoric . . . has been increasingly addressing not the hegemonic force of the 'dominant classes' but other critical theories (vulgar feminism, the Frankfurt School) inscribed as misunderstanding popular culture" (26).

21 Henry Jenkins, *Textual Poachers: Television Fans and Participatory Culture* (New York: Routledge, 1992), 86.

22 Constance Penley, *NasalTrek: Popular Science and Sex in America* (New York: Verso, 1997), 101; hereafter cited in text.

23 Constance Penley, "Feminism, Psychoanalysis, and the Study of Popular Culture," in *Cultural Studies*, ed. Lawrence Grossberg, Cary Nelson, and Paula Treichler (New York: Routledge, 1992), 484; hereafter cited in text as Penley, "Feminism."

24 As Hohendahl sees the later Adorno, especially in *Negative Dialectics*, the possibilities of totalization are already seriously compromised: "To put it differently, Adorno assumes that philosophical discourse can no longer be grounded in first principles, nor can it rely on universal concepts deduced from these principles. . . . Consequently, a positive concept of totality is no longer available. This leaves philosophy with an arduous task for which it is not quite adequately equipped: to discover how concepts and 'the nonconceptual' (*das Nichtbegriffliche*) come together" (Hohendahl, 232).

25 Yet Jameson's thought remains utopian nonetheless. If identity and the concept, for example, are associated effects of the exchange system, then to make the lineaments and limitations of one standpoint clear, one must have moved not to a neutral no place (as Jameson sometimes seems to suggest) but to another standpoint with its own now occluded (until some other thought intervenes) lineaments and limitations. In this sense, as Jameson indicates, a gesture toward the "outside of thinking" can never be more than a rhetorical or theatrical gesture within thinking's closure (*Late Marxism*, 30).

Chapter 6 The scientist: disembodied intellect and popular utopias

1 Constance Penley, *Nasa/Trek: Popular Science and Sex in America* (New York: Verso, 1997), 1–10.

2 Stephen Hawking, *A Brief History of Time: From the Big Bang to Black Holes* (New York: Bantam, 1988), 174–75; hereafter cited in text.

3 The words of his editor, Peter Guzzardi, appear in Arthur Lubow, "Heart and Mind: A Rare Glimpse at the Private Man behind the Brilliant Mind of Stephen Hawking," *Vanity Fair*, June 1992, 72; hereafter cited in text. Gregory Benford describes Hawking as a cultural icon in "A Scientist's Notebook," *Magazine of Fantasy and Science Fiction*, April 1992, 85.

4 Michel Foucault, "Truth and Power," in *Power/Knowledge: Selected Interviews and Other Writings, 1972–77*, ed. Colin Gordon (New York: Pantheon, 1980), 126. Morris speaks, at times, as if the problematics of interpretation and power that his earlier film explored had little to do with the depiction of science in *A Brief History of Time*. He remarks, for example, "I'm not one of these postmodern guys who believe that all of knowledge is subjective, that we live in some kind of deconstructive universe in which everything is just projection, transference, interpretation. I don't believe in any such thing. I mean, *The Thin Blue Line* was an essay on self-deception. Not on the unknowability of truth, but on people's vested interest in avoiding the truth. Evidence can be interpreted in many ways, but the enormous quantity of evidence in this case points to Adams' innocence and another's man's guilt." Yet Morris has also said more generally of his films that they revolve around "the idea that we're in possession of certainty, truth, infallible knowledge, when actually we're a bunch of apes running around." See David Beers, "Errol Morris, Film's Best-Known Bottom Feeder, Travels through Time with Skywalker Stephen Hawking," *Mother Jones*, May–June 1992, 47. In *A Brief History of Time* Morris seems to be examining the limits of the ape's ability to get out of its own way when it investigates the universe and searches for objective laws.

5 Marek Kohn, "Joyfully Back to Church?" *New Statesman and Society*, 1 May 1992, 32.

6 Bruce Kucklick, "The Emergence of the Humanities," in *The Politics of Liberal Education*, ed. Darryl J. Gless and Barbara Herrnstein Smith (Durham, N.C.: Duke University Press, 1992), 201–12.

7 I am indebted to Sarah Higely for conversations about androids and for her own work on science and culture. See Sarah Higley, "The Legend of the Learned Man's Android," in *Retelling Tales: Essays in Honor of Russell Peck*, ed. Thomas Hahn and Alan Lupack (Cambridge: D. S. Brewer, 1997), 127–60; and "Alien Intellect and the Roboticization of the Scientist," forthcoming in *Camera Obscura*. It may also be worth noting that of the four "minds" seated at the holodeck card table, three—in either real or imaginary history—would eventually occupy the Lucasian chair of mathematics at Cambridge: Newton, Hawking, and finally Data.

8 Roland Barthes, "The Brain of Einstein," in *Mythologies*, trans. Annette Lavers (New York: Hill and Wang, 1972), 68.

9 Michael White and John Gribbin, *Stephen Hawking: A Life in Science* (New York: Dutton, 1992), 279; hereafter cited in text.

10 For an analysis of the intertwining of empirical science and Puritan and capitalist ideology in the early modern period, see James R. Jacob, "The Political Economy of Science in Seventeenth-Century England," in *The Politics of Western Science, 1640–1990*, ed. Margaret C. Jacob (Atlantic Highlands, N.J.: Humanities Press, 1992), 19–46.

11 See, for example, Evelyn Fox Keller, *Reflections on Gender and Science* (New Haven, Conn.: Yale University Press, 1985); Nancy C. M. Hartsock, *Money, Sex, and Power: Toward a Feminist*

Historical Materialism (Boston: Northeastern University Press, 1983), esp. 240–52; Sandra Harding, *The Science Question in Feminism* (Ithaca, N.Y.: Cornell University Press, 1986), and *Whose Science? Whose Knowledge?* (Ithaca, N.Y.: Cornell University Press, 1991); and Donna J. Haraway, *Simians, Cyborgs, and Women: The Reinvention of Nature* (New York: Routledge, 1991).

12 This wish persists with remarkable force. The discovery of the so-called "top quark," the last of the six types of quarks (the elemental building blocks of the universe) to be generated in a particle accelerator was reported on the front page of the *New York Times* with sidebars that declared, "Forging a link between the physical and the metaphysical" and "Trying to understand the fundamentals of the universe" (*New York Times*, 3 March 1995, B7). The article could not, of course, explain what could be fundamental in metaphysical terms about such a discovery. Yet such announcements stir considerable excitement.

13 *The Star Trek Encyclopedia: A Reference Guide to the Future*, ed. Michael Okuda (New York: Pocket Books, 1994), 123.

14 Stephen Hawking, *Black Holes and Baby Universes and Other Essays* (New York: Bantam Books, 1993), 37; hereafter cited in text as Hawking, *Black Holes.*

15 A review of two books on cosmology that, like Hawking's *A Brief History of Time*, seek a popular audience is addressed to "believers in the tenet that science is capable, in principle, of finding solutions to some really big mysteries—the kind pondered by the mystics of Hinduism and Buddhism, Islamic Sufism, Jewish cabalism and the biblical books of Genesis and Revelation." See "Things Are Stranger Than We Can Imagine: Two Theoretical Physicists Think about Them in Ten Dimensions," *New York Times Book Review*, 20 March 1994, 3.

16 "Why Past Is Past," *Newsweek*, 28 December 1992, 53; hereafter cited in text.

17 Jean-Louis Baudry, "Ideological Effects of the Basic Cinematographic Apparatus," in *Narrative, Apparatus, Ideology: A Film Theory Reader*, ed. Philip Rosen (New York: Columbia University Press, 1986), 286–98.

18 Brian Winston, "The Documentary Film as Scientific Inscription," in *Theorizing Documentary*, ed. Michael Renov (New York: Routledge, 1993), 41–42.

19 Winston, "The Documentary Film as Scientific Inscription," 47. Citation of Leacock from James Blue, "One Man's Truth: An Interview with Richard Leacock," *Film Comment* 3, no. 2 (1965): 16.

20 Of the history of documentary and its aspirations to becoming an experiential rather than a representational mode, Brian Winston cites Michael Renov: "Every documentary issues a 'truth claim' of a sort, positing a relationship to history which exceeds the analogical status of its fictional counterpart" (Michael Renov, "Rethinking Documentary: Toward a Taxonomy of Mediation," *Wide Angle* 18, nos. 3–4 [1986]: 71). Winston continues: "These shifts in epistemology were coming into general play in sync with the development of the Direct Cinema/Cinema-Verite schools. It is somewhat ironic, then, that just as documentarists finally got the equipment to illuminate, as they supposed, the real world of externally verifiable data, that world was denied them and they were instead revealed as the constructors of particular ideologically charged texts par excellence" (Winston, "The Documentary Film as Scientific Inscription," 55).

21 Michael Renov, "Introduction: The Truth about Non-Fiction," in *Theorizing Documentary*, ed. Michael Renov (New York: Routledge, 1993), 7.

22 Quoted in Renov, *Theorizing Documentary*, 92.

23 Donna Haraway, "Situated Knowledges: The Science Question in Feminism and the Privilege of Partial Perspectives," *Feminist Studies* 14, no. 3 (fall 1988): 581.

24 "Hawking Gets Personal," *Time*, 27 September 1993, 80. His biographers have remarked

that "Hawking, despite his disabilities, commands a powerful presence," which seems to miss the point that the power of his physical presence is significantly an expression of his disabilities. See White and Gribbin, *Stephen Hawking: A Life in Science*, 284. Anecdotes of Hawking's aggressive use of his wheelchair in and around Cambridge abound.

25 Hawking is another instance of the aggressive and acquisitive tendency that materializes within what Nancy Hartsock has called "abstract masculinity." Her influential discussion of abstract masculinity may be found in *Money, Sex, and Power*, 240–47.

26 Jürgen Habermas, *The Structural Transformation of the Public Sphere: An Inquiry into a Category of Bourgeois Society*, trans. Thomas Burger (Cambridge: MIT Press, 1991), 16. Benedict Anderson has noted the importance of print capital in the identification of intellectuals with the emergence and construction of the characteristically modern state organization, the nation. See *Imagined Communities: Reflections on the Origin and Spread of Nationalism* (New York: Verso, 1983, 1991).

27 Michael Warner, "The Mass Public and the Mass Subject," in *The Phantom Public Sphere*, ed. Bruce Robbins (Minneapolis: University of Minnesota Press, 1993), 238–40.

28 This thematic is everywhere evident in Baudrillard. See, for example, *Simulacra and Simulations*, trans. Paul Foss, Paul Patton, and Philip Beitchman (New York: Semiotext(e), 1983), and "The Masses: The Implosion of the Social in the Media," trans. Marie Maclean, *New Literary History* 16, no. 3 (spring 1985): 577–89.

Chapter 7   The professional: science wars and interdisciplinary studies

1 Paul R. Gross and Norman Levitt, *Higher Superstition: The Academic Left and Its Quarrels with Science* (Baltimore: Johns Hopkins University Press, 1994); hereafter cited in text.

2 Alan Sokal, "A Physicist Experiments with Cultural Studies," *Lingua Franca* (May–June 1996): 62–64; hereafter cited in text.

3 Making a similar point, Donna Haraway attacks relativism and defends perspectivism as a more realistic form of objectivity. See "Situated Knowledges: The Science Question in Feminism and the Privilege of Partial Perspective," *Feminist Studies* 14, no. 3 (fall 1988): 584.

4 As Bruce Robbins has said, "Thanks to a supposedly direct, unmediated relation to the object or substance of his expertise . . . the expert is the one, perhaps now the only one, who is supposed to know" (*Secular Vocations: Intellectuals, Professionalism, Culture* [London: Verso, 1993], 33). Yet the public seems increasingly skeptical about what it is that experts are supposed to know and what it means to them.

5 It is easy to find evidence of crises in the sciences. For example, John Horgan, a senior writer for *Scientific American*, prepares an overview of major scientific findings of the last two decades based on interviews with many prominent researchers and publishes a book purporting to announce "The End of Science." John Horgan, *The End of Science: Facing the Limits of Knowledge in the Twilight of the Scientific Age* (Reading, Mass.: Helix Books/Addison-Wesley, 1996). *The New York Times Book Review* makes Horgan's book the cover story with the following headline: "Dark Days in the Laboratory: In 'The End of Science,' John Horgan argues that the great days of scientific discovery are over: what science now knows is about all it will ever know" (*New York Times Book Review*, 30 June 1996). Natalie Angier's review, "The Job Is Finished," appears on pages 11–12. Without arguing for or against Horgan's controversial thesis, I want to note its resonance within important segments of the scientific community and, even more important, among the nonscientific readers of the Sunday *New York Times*.

6 Dorothy Nelkin, "Responses to a Marriage Failed," *Social Text* 14, nos. 1–2 (spring–

summer 1996): 99–100; hereafter cited in text. In the same issue of *Social Text*, George Levine makes the sensible observation that "recent developments in the budget-cutting attempts to scale back government support for work in both science and the arts and humanities ought to be making it clear that our fates and our interests are entangled" ("What Is Science Studies for and Who Cares?" 113).

7   Nelkin borrows this analysis from Mary Douglas's observations about "pollution rhetoric" in *How Institutions Think* (Syracuse, N.Y.: Syracuse University Press, 1986).

8   The very idea of progress has itself become increasingly suspect. See, for example, Christopher Lasch, *The True and Only Heaven: Progress and Its Critics* (New York: Norton, 1991).

9   Such is the fear registered by many scientists. See, for example, Gerald D. Holton, *Einstein, History, and Other Passions* (New York: Addison-Wesley, 1996), esp. 3–9; hereafter cited in text. Although they don't mention either Vannevar Bush or Congress's failure to fund the supercollider project, the sense that science has fallen on hard times pervades the polemic against science studies in Gross and Levitt.

10   Nelkin describes that social contract with the sciences and its current situation. See her "Responses to a Marriage Failed," 95.

11   William Broad and Nicholas Wade, *Betrayers of the Truth: Fraud and Deceit in the Halls of Science* (New York: Simon and Schuster, 1982). Holton discusses this book and his view of what he calls its "vastly overblown" allegations in *Einstein, History, and Other Passions*, 19–22.

12   Sandra Harding, "Science Is 'Good to Think With,'" *Social Text* 14, nos. 1–2 (spring–summer 1996): 18.

13   Andrew Ross, "Introduction," *Social Text* 14, nos. 1–2 (spring–summer 1996): 3–4.

14   George Levine has noted that Ross's stated program, to encourage more fruitful interactions between science and its lay public, is similar to the aspirations Gross and Levitt claim in *Higher Superstition* ("What Is Science Studies for and Who Cares," 124). Paul Feyerabend made similar arguments and much more compelling analyses of the constructed nature of scientific knowledge two decades ago in *Against Method* (New York: New Left Books, 1975). Significantly, the book was reprinted in 1994 as *Against Method: Third Edition* (London: Verso, 1994). In the preface to the third edition, Feyerabend once again makes his position clear: "I am neither a populist for whom an appeal to 'the people' is the basis of all knowledge, nor a relativist for whom there are no 'truths as such' but only truths for this or that group and/or individual. All I say is that non-experts often know more than experts *and should therefore be consulted* and that prophets of truth (including those who use arguments) more often than not are carried along by a vision that clashes with the very events the vision is supposed to be exploring" (xiii). For reasons that we must explore, these simple, even modest ideas seem harder for scientists to receive now than they did when Feyerabend first published them twenty years ago.

15   This is, in essence, what the quintessential literary professional Stanley Fish argued in the *New York Times*. See "Professor Sokal's Bad Joke," *New York Times*, 21 May 1996, Op-Ed page.

16   Stanley Aronowitz, "The Politics of the Science Wars," *Social Text* 14, nos. 1–2 (spring–summer 1996): 192.

17   A more critical—from a scientific point of view—articulation of science in relation to other discourses may be found in Harding's work where she insists on distinguishing between more and less efficacious folk and technocratic practices. See, for example, "Science Is 'Good to Think With.'" Or as Richard Levin puts it, even if "all theories are eventually wrong, some are not even temporarily right" ("Ten Propositions on Science and Antiscience," *Social Text* 14, nos. 1–2 [spring–summer 1996]: 104).

18   Andrew Ross and Bruce Robbins, "Mystery Science Theater: Sokal vs. *Social Text*, Part Two," *Lingua Franca* (July–August 1996): 54–55.

19   Paul Feyerabend, *Science in a Free Society* (London: Verso, 1982), 79–80.

20   David Berreby, "That Damned Elusive Bruno Latour," *Lingua Franca* 4, no. 6 (1994): 26; hereafter cited in text.

21   Les Levidow, "Science Skirmishes and Science-Policy Research," *Social Text* 14, nos. 1–2 (spring–summer 1996): 200.

22   As Bruce Robbins has pointed out, such necessary appeals to the laity or to society at large are and have been a structural component of professional life. Citing work by Geison and Haskell, Robbins points out that "professions are inexplicable if one does not factor in public demand and public opinion. . . . Professions are not hermetically sealed, but porous. To associate professional language with jargon incomprehensible to outsiders is thus a serious historical error. Address to outsiders, according to these histories, is indispensable to professional speech" (*Secular Vocations*, 90–91). See Gerald Geison, *Professions and Professional Ideologies in America* (Chapel Hill: University of North Carolina, 1983); and Thomas Haskell, *The Emergence of Professional Social Science: The American Social Science Association and the Nineteenth-Century Crisis of Authority* (Urbana: University of Illinois Press, 1977).

23   C. S. Peirce, "The Fixation of Belief," in *Philosophical Writings of Peirce*, ed. Justus Buchler (New York: Dover, 1955), 5–22.

24   434a-d, *Plato's Republic*, trans. G. M. A. Grube (Indianapolis: Hackett Publishing, 1974), 99.

25   Burton Bledstein, *The Culture of Professionalism: The Middle Class and the Development of Higher Education in America* (New York: Norton, 1976), 80–81; hereafter cited in text.

26   Max Weber, "The Uniqueness of Western Civilization," in *Max Weber on Capitalism, Bureaucracy, and Religion: A Selection of Texts*, ed. Stanislaw Andreski (London: Allen and Unwin, 1983), 21–29.

27   Bledstein ends his book with the following peroration, which defines the issues that still focus and motivate our discussions today: "Perhaps never before within the last century have we as Americans been so aware of the arrogance, shallowness, and potential abuses of the vertical vision by venal individuals who justify their special treatment and betray society's trust by invoking professional privilege, confidence, and secrecy. The question for Americans is, How does society make professional behavior accountable to the public without curtailing the independence upon which creative skills and the imaginative use of knowledge depend? The culture of professionalism has allowed Americans to achieve educated expressions of freedom and self-realization, yet it has also allowed them to perfect educated techniques of fraudulence and deceit. In medicine, law, education, business, government, the ministry—all the proliferating services middle-class Americans thrive on—who shall draw the fine line between competent services and corruption?" (334).

28   Hannah Arendt, *Eichmann in Jerusalem: A Report on the Banality of Evil* (New York: Penguin, 1994), 36–55. Zygmunt Bauman makes the case as follows: "This is not to suggest that the incidence of the Holocaust was *determined* by modern bureaucracy or the culture of instrumental rationality it epitomizes, much less still, that modern bureaucracy *must* result in Holocaust-style phenomena. I do suggest, however, that the rules of instrumental rationality are singularly incapable of preventing such phenomena, that there is nothing in those rules which disqualifies the Holocaust-style methods of social-engineering as improper or, indeed, the actions they served as irrational. I suggest, further, that the bureaucratic culture which prompts us to view society as an object of administration,

as a collection of so many 'problems' to be solved, as 'nature' to be 'controlled,' 'mastered' and 'improved' or 'remade,' as legitimate target for 'social engineering,' and in general a garden to be designed and kept in a planned shape by force (the gardening posture divides vegetation into cultured plants to be taken care of, and weeds to be exterminated), was the very atmosphere in which the idea of the Holocaust could be conceived, slowly yet consistently developed, and brought to a conclusion" (*Modernity and the Holocaust* [Ithaca, N.Y.: Cornell University Press, 1989], 17–18).

29 See Andrew Ross, *No Respect* (New York: Routledge, 1989).

30 Jonathan Goldhagen has recently argued that even the Final Solution was widely popular among ordinary Germans. See *Hitler's Willing Executioners: Ordinary Germans and the Holocaust* (New York: Knopf, 1996).

31 Reynolds's remarks were published as a contribution to "Mystery Science Theater," a forum on Sokal's revelations in *Lingua Franca* (July–August 1996): 62.

32 For a number of years, Fish has been elaborating these opinions in professional literary journals and most recently in *Professional Correctness: Literary Studies and Political Change* (Oxford: Clarendon Press, 1995); hereafter cited in text. Fish's view of interdisciplinarity is not so much that it is impossible, though he notes that given the structures of professional sanction alluded to earlier, interdisciplinarity is all but impossible in any strong form. As Fish describes the usual practices that are misdescribed as interdisciplinary, they remain securely within the boundaries of one discipline or another: "Whenever there is an apparent *rapprochement* or relationship of co-operation between projects, it will be the case either that one is anxiously trading on the prestige and vocabulary of the other or that one has swallowed the other; and this will be true not only when one project is academic and the other political, but when both are housed in the academy, perhaps in the same building" (83). This description would apply to the sort of interdisciplinarity that Terri Reynolds claims. Such interdisciplinarity has been claimed by many others, notably Julie Klein and N. Katherine Hayles. See Julie Klein, *Interdisciplinarity: History, Theory, Practice* (Detroit, Mich.: Wayne State University Press, 1990); and N. Katherine Hayles, *Chaos Bound: Orderly Disorder in Contemporary Literature and Science* (Ithaca, N.Y.: Cornell University Press, 1990).

33 However subtle academic intellectuals in fields such as literary criticism, anthropology, or philosophy may be, in practical applications in other institutional contexts (and all applications are practical and tied to specific institutional matrices and cultures), they are largely, according to Fish, useless because "subtlety itself is situation-specific and its various forms do not travel well when they are transported from their (institutionally) natural habitat. When the pinch comes you want to entrust yourself to someone who knows the territory—whether the territory be the hospital room or the boardroom or the locker-room—to someone whose ways of processing information have emerged in the course of long hands-on experience rather than from the brains of self-anointed philosopher-kings" (89–90).

34 This was in fact the burden of his *New York Times* Op-Ed piece on the Sokal hoax and the anxieties within the scientific community about science studies that provoked it. Each enterprise, science on the one hand and science studies on the other, is a separate professional activity with different provinces and effects. There is no contact between them and therefore nothing for scientists to fear and no reason for animosity or anxiety.

35 Zygmunt Bauman, *Legislators and Interpreters: On Modernity, Post-modernity, and Intellectuals* (Oxford: Basil Blackwell, 1987), 145.

36 Liz McMillen, "Scholars Who Study the Lab Say Their Work Has Been Distorted," *Chronicle of Higher Education*, 28 June 1996, A8.

Conclusion: tattered maps

1 Donald Kennedy, *Academic Duty* (Cambridge: Harvard University Press, 1997), 210; here-after cited in text. Perhaps public hostility to academic intellectuals may be gauged with reference to the popularity of attacks on tenure, usually from conservative apologists and demagogues with think tank affiliations or Olin Foundation money that licenses them to violate guild codes of evidence, accuracy, and logical consequentiality. Whatever else is at stake in the struggle of tenure, right-wing demagogues seem to see in its abolition an opportunity to further their own stupefying political agenda even as academic managers see in it a way to further strengthen their hands. See, for example, George Dennis O'Brien, *All the Essential Half-Truths about Higher Education* (Chicago: University of Chicago Press, 1998).

2 Henry Louis Gates Jr. and Cornel West, eds., *The Future of the Race* (New York: Knopf, 1996), xvi.

3 Jorge Luis Borges, *Obras Completas, 1923–1972* (Buenos Aires: Emecé, 1974), 847. My translation follows.

4 Bill Readings, *The University in Ruins* (Cambridge: Harvard University Press, 1996).

BIBLIOGRAPHY

Adorno, Theodore. *Negative Dialectics*. New York: Seabury Press, 1973.

Ahmed, Akbar S. *Postmodernism and Islam: Predicament and Promise*. New York: Routledge, 1992.

Ahmed, Akbar S., and Hastings Donovan, eds. *Islam, Globalization, and Postmodernity*. New York: Routledge, 1994.

Ajami, Fouad. "The Summoning." Review of *The Clash of Civilizations*. *Foreign Affairs* 72, no. 3 (September–October 1993): 2–9.

Althusser, Louis. *Lenin and Philosophy and Other Essays*. New York: Monthly Review Press, 1971.

Anderson, Benedict. *Imagined Communities: Reflections on the Origin and Spread of Nationalism*. New York: Verso, 1983.

Ang, Ien. "Wanted: Audiences: On the Politics of Empirical Audience Studies." In *Remote Control: Television, Audiences, and Cultural Power*, ed. Ellen Seiter, Hans Borchers, Gabriele Kreutzner, and Eva-Maria Warth, 96–115. New York: Routledge, 1989.

———. *Watching "Dallas": Soap Opera and the Melodramatic Imagination*. Trans. Della Cooling. London: Methuen, 1985.

Angier, Natalie. "The Job Is Finished." Review of *The End of Science: Facing the Limits of Knowledge in the Twilight of the Scientific Age*. *New York Times Book Review*, 30 June 1996, 11–12.

Arendt, Hannah. *Eichmann in Jerusalem: A Report on the Banality of Evil*. New York: Penguin, 1994.

Aronowitz, Stanley. "The Politics of the Science Wars." *Social Text* 14, nos. 1–2 (spring–summer 1996): 177–99.

Aufderheide, Patricia, ed. *Beyond PC: Towards a Politics of Understanding*. St. Paul, Minn.: Graywolf Press, 1992.

Bamyeh, Mohammed. *The Ends of Globalization*. Minneapolis: University of Minnesota Press, forthcoming.

Barthes, Roland. *Mythologies*. Trans. Annette Lavers. New York: Hill and Wang, 1972.

Baudrillard, Jean. "The Masses: The Implosion of the Social in the Media." Trans. Marie Maclean. *New Literary History* 16, no. 3 (spring 1985): 577–89.

———. *Simulacra and Simulations*. Trans. Paul Foss, Paul Patton, and Philip Beitchman. New York: Semiotext(e), 1983.

Baudry, Jean-Louis. "Ideological Effects of the Basic Cineamatographic Apparatus." In *Narrative, Apparatus, Ideology: A Film Theory Reader*, ed. Philip Rosen, 286–98. New York: Columbia University Press, 1986.

Bauman, Zygmunt. *Intimations of Postmodernity*. New York: Routledge, 1992.

———. *Legislators and Interpreters: On Modernity, Post-modernity, and Intellectuals*. Oxford: Basil Blackwood, 1987.

———. *Modernity and the Holocaust.* Ithaca, N.Y.: Cornell University Press, 1989.

Beard, Charles A., and Mary R. Beard. *The Rise of American Civilization.* New York: Macmillan, 1936.

Beers, David. "Erroll Morris, Film's Best-Known Bottom Feeder, Travels through Time with Skywalker Stephen Hawking." *Mother Jones,* May–June 1992, 44–47.

Benford, Gregory. "A Scientist's Notebook." *Magazine of Fantasy and Science Fiction* 82 (April 1992): 85–94.

Benhabib, Seyla. *Critique, Norm, and Utopia.* New York: Columbia University Press, 1986.

Berman, Russell A. *Modern Culture and Critical Theory: Art, Politics, and the Legacy of the Frankfurt School.* Madison: University of Wisconsin Press, 1989.

Bernstein, Richard. *Dictatorship of Virtue: Multiculturalism and the Battle for America's Future.* New York: Knopf, 1994.

Berreby, David. "The Damned Elusive Bruno Latour." *Lingua Franca* 4, no. 6 (1994): 26.

Bérubé, Michael. *The Employment of English: Theory, Jobs, and the Future of Literary Studies.* New York: New York University Press, 1998.

———. *Public Access: Literary Theory and American Cultural Politics.* London: Verso, 1994.

Bérubé, Michael, and Cary Nelson, eds. *Higher Education under Fire: Politics, Economics, and the Crisis of the Humanities.* New York: Routledge, 1995.

Blassingame, John, and John R. McKivigan, eds. *The Frederick Douglass Papers: Series One.* Vol. 4. New Haven, Conn.: Yale University Press, 1991.

Bledstein, Burton. *The Culture of Professionalism: The Middle Class and the Development of Higher Education in America.* New York: Norton, 1976.

Bloom, Allan. *The Closing of the American Mind: How Higher Education Has Failed Democracy and Impoverished the Souls of Today's Students.* New York: Simon and Schuster, 1987.

Blue, James. "One Man's Truth: An Interview with Richard Leacock." *Film Comment* 3, no. 2 (1965): 16.

Boggs, Carl. *Intellectuals and the Crisis of Modernity.* Albany, N.Y.: SUNY Press, 1993.

Borges, Jorge Luis. *Obras Completas, 1923–1972.* Buenos Aires: Emece, 1974.

Boynton, Robert S. "The New Intellectuals: African American Intellectuals." *Atlantic Monthly,* March 1995, 53–56, 60–62, 64–68, 70.

Braudel, Fernand. *Civilization and Capitalism, 15th–18th Centuries.* New York: Harper and Row, 1984.

Broad, William, and Nicholas Wade. *Betrayers of the Truth.* New York: Simon and Schuster, 1982.

Brown, Wendy. *States of Injury: Power and Freedom in Late Modernity.* Princeton, N.J.: Princeton University Press, 1995.

Carpignano, Paolo, Robin Anderson, Stanley Aronowitz, and William Frazer. "Chatter in the Age of Electronic Reproduction: Talk Television and the 'Public Mind.'" In *The Phantom Public Sphere,* ed. Bruce Robbins, 93–120. Minneapolis: University of Minnesota Press, 1993.

Cheney, Lynne V. *Telling the Truth: A Report of the State of the Humanities in Higher Education.* Washington, D.C.: National Endowment for the Humanities, 1992.

Chow, Rey. *Writing Diaspora: Tactics of Intervention in Contemporary Cultural Studies.* Bloomington: Indiana University Press, 1993.

Collins, Jim. *Uncommon Cultures: Popular Culture and Post-Modernism.* New York: Routledge, 1989.

Crichton, Michael. *Rising Sun.* New York: Knopf, 1992.

"Defense and Foreign Affairs." *Strategic Policy,* 31 January 1997, 22.

Dertouzos, Michael L., Richard K. Lester, and Robert M. Solow. *Made in America: Regaining the Productive Edge.* Report of the MIT Commission on Industrial Productivity. Cambridge: MIT Press, 1989.

Dews, Peter. *Logics of Disintegration: Post-structuralist Thought and the Claims of Critical Theory*. London: Verso, 1987.

Douglas, Mary. *How Institutions Think*. Syracuse, N.Y.: Syracuse University Press, 1986.

Douglass, Frederick. *Narrative of the Life of Frederick Douglass, an American Slave*. New York: Signet, 1968.

D'Souza, Dinesh. *The End of Racism: Principles for a Multiracial Society*. New York: Free Press, 1995.

———. *Illiberal Education: The Politics of Race and Sex on Campus*. New York: Free Press, 1991.

DuBois, W. E. B. "The Talented Tenth." In *The Future of the Race*, ed. Henry Louis Gates Jr. and Cornel West, 133–58. New York: Knopf, 1996.

During, Simon, ed. *The Cultural Studies Reader*. London: Routledge, 1993.

Eagleton, Terry. *Ideology: An Introduction*. New York: Verso, 1991.

Early, Gerald. "Black like Them." *New York Times Book Review*, 21 April 1996, 7.

Eco, Umberto. *Travels in Hyperreality*. New York: Harcourt, Brace, Jovanovich, 1986.

Elias, John L. *Paulo Freire: Pedagogue of Liberalism*. Malabar, Fla.: Krieger Publishing, 1994.

Fallows, James. *More like Us: Putting America's Native Strengths and Traditional Values to Work to Overcome the Asian Challenge*. Boston: Houghton Mifflin, 1989.

Feyerabend, Paul. *Against Method*. New York: New Left Books, 1975.

———. *Against Method: Third Edition*. New York: Verso, 1994.

———. *Science in a Free Society*. London: Verso, 1982.

Fish, Stanley. "Commentary: The Young and the Restless." In *The New Historicism*, ed. H. Aram Veeser, 303–16. New York: Routledge, 1989.

———. *Doing What Comes Naturally*. Durham, N.C.: Duke University Press, 1989.

———. *Is There a Text in This Class? The Authority of Interpretive Communities*. Cambridge: Harvard University Press, 1980.

———. *Professional Correctness: Literary Studies and Political Change*. Oxford: Clarendon Press, 1995.

———. "Professor Sokal's Bad Joke." *New York Times*, 21 May 1996, 23.

———. *Self-Consuming Artifacts*. Berkeley: University of California Press, 1972.

———. *Surprised by Sin: The Reader in "Paradise Lost."* New York: St. Martin's Press, 1967.

———. *There's No Such Thing as Free Speech, and It's a Good Thing Too*. New York: Oxford University Press, 1994.

Fiske, John. *Power Plays, Power Works*. London: Verso, 1993.

———. *Reading the Popular*. New York: Routledge, 1991.

"Forging a Link between the Physical and Metaphysics." *New York Times*, 3 March 1997, B7.

Foucault, Michel. "Truth and Power." In *Power/Knowledge: Selected Interviews and Other Writings, 1972–77*, ed. Coling Gordon, 126–33. New York: Pantheon, 1980.

Foucault, Michel, and Gerald Ravlet. "Structuralism and Poststructuralism." *Telos* 55 (spring 1983): 195–211.

Fox Keller, Evelyn. *Reflections on Gender and Science*. New Haven, Conn.: Yale University Press, 1985.

Freire, Paulo. *Pedagogy of Hope: Reliving Pedagogy of the Oppressed*. Trans. Robert R. Barr. New York: Continuum, 1994.

Frith, Simon. "The Cultural Study of Popular Music." In *Cultural Studies*, ed. Lawrence Grossberg, Cary Nelson, and Paula Treichler, 174–86. New York: Routledge, 1992.

Gates, Henry Louis, Jr. *Thirteen Ways of Looking at a Black Man*. New York: Random House, 1997.

Geison, Gerald. *Professions and Professional Ideologies in America*. Chapel Hill: University of North Carolina Press, 1983.

Gilbert, James. *Designing the Industrial State: The Intellectual Pursuit of Collectivism in America, 1880–1940*. Chicago: University of Chicago Press, 1972.

Giroux, Henry. *Theory and Resistance in Education*. South Hadley, Mass.: Bergin and Garvey, 1983.

Gitlin, Todd. *The Twilight of Common Dreams: Why America Is Wracked by Culture Wars*. New York: Henry Holt, 1995.

Glen, Darryl J., and Barbara Herrnstein Smith, eds. *The Politics of Liberal Education*. Durham, N.C.: Duke University Press, 1992.

Goldhagen, Jonathan. *Hitler's Willing Executioners: Ordinary Germans and the Holocaust*. New York: Knopf, 1996.

Goodwyn, Lawrence. *Breaking the Barrier: The Rise of Solidarity in Poland*. New York: Oxford University Press, 1991.

———. *Democratic Province: The Populist Movement in America*. New York: Oxford University Press, 1976.

———. *The Populist Movement: A Short History of Agrarian Revolt*. New York: Oxford University Press, 1978.

Gouldner, Alvin. *The Future of Intellectuals and the Rise of the New Class*. New York: Seabury Press, 1979.

Graff, Gerald. *Professing Literature: An Institutional History*. Chicago: University of Chicago Press, 1987.

Gramsci, Antonio. *The Modern Prince and Other Writings*. New York: International Publishers, 1957.

Green, Hardy. "Superstores, Megabooks—and Humungous Headaches." Review of *The Clash of Civilizations and the Remaking of World Order*, by Samuel P. Huntington. *Business Week*, 14 April 1997, 92.

Gross, Paul R., and Norman Levitt. *The Higher Superstition: The Academic Left and Its Quarrel with Science*. Baltimore, Md.: Johns Hopkins University Press, 1994.

Grossberg, Lawrence. "Critical Theory and the Politics of Empirical Research." In *Mass Communication Review Yearbook*, vol. 6, ed. Michael Gurevitch and Mark R. Levy, 86–106. Newbury Park, Calif.: Sage, 1986.

Guillory, John. *Cultural Capital: The Problem of Literary Canon Formation*. Chicago: University of Chicago Press, 1993.

Habermas, Jürgen. *The Philosophical Discourse of Modernity: Twelve Lectures*. Trans. Frederick G. Lawrence. Cambridge: Polity Press, 1987.

———. *The Structural Transformation of the Public Sphere: An Inquiry into a Category of Bourgeois Society*. Trans. Thomas Burger. Cambridge: MIT Press, 1991.

Hall, Stuart. "Cultural Studies and Its Theoretical Legacies." In *Cultural Studies*, ed. Lawrence Grossman, Cary Nelson, and Paula Treichler, 277–94. New York: Routledge, 1992.

Hanchard, Michael. "Intellectual Pursuit: By Ignoring Our Social and Political History, We Have Impoverished Debate about 'Black Public Intellectuals.'" *Nation*, 19 February 1996, 22–23.

Haraway, Donna J. *Simians, Cyborgs, and Women: The Reinvention of Nature*. New York: Routledge, 1991.

———. "Situated Knowledges: The Science Question in Feminism and the Privilege of Partial Perspectives." *Feminist Studies* 14, no. 3 (fall 1988): 575–99.

Harding, Sandra. "Science Is 'Good to Think With.'" *Social Text* 14, nos. 1–2 (spring–summer 1996): 15–27.

———. *The Science Question in Feminism*. Ithaca, N.Y.: Cornell University Press, 1986.

———. *Whose Science? Whose Knowledge?* Ithaca, N.Y.: Cornell University Press, 1991.

Harris, David. *From Class Struggle to the Politics of Pleasure: The Effects of Gramscianism on Cultural Studies*. New York: Routledge, 1992.

Hartsock, Nancy C. M. *Money, Sex, and Power: Toward a Feminist Historical Materialism.* Boston: Northeastern University Press, 1983.

Haskell, Thomas. *The Emergence of Professional Social Science: The American Social Science Association and the Nineteenth-Century Crisis of Authority.* Urbana: University of Illinois Press, 1977.

Hawking, Stephen. *Black Holes and Baby Universes and Other Essays.* New York: Bantam Books, 1993.

———. *A Brief History of Time: From the Big Bang to Black Holes.* New York: Bantam, 1988.

Hayes, J. H. *The Historical Evolution of Modern Nationalism.* New York: Macmillan, 1948.

Hayles, N. Katherine. *Chaos Bound: Orderly Disorder in Contemporary Literature and Science.* Ithaca, N.Y.: Cornell University Press, 1990.

Hebdige, Dick. *Subculture: The Meaning of Style.* London: Methuen, 1979.

Herf, Jeffrey. "Money, Merit, and Democracy at the University: An Exchange." In *Higher Education under Fire: Politics, Economics, and the Crisis of the Humanities,* ed. Michael Bérubé and Cary Nelson, 149–62. New York: Routledge, 1995.

Higley, Sarah. "Alien Intellect and the Roboticization of the Scientist." Forthcoming in *Camera Obscura.*

———. "The Legend of the Learned Man's Android." In *Retelling Tales: Essays in Honor of Russell Peck,* ed. Thomas Hahn and Alan Lupack, 127–60. Cambridge: D. S. Brewer, 1997.

Hobsbawm, Eric. *The Age of Empire, 1875–1914.* New York: Pantheon, 1987.

Hohendahl, Peter Uwe. *Prismatic Thought: Theodore W. Adorno.* Lincoln: University of Nebraska Press, 1995.

Holton, Gerald D. *Einstein, History, and Other Passions.* New York: Addison-Wesley, 1996.

hooks, bell. *Ain't I a Woman: Black Women and Feminism.* Boston: South End Press, 1981.

———. *Killing Rage: Ending Racism.* New York: Henry Holt, 1995.

hooks, bell, and Cornel West. *Breaking Bread: Insurgent Black Intellectual Life.* Boston: South End Press, 1991.

Horgan, John. *The End of Science: Facing the Limits of Knowledge in the Twilight of the Scientific Age.* Reading, Mass.: Helix Books, 1996.

Horkheimer, Max, and Theodore Adorno. *Dialectic of Enlightenment.* Trans. John Cumming. New York: Continuum, 1989.

Huntington, Samuel P. "The Clash of Civilizations?" *Foreign Affairs* 72, no. 3 (summer 1993): 22–49.

———. *The Clash of Civilizations and the Remaking of World Order.* New York: Simon and Schuster, 1996.

———. "The Coming Clash of Civilizations, or The West against the Rest." *New York Times,* 6 June 1993, 19.

Ignatieff, Michael. *Blood and Belonging: Journeys into the New Nationalisms.* New York: Farrar, Straus, and Giroux, 1994.

———. "Fault Lines." *New York Times Book Review,* 1 December 1996, 13.

Jacob, James R. "The Political Economy of Science in Seventeenth-Century England." In *The Politics of Western Science, 1640–1990,* ed. Margaret C. Jacob, 19–46. Atlantic Highlands, N.J.: Humanities Press, 1992.

Jacoby, Russell. *The Last Intellectuals: American Culture in the Age of Academe.* New York: Basic Books, 1987.

Jameson, Fredric. "Always Already Cultural Studies." *Journal of the Midwest Modern Language Association* 24, no. 1 (1991): 24–38.

———. "The Antinomies of Postmodernism." In *The Seeds of Time.* New York: Columbia University Press, 1994.

———. *Late Marxism: Adorno, or The Persistence of the Dialectic*. London: Verso, 1990.

———. "On 'Cultural Studies.' " *Social Text* 11, no. 1 (spring 1993): 17–52.

———. *Postmodernism, or, The Cultural Logic of Late Capitalism*. Durham, N.C.: Duke University Press, 1991.

———. "The Vanishing Mediator, or Max Weber as Storyteller." In *The Ideologies of Theory: Essays, 1971–1986*. Vol. 2, 3–34. Minneapolis: University of Minnesota Press, 1988.

Jay, Martin. *Marxism and Totality: The Adventures of a Concept from Lukacs to Habermas*. Berkeley: University of California Press, 1984.

Jenkins, Henry. *Textual Poachers: Television Fans and Participatory Culture*. New York: Routledge, 1992.

Kamen, Michael. *People of Paradox: An Inquiry Concerning the Origins of American Civilization*. New York: Knopf, 1972.

Kelley, Robin D. G. *Yo' Mama's DisFUNKtional*. Boston: Beacon Press, 1997.

Kellner, Douglas. *Critical Theory, Marxism, and Modernity*. Baltimore, Md.: Johns Hopkins University Press, 1989.

Kennedy, Donald. *Academic Duty*. Cambridge: Harvard University Press, 1997.

Kimball, Roger. *Tenured Radicals: How Politics Has Corrupted Our Higher Education*. New York: Harper, 1990.

Klein, Julie. *Interdisciplinarity: History, Theory, Practice*. Detroit, Mich.: Wayne State University Press, 1990.

Kohn, Marek. "Joyfully Back to Church?" *New Statesman and Society* 5 (1 May 1992): 31–32.

Konrad, George, and Ivan Szelenyi. *The Intellectuals on the Road to Class Power*. Trans. Andrew Arato and Richard E. Allen. New York: Harcourt Brace Jovanovich, 1979.

Krugman, Paul. *The Age of Diminished Expectations: U.S. Economic Policy in the 1990's*. Cambridge: MIT Press, 1990.

Kucklick, Bruce. "The Emergence of the Humanities." In *The Politics of Liberal Education*, ed. Darryl J. Gless and Barbara Herrnstein Smith, 201–12. Durham, N.C.: Duke University Press, 1992.

Lasch, Christopher. *The New Radicalism in America, 1889–1963*. New York: Norton, 1965.

———. *The True and Only Heaven: Progress and Its Critics*. New York: Norton, 1991.

Lauter, Paul. " 'Political Correctness' and the Attack on American Colleges." In *Higher Education under Fire: Politics, Economics, and the Crisis of the Humanities*, ed. Michael Bérubé and Cary Nelson, 73–90. New York: Routledge, 1995.

Lentricchia, Frank. *Ariel and the Police: Michel Foucault, William James, Wallace Stevens*. Madison: University of Wisconsin Press, 1988.

———. *Criticism and Social Change*. Chicago: University of Chicago Press, 1983.

Lerner, Max. *America as a Civilization: Life and Thought in the United States Today*. New York: Simon and Schuster, 1957.

Levidow, Les. "Science Skirmishes and Science-Policy Research." *Social Text* 14, nos. 1–2 (spring–summer 1996): 199–206.

Levine, George. "What Is Science Studies for and Who Cares." *Social Text* 14, nos. 1–2 (spring–summer 1996): 113–28.

Levins, Richard. "Ten Propositions on Science and Antiscience." *Social Text* 14, nos. 1–2 (spring–summer 1996): 101–11.

Livingston, David, ed. *Critical Pedagogy and Cultural Power*. New York: Bergin and Garvey, 1987.

Lovejoy, A. O. *The Thirteen Pragmatisms and Other Essays*. Baltimore, Md.: Johns Hopkins University Press, 1963.

Lubow, Arthur. "Heart and Mind: A Rare Glimpse at the Private Man behind the Brilliant Mind of Stephen Hawking." *Vanity Fair*, June 1992, 72, 74, 76, 78, 80, 83, 85, 86.

Lyotard, Jean-François. *The Post-modern Condition.* Minneapolis: University of Minnesota Press, 1984.

———. *Tombeau de l'intellectuel et autres papiers.* Paris: Gallimard, 1984.

Martin, Waldo F. *The Mind of Frederick Douglass.* Chapel Hill: University of North Carolina Press, 1984.

Mazarr, Michael J. "Culture in International Relations: A Review Essay." *Washington Quarterly* 19, no. 2 (spring 1996): 177–97.

McMillen, Liz. "Scholars Who Study the Lab Say Their Work Has Been Distorted." *Chronicle of Higher Education,* 28 June 1996, A8.

Michael, John. "The Intellectual in Uncivil Society: Michnik, Poland, and Community." *Telos* 88 (summer 1991): 141–54.

———. "Making a Stand: Standpoint Epistemologies, Political Positions, Proposition 187." *Telos* 108 (summer 1996): 93–104.

Modleski, Tania. *Feminism without Women: Culture and Criticism in a "Postfeminist" Age.* New York: Routledge, 1991.

Morgan, Philip D., ed. *Diversity and Unity in Early North America.* New York: Routledge, 1993.

Morley, David. *The "Nationwide" Audience: Structure and Decoding.* London: British Film Institute, 1980.

Morris, Meaghan. "Banality in Cultural Studies." In *Logics of Television: Essays in Cultural Criticism,* ed. Patricia Mellencamp, 14–43. Bloomington: University of Indiana Press, 1990.

Morrison, Toni. *Playing in the Dark: Whiteness and the Literary Imagination.* Cambridge: Harvard University Press, 1992.

Naipaul, V. S. *Among the Believers: An Islamic Journey.* New York: Knopf, 1981.

Nairn, Tom. *The Breakup of Britain and New Nationalism.* New York: New Left Books, 1977.

Nelkin, Dorothy. "Responses to a Marriage Failed." *Social Text* 46–47 (spring–summer 1996): 93–100.

Nelson, Cary. *Manifesto of a Tenured Radical.* New York: New York University Press, 1997.

Nelson, Cary, and Dilip Parameshwar Gaonkar, eds. *Disciplinarity and Dissent in Cultural Studies.* New York: Routledge, 1996.

Norris, Christopher. *Uncritical Theory: Postmodernism, Intellectuals, and the Gulf War.* Amherst: University of Massachusetts Press, 1992.

———. *What's Wrong with Postmodernism: Critical Theory and the Ends of Philosophy.* Baltimore, Md.: Johns Hopkins University Press, 1990.

O'Brien, George Dennis. *All the Essential Half-Truths about Higher Education.* Chicago: University of Chicago Press, 1998.

Okuda, Michael, ed. *The Star Trek Encyclopedia: A Reference Guide to the Future.* New York: Pocket Books, 1994.

Painter, Nell Irvin. "The Future of the Race." *Nation,* 6 May 1996, 38–39.

Peirce, C. S. *The Philosophical Writings of Peirce.* Ed. Justus Buchler. New York: Dover, 1955.

Penley, Constance. "Feminism, Psychoanalysis, and the Study of Popular Culture." In *Cultural Studies,* ed. Lawrence Grossberg, Cary Nelson, and Paula Treichler, 479–500. New York: Routledge, 1992.

———. *NASA/Trek: Popular Science and Sex in America.* New York: Verso, 1997.

Piper, Richard. "The Clash of Civilizations?" *Commentary* 103, no. 3 (March 1997): 62.

Plato. *Plato's Republic.* Trans. G. M. A. Grube. Indianapolis: Hackett Publishing, 1974.

Poster, Mark. *Critical Theory and Poststructuralism: In Search of a Context.* Ithaca, N.Y.: Cornell University Press, 1989.

Radway, Janice. *Reading the Romance: Women, Patriarchy, and Popular Literature.* Chapel Hill: University of North Carolina Press, 1984.

Readings, Bill. *The University in Ruins*. Cambridge: Harvard University Press, 1996.

Reed, Adolph L., Jr. *W. E. B. Du Bois and American Political Thought: Fabianism and the Color Line*. New York: Oxford, 1997.

———. "What Are the Drums Saying, Booker? The Current Crisis of the Black Intellectual." *Village Voice*, 11 April 1995, 31–36.

Reich, Robert. *The Work of Nations: Preparing Ourselves for 21st Century Capitalism*. New York: Random House, 1992.

Renan, Ernest. "What Is a Nation?" In *Nation and Narration*, ed. Homi K. Bhabha, 8–22. New York: Routledge, 1990.

Renov, Michael. "Introduction: The Truth about Non-Fiction." In *Theorizing Documentary*, ed. Michael Renov, 1–11. New York: Routledge, 1993.

———. "Rethinking Documentary: Towards a Taxonomy of Mediation." *Wide Angle* 18, nos. 3–4 (1986): 71–77.

Reynolds, Terri. "Mystery Science Theater." *Lingua Franca* (July–August 1996): 62.

Robbins, Bruce. "Introduction: The Grounding of Intellectuals." In *Intellectuals: Aesthetics, Politics, Academics*, ed. Bruce Robbins, ix–xxvii. Minneapolis: University of Minnesota Press, 1990.

———. *Secular Vocations: Intellectuals, Professionalism, Culture*. London: Verso, 1993.

Rorty, Richard. *Achieving Our Country: Leftist Thought in Twentieth-Century America*. Cambridge: Harvard University Press, 1998.

———. *Contingency, Irony, Solidarity*. Cambridge: Cambridge University Press, 1989.

———. "Cosmopolitanism without Emancipation: A Response to Jean-François Lyotard." In *Objectivity, Relativism, and Truth: Philosophical Papers, Vol. 1*. New York: Cambridge University Press, 1991.

———. "On Ethnocentrism: A Reply to Clifford Geertz." *Objectivity, Relativism, and Truth: Philosophical Papers, Vol. 1*. New York: Cambridge University Press, 1991.

Ross, Andrew. *No Respect: Intellectuals and Popular Culture*. New York: Routledge, 1989.

———. *Real Love: In Pursuit of Cultural Justice*. New York: New York University Press, 1998.

Ross, Andrew, and Bruce Robbins. "Mystery Science Theater: Sokal vs. Social Text, Part Two." *Lingua Franca* (July–August 1996): 54–55.

Rubenstein, Richard E., and Jarle Croker. Review of "The Clash of Civilizations?" *Foreign Affairs* 96 (22 September 1996): 113.

Said, Edward. *Representations of the Intellectual*. New York: Pantheon Books, 1994.

Sajoo, Amyn B. "Latent Contests of Culture Are Surfacing." Review of "The Clash of Civilizations?" *Bangkok Post*, 30 March 1997, 2.

Shafer, Boyd C. *Nationalism: Myth and Reality*. New York: Harcourt, Brace and World, 1955.

Shapiro, James. "From Achebe to Zydeco: Two African-American Scholars Have Produced a 'Dictionary of Cultural Literacy' for the 1990s." *New York Times Book Review*, 2 February 1997, 7.

Schlesinger, Arthur. *The Disuniting of America: Reflections on a Multicultural Society*. New York: Norton, 1992.

Scholes, Robert. *The Rise and Fall of English: Reconstructing English as a Discipline*. New Haven, Conn.: Yale University Press, 1998.

Schroeder, Ralph. *Max Weber and the Sociology of Culture*. London: Sage Publications, 1992.

Shuffelton, Frank. Introduction to *A Mixed Race: Ethnicity in Early America*, ed. Frank Shuffelton, 3–18. New York: Oxford University Press, 1993.

Smith, Paul. *Millennial Dreams: Contemporary Culture and Capital in the North*. London: Verso, 1997.

Smith, Thomas M., ed. *The Condition of Education, 1996*. U.S. Department of Education, National

Center for Educational Statistics. Washington, D.C.: U.S. Government Printing Office, 1996.

Sokal, Alan. "A Physicist Experiments with Cultural Studies." *Lingua Franca* (May–June 1996): 62–64.

Spivak, Gayatri. "Can the Subaltern Speak?" In *Marxism and the Interpretation of Culture*, ed. Cary Nelson and Lawrence Grossberg, 271–313. Houndmills: Macmillan, 1988.

Storey, John. *Cultural Studies and the Study of Popular Culture*. Athens: University of Georgia Press, 1996.

Takaki, Ronald. *A Different Mirror: A History of Multicultural America*. Boston: Little Brown, 1993.

Taylor, Paul V. *The Texts of Paulo Freire*. Bristol, Pa.: Open University Press, 1993.

Vattimo, Gianni. *The Transparent Society*. Baltimore, Md.: Johns Hopkins University Press, 1992.

Walker, Peter F. *Moral Choices: Memory, Desire, and Imagination in Nineteenth-Century American Abolition*. Baton Rouge: Louisiana State University Press, 1978.

Wallace, Michelle. "Bell Hooks, Line, and Sinker: Black Feminist or Poststructuralist Oprah?" Review of *Killing Rage: Ending Racism*, by bell hooks. *Village Voice Literary Supplement*, 7 November 1995, 19–24.

———. *Black Macho and the Myth of the Super Woman*. New York: Dial Press, 1978.

Warner, Michael. "The Mass Public and the Mass Subject." In *The Phantom Public Sphere*, ed. Bruce Robbins, 234–56. Minneapolis: University of Minnesota Press, 1993.

Weber, Max. *The Protestant Ethic and the Spirit of Capitalism: The Relationship between Religion and the Economic and Social Life in Modern Culture*. New York: Charles Scribner's Sons, 1958.

———. "The Uniqueness of Western Civilization." In *Max Weber on Capitalism, Bureaucracy, and Religion: A Selection of Texts*, ed. Stanislaw Andreski, 21–29. London: Allen and Unwin, 1983.

Weber, Samuel. *Institution and Interpretation*. Minneapolis: University of Minnesota Press, 1987.

West, Cornel. "Black Strivings in a Twilight Civilization." In *The Future of the Race*, ed. Henry Louis Gates and Cornel West. New York: Knopf, 1996.

White, Michael, and John Gribbin. *Stephen Hawking: A Life in Science*. New York: Dutton, 1992.

"Why Past Is Past." *Newsweek*, 28 December 1992, 53.

Wiggershaus, Rolf. *The Frankfurt School: Its History, Theories, and Political Significance*. Trans. Michael Robertson. Cambridge: MIT Press, 1995.

Williams, Patricia. *The Alchemy of Race and Rights: Diary of a Law Professor*. Cambridge: Harvard University Press, 1991.

———. *The Rooster's Egg: On the Persistence of Prejudice*. Cambridge: Harvard University Press, 1995.

Wilson, John K. *The Myth of Political Correctness: The Conservative Attack on Higher Education*. Durham, N.C.: Duke University Press, 1995.

Winston, Brian. "The Documentary Film as Scientific Inscription." In *Theorizing Documentary*, ed. Michael Renov, 37–57. New York: Routledge, 1993.

Wood, Donald N. *Post-intellectualism and the Decline of Democracy: The Failure of Reason and Responsibility in the Twentieth Century*. London: Praeger, 1996.

Yaakov, Daniel Ben. "Conflictual Relations." *Jerusalem Post*, 6 March 1997, 3.

Yack, Bernard. *The Fetishism of Modernities*. Notre Dame, Ind.: University of Notre Dame Press, 1997.

INDEX

Glass, Philip, 141
Globalization, 83–84, 87–88, 183 n.6, 188 n.21, 190 n.11
Goldhagen, Jonathan, 200 n.30
Goodwyn, Lawrence, 178 n.9
Gouldner, Alvin, 4–5, 8, 13, 179–80 n.24
Graff, Gerald, 54–55, 186 n.2
Gramsci, Antonio, 2–9, 23, 115, 178 n.10, 179 n.15
Gravity, the law of, 159–60
Green, Hardy, 189 n.3
Gross, Paul R., 149, 150, 154, 155, 158, 166, 167, 179–80 n.24, 198 nn. 9, 14; and gender, 154–55
Guillory, John, 170–71, 182–83 n.4

Habermas, Jürgen, 17, 143, 177 n.1, 180 n.27, 186 n.11
Hall, Stuart, 7–8, 23, 59, 101, 178 n.10
Hanchard, Michael, 24
Haraway, Donna, 141, 197 n.3
Harding, Sandra, 153–54, 198 n.17
Harris, David, 178 n.10, 180 n.1
Hartsock, Nancy, 197 n.25
Harvey, David, 129
Hawking, Jane, 138, 144
Hawking, Lucy, 144
Hawking, Stephen, 18, 131–47, 148, 196–97 n.24; and gender, 132, 135, 137, 142, 145, 147; and law, 133, 134, 136–37, 146–47; popular fantasies about, 135, 137–38, 141–42; as universal intellectual, 131–33, 139, 142, 143, 144, 145–47
Hayles, Katherine, N., 200 n.32
Hebdige, Dick, 115–16
Hegel, G. W. F., 151
Heidegger, Martin, 160
Heisenberg uncertainty principle, the, 140
Herf, Jeffrey, 49
Higley, Sarah, 195 n.7
Hirsch, E. D., 69
Hohendahl, Peter Uwe, 111, 128, 192 nn. 2, 3, 193 nn. 4, 5, 194 n.24
Holton, Gerald, 153, 198 nn. 9, 11
hooks, bell, 25, 31, 34, 36–37, 38, 39, 181 n.12, 181–82 n.17
Horgan, John, 197 n.5
Horkheimer, Max, 6, 12, 47–48, 112, 123, 172–73, 193 n.5

Humanities, the: cultural capital of, 44–45, 170–71, 174–75, 182–83 n.4; and democracy, 170–71; and elitism, 170
Hume, David, 151
Hunter, Kendra, 120
Huntington, Samuel P., 89–107, 189 nn. 2, 3, 189–90 n.8, 190 nn. 11, 14, 190–91 n.17, 191 n.19, 192 nn. 25, 27; and the betrayal of the West, 105–7; and the Cold War, 89, 92, 97; and cultural studies, 98; and fear of the West's decline, 96–97, 100; and multiculturalism, 100–101; and political-ethico commitment, 98; and religion in the New World Order, 96–97; and world models or maps, 95–96

Identity politics and "white" Americans, 28–31
Ignatieff, Michael, 99–100
Imaginary time, 146–47
Immigration and community, 85–87
Imperialism, 174
Intellectuals, 23–46, 157–58, 160, 162–63; and academics and the public trust, 1–3, 9–11, 18–19, 42–43, 57–63, 169–70; African American, and authenticity, 23–26, 36–37, 40–41; African American, and community, 23–25, 26–29, 33–43; African American, and elitism, 35–36; African American, and gender, 35–36; African American, contrasted to New York intellectuals, 24–25; African American, and U.S. national identity, 29–32, 39; and anxiety, 76–77; black intellectuals as, 23–26, 27, 36–37, 40–41; and collectivism, 7; and community, 64–67, 82–83, 87–88; critical, 2–4, 8, 11; and cultural difference, 98–99; and cultural studies, 93–94; and culture, 89–90; and democracy, 162–63; and empiricism, 117–18, 123; as experts, 10, 13–14, 149, 150, 153, 156; as fans, 112, 117–18, 120–30; and the Frankfurt School, 112–14, 116; as a New Class, 2, 4–5, 7, 8, 13–14, 19, 114; organic, 5–6, 7–9, 18, 23, 59–60, 94, 101–2, 115, 116, 178 n.10; and politics, 60–61, 145–47, 150, 171; and populism, 94; and the problem of the university, 171–75, 185–86 n.1; and projection, 116, 118, 119–21,

Newton, Isaac, 134, 135–37
New York intellectuals, the, 24–25, 60
Nietzsche, Friedrich, 48
Norris, Christopher, 10, 189 n.5

O'Brien, George Dennis, 201 n.1

Painter, Nell, 35
Pedagogy: and Enlightenment, 53–54; and manipulation, 51–53; oppositional or critical, 50–56, 63, 174–75
Peirce, Charles Saunders, 74–75, 160; on community, reality, and conflict, 75
Penley, Constance, 121–22, 124, 126–28, 131, 177 n.1
Pfaff, William, 189–90 n.8
Phillips, Wendell, 30
Piper, Richard, 189–90 n.8
Plato, 48, 70, 71, 146, 161–62, 163; and democracy, 162; and interdisciplinarity, 161–62; and totalitarianism, 163
Pope, Alexander, 134
Popular politics, 2–3
Populism, 3–9, 11, 12–14, 23, 50–51, 54–55, 60, 93–94, 112, 114–16, 155, 171, 178 n.9, 179 n.19, 180 n.1, 192–93 n.15, 194 n.20, 198 n.14; as anti-Jacobinism, 94; as an ideology of intellectuals, 94
Poster, Mark, 192–93 n.3
Postmodernity, 14–15, 16, 47, 112, 129, 145–46, 177 n.1, 188 n.25
Poststructuralism, 112
Pound, Ezra, 60
Pragmatism, 74–78, 80–81, 187 n.13
Professionalism, 162–64, 199 nn. 22, 27; and anxiety, 76–77; and democracy, 163; and disciplinarity, 68–69, 71–72, 76–77, 158–59, 164–67
Professors, humanities: as experts, 157–58, 160, 165–67; popular images of, 147–49; as professionals, 158–59, 164–67; and science, 148
Public sphere, 143–44, 166–67, 170

Quiz Show (film), 169

Radway, Janice A., 117, 177 n.1
Rahv, Philip, 60
Reading: and politics, 58–59

Readings, Bill, 15, 17–18, 64–65, 173–74
Reagan, Ronald, 59–60
Reed, Adolph, 6, 24, 25–27, 28, 34–45, 38
Relativism, 10–11, 44–49, 65–66, 68, 93, 94, 96, 98, 107, 111, 150–51, 155–56, 157–58, 163, 170, 185–86 n.1, 189 n.5, 197 n.3, 198 n.14; conservative and progressive critics of, 64, 66, 83, 87–88, 90; and global politics, 89–93, 96, 98; and imperialism, 90–91, 98, 102; and professionalism, 165–67; and social constructivism, 150–51, 156; and totalitarianism, 163; and the West, 44–45, 48, 55, 61, 66–67, 83, 87–88, 90–91
Religion and culture, 96–97
Renan, Ernst, 29–30
Renov, Michael, 140
Reynolds, Terri, 164, 165, 200 n.32
Richards, I. A., 80–81
Robbins, Bruce, 4, 11, 25, 93–94, 157, 177 n.1, 179 n.21, 184 nn. 14, 22, 188 n.19, 197 n.4, 199 n.22
Robbins, T. M., 148–49
Rorty, Richard, 14, 15, 84–87, 91, 98–99, 190–91 n.17, 192 n.27: and community, 85–87; and ethnocentrism, 86–87; and immigration, 85–86; and liberal ironists, 84, 85; and liberalism, 86
Ross, Andrew, 4–5, 57, 62, 90, 113–14, 155, 157, 166, 177 n.1, 198 n.14
Rubenstein, Richard E., 189–90 n.8
Ryan, Meg, 148–49

Said, Edward, 5, 9–10
Sajoo, Amyn B., 189 n.3
Schlesinger, Arthur, 28–30, 179–80 n.8
Schroeder, Ralph, 190 n.16
Schwarzenegger, Arnold, 143
Science: and the Cold War, 151–52; crisis in, 151–52, 197 n.5; and cultural studies, 148–49; and democracy, 155, 157, 161, 162; and empiricism, 156–57; and epistemology, 140–41; and gender, 137, 140, 142, 144–45, 146–47, 149, 153–54; and the humanities, 151; and the law, 133, 134, 136–37; and philosophy, 134, 135, 139–40, 150–51, 156–67, 160–61; and politics, 133–34, 143–44, 146–56; popular fascination with, 169–70, 171, 174–75,

Science (*continued*)
196 nn. 12, 15; and populism, 155; and the
public sphere, 134, 143–44, 150, 153, 154,
166–67; and representation, 141, 142, 147
Science studies, 148–68; and populism,
155–56; and social constructionism,
150–51, 155–56
Science wars, 148–68; and anxiety, 157–59,
167–68
Scientists: as experts, 156, 157–58, 160,
165–67; as intellectuals, 131–47; popular
images of, 148, 149, 152, 153–54, 163–64;
as professionals, 158–59, 164–67
Self-reflection and rhetoric, 74–75, 77, 78
Shapiro, James, 103
Shuffelton, Frank, 29, 192 n.26
Slash fiction, 126–28
Smith, Barbara-Herrnstein, 185–86 n.1
Social constructivism, 150–51, 156
Social Text, 149–50, 157
Sociology, orthodox consensus in, 96
Socrates, 160
Sokal, Alan, 149–51, 152, 156, 157, 159–60,
164, 165, 167, 168, 179–80 n.24, 200 n.34
Spivak, Gayatri, 5, 184 n.14
Steele, Shelby, 25, 38
Subcultures, 155–56
Szelenyi, Ivan, 4–5, 11–12, 27, 178 n.5

Takaki, Ronald, 192 n.25
Talk shows, 46
Taylor, Paul, 51
Thatcher, Margaret, 59–60
Theory, and pragmatism, 68–69, 70, 71,
77–78, 80–81, 82–83, 84
Thin Blue Line, The (film), 133, 140
Totalitarianism, 163

Totalization, 91, 93–94, 95, 100, 105–7, 111
Transcendence (local) 11–12, 42–43, 85
Trekkies, 120–30
Trinh T. Minh-ha, 141
Twain, Mark, 31

Universal (specific), 11–12, 42–43, 85
Universities, 2–3, 6, 10, 169–75; and Enlightenment values, 172–73, 182 n.2,
182–83 n.4, 184 n.13, 185 n.1, 201 n.1;
and national identity, 64–65, 88

Wallace, Michele, 25, 143–44, 181–82 n.17,
182 n.20
Warner, Michael, 55, 56, 143
Weber, Max, 95–96, 102, 162, 190 n.16,
190–91 n.17
Weber, Samuel, 186 n.5, 187 n.16, 188 n.20
West, Cornel, 24, 25, 26–27, 28, 31, 34, 35,
36–38, 39, 171
West, the, 173–74; and the rest of the world,
91–92, 95–101, 102–4; and values, 90–91,
98–99, 104–5
Wheeler, John, 144
Wiggershaus, Rolf, 112–13
Williams, Patricia, 25, 32–33, 34, 35, 37, 46,
180–81 n.8
Williams, Raymond, 60
Williamson, Judith, 116
Willis, Bruce, 132
Winston, Brian, 139–40, 196 n.20
Wolpert, Lewis, 158
Wood, Donald N., 177 n.1
Wood, Robert, 133

Yaakov, Daniel Ben, 189–90 n.8
Yack, Bernard, 14–15